Praise for Mc

"Some of her writings bring a tear to my eye. Others are knee slapping funny. She knocks it out of the park." **Don Wozniak**, Educator, Grand Rapids

"Maureen has a quirky way of looking at the world. She thinks and writes about things most other people do not . Sometimes her words are funny, sometimes sad, sometimes deeply thoughtful and sometimes a little naughty. When you finish one of her columns, and I've read them all, her words stay with you. She makes you laugh and cry and wish you'd said it yourself. And, maybe, like me, you'll find yourself repeating her stories to others." **Beverly Geyer**, President, Management Innovations

Maureen's writing is a beacon of positive energy with an amazing and consistent sense of humor and look at life which inspires many and makes people laugh - and that's a good thing." **Susan McFarland**, Professional Speaker, Grand Rapids

"Maureen's columns are the best. I value the insights, ideas, chaffing observations and sincere concern for the readers. I laughed and laughed." **Nancy Wills**, Nebraska

"Maureen always sees the humor in human nature and I love it. She's a hoot and her writing makes me laugh out loud." **Diana Jones**, Employment Training Manager, Greenville

"Maureen's writings are so personal, funny and daring - beautifully written. I love them." **Skeet Slocum**, Educator, Greenville

"OMG - I can easily relate to Maureen's writing. I laughed so hard I got tears in my eyes. It made my day!" - **Sandy Quist**, Greenville

"I love, love, love her writing. It resonates with me and perks up my day." **Terri Handlin**, Career Counselor, Grand Rapids

"Maureen is a great difference maker with her talented writing and delightful sense of humor that flows through her. She easily expresses the seriousness of life and those things that should not be taken so seriously." **Duane Putnam**, Educator, Greenville

Also by Maureen Burns

Looking and Laughing at Life

Forgiveness / A Gift You Give Yourself

Getting in Touch / Intimacy

Cara's Story (written with Cara Burns)

Run With Your Dreams

On my mind . . . or what's left of it!

Maureen Burns

First Printing November 2012

ISBN: 0-978-1-4675-5136-6

Published by:
Empey Enterprises
Greenville, Michigan

maureenburns@maureenburns.com

This book is dedicated to my delightful grandsons, Danny and Louie, who add so much joy to our lives and fodder to my writing. I love them sooooooooo much!

Danny and Louie Burns

In memory of our dear Aunt Julie Burns who was one of my greatest encouragers. She led by example when she wrote her own books and showed me it could be done.

Acknowledgements:

First, I would like to thank my daughter, Colleen, for being my editor. Whether she has time or not, she always takes time to do her clear honest critique. I trust her. I love her and I am most grateful.

A special thanks to my husband, Don, who is truly my better half. I have been blessed to share the last 45 plus years with him.

Thanks to my daughter, Donna, my daughter, Cara, my son, Dan, and my daughter-in-law, Ann-Drea, who continue to encourage me with their love, support and appreciation. It means the world to me and more than they will ever know.

Thanks to Mary Stek who always seems to know what is wandering around in my brain. I appreciate her fabulous artistic ability and am grateful to have been able to do the last five books with her. Thanks to Dotti Rackliffe who helped me "run with my dreams".

Thanks to Julie and Rob Stafford who have encouraged me on this journey of writing weekly columns, to Camille Beecroft who has added a new dimension to that experience and to Darrin Clark, my fun newspaper editor.

Thanks to Beverly Geyer who is always there for me with praise, prayer, honest words and clear guidance. She makes soul sister a reality.

Thanks to my great friends and family who continue to give me ideas and encouragement. Thanks to Aunt Mary Empey, Norm Nickle, Julie Bowers, Don Wozniak and Gail Walsh for their continuous and much appreciated comments.

Thanks to all the readers who not only take their precious time to read my "stuff" but then take the time to email, write and call with their comments. They honor me and I am very grateful. Without a reader, writing is only half done.

Introduction

As a speaker and writer I try to balance humor and depth. I believe strongly that laughter is the sunshine of the soul and the main ingredient of mentally healthy people.

I hope you get a laugh or two or three. I hope you shed a tear or get a lump in your throat. And I hope you gain a new insight or perspective. If any of these hopes come true, this project will have more than fulfilled my dreams.

Wishing you the best –

Maureen Burns

Foreword

For those of you who have had the pleasure of hearing Maureen Burns speak, reading her weekly columns, or breaking bread with her at one of a myriad of community related events, I'm sure you will agree with me that it is a sheer delight to learn what's on her mind, or what's left of it!

Ms. Burns is witty, insightful, creative, transparent, direct, and incredibly human. Her stories evoke laughter and tears, reflection and action, empathy and grace. I've had the delightful privilege of working closely with Maureen in One Book, One County – Montcalm, a movement that she founded several years ago and continues to this day. In that role, I've become keenly aware of her passion to connect with others and make a difference in the community. Her drive, attention to detail, and commitment to "the personal touch," have endeared her to many from all walks of life.

In this meaningful collection of columns first published in The Daily News of Greenville, Michigan, along with several of her articles in Faith Magazine, Maureen will touch your heart, soul, and funny bone. This is likely to be one of those books you'll want to read more than once, and pass on to friends as well.

Fasten your seatbelt, and enjoy the ride!

Gary L. Hauck, Ph.D.
Author, Dean of Instruction

Contents:

Just Keep Laughing

Married With Children

The Way We Talk

The Times They Are A Changing

That's Life

Goin' For It

On Living A Better Life

Young Fun

Glorious Food

The Way We Were . . . And Are

In The Spirit

Real Role Models

Near And Far

Holidaze Through The Year

On America

For Your Reading Pleasure

Relevant Recipes

Just Keep Laughing

Looking for Gold

I like to think of myself as a "good wife". For the last 42 years I have tried to make that a true fact. Now, I'm not quite sure I'm going to make it.

My spouse almost never complains. Unlike me, who could win awards for complaining.

So when he starts in a few days ago, complaining of a bad toothache, I take notice. This has to be serious. I try to be a good wife by feeding him drugs.

The drugs don't touch the pain so after a couple of days we decide he has to call the dentist.

This call doesn't get made as planned. He thinks I will do it, but I end up watching our grandsons all day and never get the call made. On Friday he gets up early. The pain is still there so he makes the call himself.

The recording says (don't you just love those?), that "The office is closed Friday, Saturday and Sunday. If you have an emergency, call this number . . ."

We discuss whether this is an emergency. I think it has grown into one so he makes the call. After a while, my dentist calls him back. It seems his dentist is not on call, but, of course.

They discuss the problem and decide he has lost a gold crown off his tooth. They set up an appointment for Monday. Though he is in constant pain and has been for days now, that is not enough to bring in the doc.

The dentist asks him where the gold is. My husband replies he assumes he swallowed it.

The dentist assures him with an odd comment. "Oh, don't worry. It should work its way through you." Sigh. Gulp. Say it ain't so.

And that is when the dentist comes up with the horrific idea.

"You will want to look for it," he says. He says this like he might say, go find your book or go find the dog. But, as we think about it, this is clearly a different kind of "go look for".

We both went, "Uuuwwwwwwww". And I thought to myself, "Oh, heck no." But I probably thought that in stronger terms. I also thought of that song from Urban Cowboy, "Looking for Gold in all the Wrong Places." Well, maybe it wasn't gold, but you know what I mean.

It is now obvious to the dentist that my husband isn't excited about this prospect. It is a kind of "prospecting for gold" that he clearly does not want to do.

The dentist sweetens the pot. (No pun intended.) He says, "Let me sweeten the deal, here. If you find the gold, it will save you about a thousand bucks." My mate sighs. Talk about a dilemma.

The dentist senses his hesitancy and then suggests, "Maureen will probably be happy to search for you." This is followed by gales of loud laughter that I can hear across the table. It seems the dentist knows me quite well. My mate is also laughing but has a hopeful look on his face as he does so.

In my mind I am thinking, 'hope all you want, buddy. While you are hoping, you might also want to hope for a pet unicorn. Because neither are going to turn into reality'.

And that is how I quit becoming a "good wife". Unfortunately, just as there are some things that money can't buy, there are also some things a good wife just won't do.

****

*Later two friends wrote. Al said, 'Where's the tooth fairy when you need him?" Ted reminded us that what we really had needed was a metal detector. Fun!

(This column won an Associated Press award.)

I Feel Lucky

Yesterday at my grandson's preschool Halloween program, I watched him with glee. Not knowing that, for me it was the calm before the storm. As I left his farm school, I slipped on some leaves in the midst of a nasty rain and slid into a ditch of yucky mud.

Falling into a bunch of mud is not as glamorous as it sounds. I laid there stunned and actually covered in mud – my clothes, my hands, my jewelry, my camera. I was going to take a cute picture of my grandson and his mom in the rain. Forget that.

I was slick, wet, dirty and downtrodden. And then there was the fact that I could hardly move. I kept thinking of the Doctor telling me after I had both knees replaced. "Just don't fall on them." Boom.

My positive husband chattered like a parrot. "What a lucky fall. How lucky. You could have broken something. How great. What luck." Until my daughter-in-law gave him the high sign: *Enough with the luck, dude.*

The night went on. I could barely take a step. I thought, how lucky can a girl get? Should I go buy a lottery ticket?

The luck continued. Halloween morning we got up and headed off to Michigan State University for a live National Public Radio show. We didn't, but we should have, had the Mary Chapin Carpenter song, I Feel Lucky, playing on the CD player. That would have been most appropriate for our lucky weekend. Especially when the huge buck plowed into my nearly brand new car as we had just barely pulled out of town going east on M57.

Boom again. Wow. "What was that?" I asked. Of course I had been reading the *Greenville Daily News* so I wasn't looking up to watch this luck happen. By the time I looked up, the deer was gone. We weren't sure if he was alive or dead. He had flown into a cornfield. We were sure, however, that the car wasn't a pretty sight. Our eyes filled with mucho dollar signs as we thought of the upcoming repair bill. I tried to get out of the car. Not so fast, lucky girl. My door wouldn't open at all.

I took my gimp leg and ambled over the gear shift to exit on the driver's side. It turned out the gear shift was not my friend. I confess. I did not feel lucky, even though I knew I was. But then I heard my positive partner again. "How lucky was that! That could have been so much worse. Wow, what luck!"

Yep, that was one way to look at it, for sure. It could have been worse. I knew that to be true. Yessirreee, Donald, I thought. We are having one lucky break after another. I was not sure I could take much more luck, though.

I then wondered if instead of continuing on to Michigan State, we should head on up to Mount Pleasant and the Casino. We have never really been "into" casinos but we were on such a lucky streak, don't you know. It almost seemed crazy not to play this sucker out.

We did go on to Michigan State University, though, and the Michael Feldman show, where he quipped, "Michigan people need deer crash helmets". True dat, I thought.

4

As I considered this sorry, but lucky, state of affairs, I thought of another lucky thing. As I limped along with my leg that wouldn't bend, I did resemble Frankenstein. At least I walked like him. And it was Halloween. How lucky was that? I didn't even need a costume. It was just luck, luck, luck, all over the place.

Garrison Keillor said, "Some luck lies in not getting what you thought you wanted but getting what you have, which once you have got it you may be smart enough to see is what you would have wanted had you known." Whew, I guess he is right and that explains our lucky weekend.

Marshall Brickman put it another way. "When something good happens it's a miracle and you should wonder what God is saving up for you later."

Now that was something to ponder. I decided to go ponder that for a few hours with my stiff leg up, some ice on it, some mindless TV and a glass of medicinal vino. And I hoped lightning wouldn't strike the house as I sat there. If it did, though, I thought this string of good luck would likely hold out and the house wouldn't burn down.

Oh, yeah. Luck be a lady tonight!

Flirting With Disaster

Sometimes life is so challenging. Last week I was on my way to Lansing with my usual traveling companion, a large latte. I sailed through Ionia without any thought of needing a bathroom. Then I landed at the bottom of a big hill and sat in a traffic hold. I assumed it was due to construction and that we would be moving shortly. I assumed wrong.

We sat and sat and sat. A big semi on my left kept inching ahead of me, bugging me. I was suddenly reminded of that joke. "What is stress? It's having a large coffee and a bran muffin and then getting stuck in traffic." It seemed humorous once, but reality wasn't nearly as witty.

That darn truck kept trying to get in. I wanted to yell, "Hey buddy, fugeddaboutit, I need a potty so get in line like everyone else." We continued to sit and sit. I had been on time for my meeting but now time was ticking along and I was not. I was just getting ticked.

I tried mind over matter. That means I tried to hold on to my feeble mind and not do matter in my pants.

The next thing I knew, a kind looking man appeared out of nowhere. I rolled the window down and it was the jerky trucker who turned out not to be jerky at all. Once again, so much for judging people. He kindly told me, "There's a head on collision ahead. Traffic won't be going anywhere for a long time. They're bringing ambulances."

I said some kind things back to the nice trucker man but what I really wanted to do was scream, "Got a toilet on ya, good buddy? Ten four." I did not say this, however. I was surprised, though, that he couldn't read it in my tightly controlled expression.

I now felt like a jerk for my impatience yet hugely grateful that I hadn't been in the collision. However, I was getting later by the second and my body was urging me to move along little doggie with the gentle nudging of a tornado.

I asked him if there was another way to Lansing. He got his map. I also called my husband. They got me turned around and I took off out of Ionia, happy to be moving at last.

I sped along and my husband asked which direction I was going. I thought, 'how the heck would I know.' He suggested I look at the bright thing on my dash which tells me. I couldn't find it and I knew that even if I did, it would mean nothing to me. I looked and I looked but found no direction. Then I glanced in my rearview mirror and spotted a letter, S. I was pretty sure this did not mean Michigan State so I told him, "south." He sighed, "You should be going east," but always the encourager, he went on, "That's o.k., just keep going, you're all right."

I knew I was not alright. I still had to go potty, don't you know. He said, "If you see a sign that says left to Lions, go right." I replied, "And if I see a sign that says 'potty here', I will be sure to stop." I could tell by his sigh that he wished he had not picked up the phone call.

My mate suggested I get out the GPS and use it. I complained, "If I do, it will just send me down dumb country roads." He sensibly replied, "You are already on dumb country roads. Use the Garmin."

I got it out. It said low battery and wouldn't turn on. I now began my mantra. It is usually the serenity prayer. Today I adjusted the words to my reality and said over and over. "I don't have to potty. I don't have to potty." I was desperately trying to be serene and desperately trying to figure out where I was. I remembered the phrase, I don't know where I'm going but I'm making good time. It had never been truer. Dirt roads. Dead ends. Roads with no signs. It went on and on and so did I.

I was now reminded of the lady from NASA that drove across country in a diaper. They made such fun of her but I was now beginning to see her side of the story. A friend commented later, "What we need is a pill to relieve our anxiety while we wet our pants." Right on!

At last I saw the most beautiful sign I had ever seen, "Welcome to Portland". I joyfully thought, 'I can potty in Portland. Yeah. Happy days are here again'. I had now nearly forgotten my appointment. I was flirting with disaster, after all.

I took the wrong road in Portland and ended up on the road with no fast food places and no place to potty. Before I knew it, I was on the expressway. Lucky me. I picked up my speed and before long was at my meeting place. I was only 30 minutes late, a miracle.

I rushed in to find I no longer had to potty. All the nagging urges had stopped. I was normal. I was free. All I could think was, 'Bodies are SO stupid!'

This Be Da Truth

Ah, every once in a while, a blast from the past comes in. Recently on my answering machine was a message from Larry. He kindly said he liked my column but wondered if I was ever going to share the traumatic experience he and I had shared. Then he ended the message with lots of chuckling.

Larry and I don't really know each other very much at all. He worked at Meijer forever and I have shopped there forever. That is our relationship. However, on a fateful day in the seventies, we bonded.

We bonded in a way that two people bond when they go through something together that no one else is going through. This is even a deeper bond when no one can really believe what you went through. And Larry and I would both agree, it was unbelievable.

I think Larry retired awhile back and I never see him at Meijer or anywhere else. But a few months ago we ran into each other at the self check-out at Meijer. We looked up, saw each other, started laughing and said, "No one would believe it." We were both still traumatized by our shared experience.

Here's how it played out and I share this with a shout-out. This one's for you, Larry.

It was somewhere in the late seventies. It was a Sunday morning on a lovely spring day. I remember it well.

I had been working on a volunteer project. It was a huge event and had taken all of my time and attention for months. It was the day after the event and I was at Meijer to have some bonding time with my three daughters. They were about 7, 4 and a little one in the baby seat of the grocery cart. We were on a mission. We were going to buy a swing set for them. We were full of excitement and joy.

As we entered the store, I began talking to Larry. There were all kinds of swing sets hanging above the entrance and I was asking him about them. The two little ones were in the cart but Colleen, the 7 year old, was standing at my side. After we had been looking up and talking for a while, Colleen began to pull at my arm, "Mom. Mom. Mom. Mom."

Like any seasoned Mom, I ignored her and kept talking with him about the swings and kept looking up at them. Colleen would not stop. Finally, I told her, "Please don't be rude." As I said this, Larry and I both turned our heads and eyes from the suspended swings down into the area directly in front of our cart. This was directly in front of the main door entrance.

Now what I am about to tell you will sound absurd. You will think I have made this up, but you can't make stuff like this up. You really can't.

Also, you could give lie detector tests to Larry, myself and my three daughters and it would show the same. This be da truth.

What we saw was a very large lady. She was bent over, hands on the ground in front of her. She had dropped a bag of jelly beans and they were scattered all over the floor. Not so odd, right? Just wait.

The odd part happened next. In slow motion, I swear. She was wearing pants with an elastic waist and the elastic must have given out as we looked because they fell completely to the floor and lay like a puddle around her feet.

The really traumatic part was that she had no undergarments on and was as bare as a newborn babe. This was the part facing us. Now one would think that she would have yanked her pants up and run out of the store for dear life, but you would be wrong. Oh, no. She just stayed there, as she was, in all her un-glory and slowly picked up every single jelly bean.

The 5 of us were so very stunned. We stood there with our mouths gaping. My daughter's eyes were nearly popping out of their cute little faces. It was horribly horrible and no one knew what to do. So I looked back up to the swings and asked Larry, "Well, which one do you think is best?"

When the lady got all her beans retrieved, she grabbed up her pants and headed on over to the courtesy counter. Believe me. I swear this is all fact.

And then it happened. Larry and I began to laugh loudly and hysterically and we could not stop. I quickly steered the girls off into the aisles and laughed for so long, so hard that I couldn't get any shopping done. We had to go home and bond another way. I also had to find a way to ease them out of the trauma.

It is now many years later and I would like to say I have recovered but you really don't get over an experience like that. And so forever, Larry and I are bonded through no fault of our own. And the punishment for that is, whenever we see each other, even some thirty years later, we immediately begin to laugh and shake our heads.

So if you ever sit back and say to yourself, "Self, is truth really stranger than fiction?" I say to you, "Yes, my friend, yes it is. Truth is really, really, really stranger than fiction.

This one's for you, Larry. Chuckle. Chuckle.

My Two Black Thumbs

Lies, lies - nothing but lies.

Okay, I'm probably naive. Some would say I'm ignorant. And I am, ignorant of lots of things, that is. I prefer to think I have faith - faith in people, faith in our country . . . and faith in fertilizer companies. Ah, you didn't expect to see country and fertilizer companies together in that sentence, did you?

Kathy Jo and I just took a class together at Aquinas College. In it, we had to list our core values. My top one was honesty. Obviously lying doesn't fit into that category.

So, and I know you are wondering where this is going, when I go to fertilize my beautiful flower pots, I believe. I believe what the label on the fertilizer says. Call me naive. Call me ignorant. Just don't call me late for dinner. Oops, I digress.

Let me backspace here a bit. My flowering pots have been so beautiful this year, you would swear they could not possibly be mine. Mine never look this good. Because of their beauty, I have been basking in the glow of their blooms and loving the praise I've been getting from people walking by.

Because I am wiser than I used to be, I know it is important and time to fertilize my flowers. I learned this lesson the hard way. I also know that fertilizer is easy to use. Just add to water and pour. Oh, be sure to take that foil off the end of the spout. The first year I didn't remove it and had some humiliating and sad experiences. Suffice it to say, I fertilized forever and with gusto and never got any results. If you don't count the guffaws from my fertilizing smarty pants friends who figured out I had never taken off the spout foil. In my defense, I don't think there were any directions to do so. I need to be told every single detail when it comes to this gardening stuff. One should never ever assume that I will figure this stuff out on my own.

In preparation for my simple task, I purchased the fertilizer. I won't say the name because that would not be nice. I'll just say it rhymes with lyrical moe.

I read the label and I thought I read that it said, "No danger of over fertilizing". I loved that idea. I cheered to myself. Now when I think of it, I say to myself, "Hah!" I also say, "Liars!"

Because I hate gardening, I decided to do it in one fell shot. I fertilized all my flowers way more than I ever had before - way, way more. Why not, I thought? Why not make my already beautiful blooms more beautiful-er? I know that isn't a real word, but it was how I was thinking - slightly off base.

After the hearty dose of fertilizer, I added some new dirt, some water and presto - I felt proud. I'd done good, real good.

I left for three days and when I returned, half of my beautiful posies looked like someone had sucked the life out of them. They laid there limp. No more perky blooms. Their green leaves had turned yellow, some even brown. Some had turned crisp, which I didn't think was even an option. They had lost their pizzazz and, basically, given up the fight.

What's a gardener to do? Oh, you think I use that term lightly? Maybe so.

Now, if you can't believe what you read on product labels, what is next? Is someone going to rock my boat further by telling me political ads aren't 100% truthful?

Clearly, though, even I realize the fertilizer label and I had a major communication gap. Either I read it wrong or they printed lies. I am guessing it was them. You keep your guesses to yourself, please.

I have a wonderful woman who comes a bit to help with our unpotted flowers. She is a master gardener and full of exuberance and gusto about gardening. She is my hero. She examined the remains of my catastrophe and told me not to worry. "You haven't actually killed all of them. You just need to have patience and they will come back."

"For heaven's sake," I exclaimed to her, "I'm already 65. I don't have that much time left."

No matter how hard I tried, I just couldn't come up with her kind of optimism. I decided to toss the suckers and go buy new. And then I remembered all the money I had spent on the ones I had killed. Oh, man, that wasn't in my original plan. I needed a new plan, one with a heavy dose of rationalization.

So, in the end (can it be the end if it is only the week of July 4th?), I got rid of all evidence and bought new blooms. Things look lovely again, though not as good as before. I am sad about all the extra money I had to spend, though. But then I remember and am comforted by the fact that I personally gave birth to an attorney. I am thinking and hoping that for a large fee, he might just sue that fertilizer company for me.

If I can get some coin back, then I can go buy more plants and continue my great gardening saga. What is that famous bit of wisdom? Try, try, try again. Maybe that wasn't meant for me and my black thumbs.

Get Your Group On

Telethon, readathon, bikeathon, MoveOn – the list goes on and on and I find it hard to keep up. The latest to hit my world is Groupon. Groupon is going gang-busters across the country. Everyone is on their emails getting daily bargains. It is such a deal. You buy, buy, buy because it is so great, even if you really don't need it now. Someday you might. One never knows.

I don't do things like this on my computer very well. I mean, I hardly do Facebook. I am on Facebook but only look at it every couple of months, which kind of defeats the whole purpose. So, adding Groupon to my routine is just another thing to tend to. If I tended to things daily, I wouldn't have all artificial plants in my home.

But my daughter and nieces were raving about Groupon this and Groupon that. What a deal! What a bargain! Wow! Ya gotta get on the band wagon. So, on I jump.

I sign up for Groupon Grand Rapids. Slick. Not hard at all and I do go to Grand Rapids often so it all made sense. Then I thought I should get on Groupon Greenville too. So I did. Presto! Sometimes I amaze myself at how with it I can be.

I immediately began getting Greenville daily bargains – such fun. I can't figure them out, though. They offer 18 cupcakes from a shop I have never heard of. When did that come to town, I wonder, and how come I have never seen it? Hmmmm. Still no light bulb goes on. My brain lives in a dim light, for sure.

I do notice and wonder at the absurdity that the cupcake store is in South Carolina. I think – don't judge me – that it must be a mail-order bargain put on by a local bakery.

This kind of bargain continues on a daily basis: spa treatments in South Carolina; restaurants in South Carolina; all kinds of Carolina specials. As I said before, hmmmmm, how odd is that?

The light bulb remains dim. I run into my niece, Rachel, and tell her I am on Groupon Greenville. She is amazed as she didn't know Greenville had one. She is excited and rushes home to get on it. She thinks I am mighty slick to have figured this out ahead of her. So do I. Dimness has lots of illusions.

After a couple days, dear Rachel calls me. "Auntie Moe, I think you have joined Groupon in Greenville, South Carolina. "No," I laugh/scream, "No wonder every bargain has to be gotten there! I kept wondering why our city was sending all their potential buyers to South Carolina." As the rest of you are probably saying, "Duh!"

As I always say with life, you don't see what you aren't looking for. I had signed up for Greenville, Michigan, and by golly, that's what I was looking for.

In my measly defense, the Groupon Greenville website never said what state it was in. I rest my measly case. The light gets dimmer.

I finally had to sign off Groupon Greenville. I have never been to South Carolina and have no idea if I'll ever go. I really don't need to know their deals. In the meantime, I wonder to my poor wounded self-esteem and mind, how'd I get so dim and what else is going on right under my nose that is not real but just an illusion in my mind. Perhaps it is better not to know. Reality bites. And . . . it's not always a bargain either!

Just When You Think You've Seen It All

I tell ya – just when you think you've seen it all . . . along comes something to surprise you. Surprise, surprise. That is how I felt when I was reading an English newspaper in Spain. Let me state here and now that it was an upstanding newspaper. It was full of world news and all that good kinda stuff. Then, as I was hardly even glancing at the last couple pages, which of course were just classified ads, an add leapt out at me.

Yes, it leapt out. It had some extra border on it and it was black background with white print so it set itself apart from all the rest of the ads. The headline was bolder and larger than the other ads and it read,"Nude Housekeeping". Say what? Did I read that right? Could that be possible? Right here in this normal newspaper. Right here for all the world to see. Yepper. It was right there.

I know ladies who do housekeeping as a career. They don't do it nude. When they want to market their business, they do different creative things for promotion. Perhaps a clever ad or a discount. One takes people banana bread as a friendly gesture.

This whole idea brings up so many thoughts. How do they get from the car to the house? What if they get stopped for speeding? Would they take the bus or a taxi or a bike? They couldn't walk to work. Could they? These visuals are too much. Way too much!

I wondered. Would you still need an apron? Should you wear a belt to hold rags or your tools?

I am sure this ad was placed by a woman. A man might place it, but probably wouldn't have many takers. Likely the excitement this would bring to a woman would only be the excitement of the house cleaning being done . . . by anyone other than herself. What the house cleaner was wearing or not wearing would not matter one bit.

I thought of the problem that the vacuum cleaner could present. There would be too many things that could get sucked into the machine. It for sure would give new meaning to the phrase, "This job sucks." There would also be the danger of drawers and cupboards slamming shut. Yowser!

This whole idea seems quite absurd, yet there it was in black and white. I am thinking this could be a cover story in that magazine, "Bad Housekeeping". Isn't that the rival of *Good Housekeeping*? It may have a higher circulation than the one we know of. More people can relate to it, after all.

Do you think hiring a nude housekeeper would be a one-time thing? I mean, housekeeping never ends. As Joan Rivers says, "You make the beds, you do the dishes, and six months later you have to start all over again." It's never-ending.

And, thinking about housekeeping made me think of that famous comment by Zsa Zsa Gabor. "I am a marvelous housekeeper. Every time I leave a man I keep his house." She has been married nine times.

Yes, this is all too much to imagine. And it proves one thing to me, for sure. I gotta be more discerning about reading the paper. Who knew it could be so wild?

Should You Or Should You NOT . . . Take Your Dog To The Movie

My husband and I gave ourselves a treat. We went to see the film, The Help. We, along with many of you, read the book and loved it. We were thrilled that the movie was even better than the book. How rare is that! We highly recommend it.

What we do not recommend is taking your dog to see it. I mean, who would? So, here is what you need to be careful of. That is, if you are considering taking your dog.

If your dog gets all freaked out in storms, you might want to leave him home with his bone. The movie has a long sequence of lightning, thunder and rain. I'm just saying. If your dog has seizures, you might not want to take him. It is quite hard to handle a dog having a seizure while he is hidden, especially if he moans at the beginning of the seizure. Of course, you could act like it is you moaning, but then you have to deal with that.

If your dog gets hot and pants a lot loudly, you might not want to take him. Of course, you could pretend it is your mate panting. That, too, has its problems. Add that to the moaning and you could get thrown out on your ear, or rear.

And, one more thing, if your dog has recently begun to bark like a seal, that could be another problem. Even if your kind mate begins to cough a lot during the seal like bark/coughs, it is hard to have them sound like normal human sounds. They kinda end up sounding like a guy fake coughing to cover up a dog coughing like a seal bark. Then again, who would expect such a thing in a movie, so it might work for ya. But, if the man two rows up turns around and gawks, that could be another problem. And this could be even more of a problem if this seal like bark/cough happens in several bouts during the film. Yeah, it would be a good idea to leave rover at home.

Now, of course, this is all silliness. No one takes a dog to the movie. But, just in case you are considering it, you might want to get "the help" first. That would be psychiatric help, of course.

Mulligan Burns

But, then again, I think he liked the movie.

I'm No Loser

I swear to you, I am not a loser. I just lose things once in awhile, not every day or week, not all the time, just occasionally. But when I do, boy oh boy, it drives me wacko. Someone said, "Show me a good loser and I'll show you a loser." Leo Durocher said, "Show me a good loser and I'll show you an idiot." I don't like either of them. I like Bill Lyon just a bit better. He said, "If at first you don't succeed, find out if the loser gets anything." I'm pretty sure he wasn't talking about the same kind of loser I am, but at least his thought is promising.

This morning I asked my friend, Pat, if she ever loses anything, like keys, for instance. She said, "No, never." I'm not sure we can still be good friends. I'm not sure she can really understand someone like me. And I can't really understand anyone who never loses anything.

Let's see. The list of things I lose is long. I lose shoes. I run around, always in a frantic state as I am about to go somewhere. I can't find the dang shoes anyplace. Where did I take them off? That could be anywhere in the entire house. They could be under the table, under the desk, by the door, in the closet, in the kitchen. The list goes on and on. In all our years of marital bliss, I am quite sure my husband has never lost his shoes. They are always in one of two places – on his feet or where they belong. How crazy is that? Once I found mine where they belong and it was absolutely shocking to me. I never look there!

I lose my glasses. I need my glasses to see just about everything, so when I lose them, I can't see to find them. Life is so hard for folks like me.

I often hear people say they have lost their cell phones. I don't do that, but I do lose the many portable phones we have in our house. The phone rings and we yell, "Where's the phone?" It keeps on ringing and I keep on yelling and looking. When I do find it, I am always delighted to have it be a political call or courtesy call. Courtesy to whom, I wonder? And my political persuasion never seems to ringy ding me. Slamming the receiver down always seems like a great way to end those kinds of calls. At least I like the feeling. Hummmpf! That is if I find the phone in time.

I lose recipes often. I keep them in a bushel basket filled to the brim. It is one of my many to do projects that I never actually do. Someone said, "Why do you bother to look? You can find any recipe you want on the internet." I look and look and look because I want my old favorite recipes and nothing else will do. One of my very favorites I lost forever. It has been years and I have given up the dream of finding it. It was for my Spanish Risotto, just in case a miracle happens and some reader has it and can send it on to me. I believe in miracles so I gotta keep the faith, don't you know.

I lose shopping lists. I spend lots of time figuring out what I am going to make, what I need to buy, what I have already. I make my list. I check it twice. I look around for who's naughty or nice – nah, that ain't it. But I high tail it to Meijer to buy, buy, buy and when I get in the door and grab my cart, I can't find the darn list. I call my husband, but of course, he can't find the phone. So I'm left to fend for myself with my feeble memory. That is never a good thing.

Ever since we moved to the lake, we lose our electricity quite often. At least I can't be blamed for that.

Perhaps I'm not really a loser, after all. I don't want to lose things. It really wastes my time and my already fading energy. It really adds to my stress level.

There are things I never ever lose, though. Things like weight, wrinkles, aches. You get the picture. It ain't pretty, I tell ya.

So, here I am. I lose things I don't want to lose. I can't lose things I do want to lose. What's a gal to do??

My daughter called me with a quote we love. "People aren't born winners. People aren't born losers. They're born choosers."

Yeah, right. I'm pretty sure if I choose to not lose things anymore, I'm still gonna lose 'em. As Lady Gaga sings, "Baby, I was born this way!"

And that reminds me of that great Mark Twain quote. "Of all the things I've lost, I think I miss my mind the most." He gets me, that Mark. I really gotta find that mind of mine soon. I'm gonna look as soon as I find my glasses and my shoes and my keys ...

Oops

Years ago we had friends visit from Grand Rapids. I remember I returned into the room after a bathroom break and my beautiful, always looking perfect friend said, "You've got something on your foot." I looked down and to my chagrin was a very long strip of toilet paper. Sigh. Dang. Oops.

As Tartakower said, "The mistakes are all there waiting to be made." Many of us have oops experiences. They shame us. They give us pause. If we are lucky, they make us laugh.

I am a tearer. Not a holy tearer, but a magazine tearer. I tear out snippets guaranteed to improve my life; help my house stay clean; ideas on fashion, aging, health,; movies to see, books to read; how to keep my marriage happenin'. The list goes on and on. You might think that with all this helpful hint info, I would have it all together by now. That would show you don't know me.

Unfortunately, my children, in spite of their preventative measures, have turned out more like me than they wish. My daughter, Donna, has also turned into a tearer.

She called the other day and kind of whined. "I had this thing I tore out of a magazine. It said to take the water I boil my vegetables in and put it in my plants and that they would thrive from all the wonderful nutrients. I finally remembered to do it. I cooked broccoli. Oops. You know how broccoli makes your house smell? When I returned from work, my whole house smelled nasty. I have no way to get it out because it is in all the soil." Shouldn't the magazine writers have kindly mentioned vegetables you might not want to use?

I began to do some investigative work looking for other peoples oops moments.

Yesterday after water aerobics class, one gal realized she had forgotten her bra. Oops. Turned out this is not an uncommon practice. Women often forgot their underwear at class and have to leave commando. Yesterday, though, another woman had an extra bra in her bag and saved the day. What I wonder is, why does anyone carry around an extra bra?

During this scenario, another member was looking for the bathing suit she had just removed. We all turned into instant detectives. We discovered another lady had taken the suit home along with her own. Oops. As I went to leave, I asked. "Has anybody seen my glasses?"

"They're hanging from the front of your shirt." Oops.

Someone once said, "Experience teaches you to recognize a mistake when you've made it again."

My friend, Carol, lost her glasses. Finally, she noticed a thing front and center in her refrigerator - her glasses. Her husband had put them there for her to find but she had never noticed as she hauled food in and out for days. Oops.

Holly and I both have had oops moments putting in way too much of the wrong ingredient into our batches of chili. I am sure lots of you have done these kinds of oops, right? Say yes, please.

Yesterday I wasn't paying much attention to what I was doing. I was at my desk and grabbed the lip balm to put some on. At the last possible moment I realized it was not lip balm. It was a glue stick. Nasty. Uwwwww.

Barbie just had a painter forget about the open can of brown paint on her ladder. He moved the ladder and dumped brown paint all over her carpet and walls. Oops. Yuck. Call the stain squad.

Elaine came into the house and left her car running in the garage for an hour. Likewise, my husband left our car running and unlocked during an entire Pistons game at the Palace. Oops. Multi tasking can be such a burden.

Men get a break in the oops department. Red Skelton said, "All men make mistakes, but married men find out about them sooner."

Sending emails to the wrong person can be major oops.

My friend, name withheld because of her self-esteem, was asked if she was pregnant when she wasn't. I have been in that boat, sister. Oops. This goes along with people who ask if you are someone's grandparent, when you are the parent; asking if you are the oldest, when you are the youngest; asking if you are the parent, when you are the girlfriend.

My aunt just told me I was too old to dye my hair this dark. I told her, "I may be too old, but I don't dye my hair." She replied, "Oh, and I was just thinking you needed a touch up." Oops.

Beth had one that made me laugh out loud. She has ordered food at a drive-thru and driven home without stopping at the second window to collect it. Oops. That would never happen to me. I never forget my food.

Sally McDonald looked all over for her slacks one morning and couldn't find them. At last she realized she was wearing them. Oops.

My daughter may have the best (or worst) oops of all. Halloween week her office group decided to dress up in costumes. She went as "herself at night". She wore her pajamas, her slippers and was armed with her T.V. remote and her current Oprah Magazine. She thought her costume was funny but had no idea how funny. On Thursday when she got to work, she realized the costume day was Friday. She was the only one dressed up like a goofball and had to stay that way all day, meetings and all. Yup, she gets the award, for sure!

So, here's to all of us oops people. George Bernard Shaw said, "A life spent making mistakes is not only more honorable but more useful than a life spent doing nothing." I like that much better than Robert Byrne who said, "To err is human and stupid."

Sharing Silliness And Snickers

I read the whole Harry Potter series and saw the movies. Many of you did too, I'm sure. I felt I had to do it because I needed to stay current. So, when I read a quote by Ellen Degeneres last week, it made me laugh out loud and want to share it with others. Ellen said, "I can't believe this is the last Harry Potter movie. It's the end of an era. Who knows, maybe someone will turn it into a book."

That kind of humor that comes out of nowhere and is just darn silly – well, it's golden. We all need it and we need to share it when we hear it.

For many, many years, I have done a Christmas letter that is mostly cartoons. I search for cartoons all year. Some years are bountiful, some not so much.

I'm sure that some get our letter and think, 'How irreverent!' Some likely don't even read it. (I need their names so I can cut them from the list.) It is getting, though, that people thank us for it. They say how hard and serious their daily lives are and how very much they need that ridiculous, silly collection of humor.

I have decided to share a few with you. Granted, they lose something without the artwork, but, hey, try and visualize. You can, hopefully, still get a chuckle out of them. If you do, be sure and share it that with someone else who needs a laugh.

A dog is in a store, looking at a display of aroma therapy candles. The candles are all colors and sizes and are displayed on shelves. Each candle is of a dog's butt.

A nurse calls a patient into the doctor's office and says, "The doctor will see you now. Please try not to upset him with all your medical problems." Another doctor is in with a patient who is sitting on the table. The patient has one leg on a stool. The doc says to him, "Have you tried limping?"

Another doc says to his patient, "Your insurance won't pay for an expensive procedure, so we'll be doing your colonoscopy with my cell phone camera."

We are all aware of the new meager services that the airlines now offer. A stewardess is reciting her spiel to the passengers and says, "In case of cabin pressure, oxygen masks will drop down in front of you for two dollars." I expect that may be a reality anytime soon. Another is of a passenger at the ticket counter. The clerk says to him, "I'm sorry, sir, but all of your frequent-flier miles have already been used up by your lost luggage."

A wife spouts off to her husband, "While you're renting the wallpaper stripper, the cutter and the floor sander, ask about renting someone who knows what he's doing." Aha.

A parent says to his child, "Go to bed and I'll text you a story."

One rings true at our house. The parent calls their grown kid for help. "Hello, Bob? It's your father again. I have another question about my new computer. Can I tape a movie from the cable TV, then fax it from my VCR to my CD-ROM, then E-mail it to my brother's cellular phone so he can make a copy on his neighbor's camcorder?" We have actually had discussions that feel like this. Somehow, the kids always have to go and refer us to someone else, or even worse, the manual.

A guy is in a job interview and the interviewer says to him, "It says here you're intelligent, honest and reliable. What makes you think you'd be an asset to this company?"

As I go through past Christmas letters, I realize how cartoons are really a sign of the times. What was funny ten years ago, isn't necessarily funny today. An example of one relevant today, but not necessarily funny years ago, is a woman who says of her husband, "Sean can say, 'I'm unemployed in seven languages.' "

The other day a friend asked me if I wanted to take a concealed weapons class with her. I said, "Are you nuts? The last thing I need is a gun. I'm sure I'd shoot myself, or even worse, my dog or my husband." One cartoon is a gun store salesman holding a rifle. He says to the customer, "O.K., but let's say you have up to 600 intruders per minute." Yeah, for sure.

And what good joke collection would be good without something on aging? One I relate to, "I guess I never realized that growing old was such a big part of the aging process." A guy shares, "I'm at that awkward age – I can't decide whether to get a hearing aid or an earring."

And I guess I'll close with one which is way too close to home. A couple is standing in the kitchen. She's cooking. They both have a glass of wine. The man says, "If they don't show up, I'll have to admit I forgot to invite them." Sigh. I suppose the thing that makes us laugh at cartoons is that they mirror our lives. We might as well laugh. It's too painful to cry.

To Look Or Not To Look

A comedian I really enjoy is Rita Rudner. She wrote a book called, *Naked Beneath My Clothes*. Aren't we all?

Last week I had an unusual experience. We were in Spain with two of our daughters. One day we went to the most beautiful beach on the Bay of Biscay, a glorious spot touted as one of the best beaches in Europe.

When I got there, the rest of my family was already settled in, basking in the nearly 100 degree sun. The beach was wall to wall beach towels covered with people. Occasionally there was a beach chair. It was full of men and women of all ages, all sizes and shapes. This, then, is how I experienced it, voyeuristically, or as I prefer to think of it, as a writer. When I think of it that way, it helps me feel less shame.

Everywhere I looked I saw them – all sizes, all states of skin elasticity, all ages. Nearly everyone I saw was topless. What I didn't see were any signs to warn folks. It was obvious this was normal there. No one was uncomfortable except me, the American gawker. I couldn't stop myself.

I have been to beaches before where women were topless. I just have never been to a beach where almost every woman was topless.

Toddlers were playing naked in the sand. Oh, did I say they were naked? They really weren't. They were wearing hats.

Next to us was a woman lying asleep on her back, mouth open, tatas saluting the sun. Well, in reality, it wasn't much of a salute. It was more of a low bow or a shrug.

She did not stand out. We stood out. We did not belong. I estimated there were a couple thousand bathers on this very crowded beach. I was quite sure, as I examined all I could examine within my vision field, that we were the only women not in bikinis. Oh, there could have been another one piece bathing suit, maybe, perhaps . . . but mine was definitely the only one with a skirt. Women only wear suits with skirts to hide things, things we don't want the world to see, things we don't want to see ourselves. Obviously this is not a European concept. No one there was hiding anything. We so didn't belong.

I think back on my life. I have only seen the "girls" set free like this in the shower in high school gym class. I remember, with a sick feeling in my stomach, how a classmate slipped and fell coming out of the shower. She laid there on the floor, on her back, naked as a jay bird. (Why do we say that phrase? Don't jay birds wear feathers?) We all gawked silently. No one would touch her or offer help. I am pretty sure we were all thinking the same thing, 'Oh, my God, that could have been me. I'd rather die.'

But I digress. It was so very, very hot at the beach that we went into the water. As I walked out, young women passed me. They were out for their morning beach stroll, walking and talking with friends, moving right along at a fast pace. They were all just wearing bikini bottoms. I tried so hard to act like I saw this all the time, but I failed.

The other shocker for me was that women changed their clothes on the beach, right there in front of God and everybody. They took their bras off. They put their bras on. They took their bottoms off and put other bottoms back on. No one blinked an eye, except for you know who.

I think when folks think about going to a topless beach, they think perky thoughts. They imagine the bodies will be young and like models in magazines. All I can say after being there and witnessing this is, "Hah!" Reality is not always pretty or perky.

I saw another thing I have never seen before. Two men wearing T-shirts emblazoned with a red cross pushed a woman in a beach wheel chair through the sand out into the water. When they got out a ways, they dumped her into the water where she immediately began to swim. After a long time, they reversed this and she was able to lie in her beach wheelchair in the sun to bask in the rays. How wonderful that must have felt to the lady in the wheelchair. Why have I never seen anything like that before?

Sometimes we Americans make the mistake of thinking our world is the world. It is so clearly not. There are many ways of living life and many ways of enjoying a day at the beach.

Really? Really?

In December we took our grandsons to see The Nutcracker ballet. It was little Louie's first time to see the whole very long show. He had just turned 5. After about eight minutes, he whispered to me, "Nina, when do they talk at ballet?"

I hated to tell him. I knew it would be hard to imagine, but I said, " They don't talk at ballet." His big blue eyes got bigger and without words he gave me a look - Really? Really?

At Christmas we gave our grandsons super hero capes with their names on. The boys loved them. They immediately put them on and began playing. All the adults were busy talking and basically ignoring the super heroes.

All of a sudden we heard a huge bang/crash/boom. We couldn't see anything. And then Louie, from a heap on the floor, uttered quietly to himself, "Ugh, I sought I could fly!" Really?

I asked others for their "Really?" moments.

Gayle read in the newspaper about the Amish house fire. "The cause of the fire is under investigation but electrical problems have been ruled out." Really?

Dan said, "When I see a billboard and TV ads for casinos, they show the clientele as young, attractive, well-dressed and ecstatic with their casino experience. When I go, all I see are a bunch of baggy-eyed baby boomers dressed in sweat pants and sweatshirts smoking cigarettes, sometimes even dragging oxygen along behind them. I know many of them are spending their rent and grocery money. The next time you see one of those ads, think - Really?"

Hollie saw a guy at the play, The Sound of Music. He was wearing a T-shirt that said,

"SEX", in letters about 8 inches high. Below it said, "One of us is thinking about it. OK, it's me." Everyone looked at him and thought - Really?

She also said there is an SUV that drops kids off to her school. It has a giant logo across the back window that says, "Boobies make me smile." Really?

In the last couple of weeks, I have had about 5 letters from people I know who have been stranded in Europe and need me to send them a lot of money quick. Do people really fall for this stuff? Really? I just got one from a friend who is in Florida. He wrote and apologized and said said that had been a bogus letter. I replied, "Oh, darn, and I just sent you a big bunch of money!"

Beth said, "When I go to a drive-thru restaurant, order, pay and then drive on home without collecting my order, I say to myself - Really?"

Cheryl recently ordered french fries at a restaurant The young waitress told her they didn't have french fries. Cheryl was confused. Then someone in the kitchen yelled out, "She means fries." Really?

Alison works at a court house in San Diego. "When I see people going to court, waiting to go through the metal detectors and they are wearing wife-beater T-shirts and baggie pants or flip flops, very, very hot pants and short belly shirts, I think - Really? One guy even had bare feet! You gotta love California."

Beth was subbing at a school. A student came up and asked, "Will you help me with the deer orgasm?" She tried to contain herself and thought - Really? The child meant organism.

Harriette sent me this. "I've just heard from a friend in northern Wyoming. He says it has been snowing heavily for three days now. His wife has done nothing but stare through the window. If it doesn't stop soon, he'll probably have to let her in." Really? Nah!

Where North Is?

I know she hates me. I mean you can tell when someone doesn't like you. It's so obvious. Her tone is always cold, emotionless - never a smile in her voice. I don't know what she's got against me but it's clear, we're not friends, just mere acquaintances. She has to deal with me. She doesn't choose to.

On top of her rude attitude, she acts like I'm stupid. And she repeats herself over and over and over – like I am too dumb to understand what she is saying.

I am talking about my GPS navigational device, of course. My husband calls her Sally. I don't know why. I don't call her anything, except irritating. And I don't trust her either. Oh, yes, sometimes she gets me right where I need to go and makes it seem easy. But there are other times she screws it all up and leaves me fumbling. My friend, Diana, says sometimes when hers starts in she just says to it, "Liar".

Now I'm gonna come clean here. I have a serious handicap. I am directionally challenged. And I mean completely challenged. When I was put together, they did something wrong inside of me, all wrong. Whatever direction I feel I should go in is always, always, always completely wrong. You can bet your sweet bippy on it.

I get to a dead end. I know deep inside me I should turn left, so of course, I turn right as my internal system is 100 % wrong, each and every time.

My family knows this to be true but they still laugh at me. That's no way to treat someone with a problem.

I don't think counseling would help, nor medication. I am just plain up a creek without a paddle when it comes to a true sense of direction. And, as life would have it, my mate has one that is never wrong. He thinks direction. He has this weird thing where he always has to know which way is North. I have never given one thought to where north is in my whole life. I could live the rest of my days without ever thinking about it or caring.

We will land by plane in a new town and he will ask the first person he sees, "Which way is North?" I think, are ya kiddin' me? I swear that thought would never cross my brain. I mean, who gives a rip? Why would anyone care? North, South, East, West – they are such enigmas.

When I have to think North in Greenville, I mentally have to go back to Grand Rapids and think it through from there. When I lived in Grand Rapids, for some odd reason, I really did know North, South, East and West. It was so easy. But never after that.

I know we lived in East Lansing, because it was called East Lansing. When people would ask what part of Spain we lived in, I would reply, "middle". North, South, East, West was never on my radar.

There are others who have problems with their GPS ladies. When David Letterman had his "problem", he said even his navigation lady wasn't speaking to him. Last summer in a heat wave he said that on the way home from work she said to him, "Hey, wanna stop for a beer?" At least they have a relationship.

I think it is irritating to hear the same voice all the time. And why is she a woman? Perhaps it would work better if it was a man. It could be a pirate. "Hey, matey, turn this vessel around." Kinda cute.

Perhaps a voice like Sean Connery would be nice. I wouldn't want to have it sound like Woody Allen. Nah, that wouldn't ease me on down the road very well. Perhaps a jersey accent. "You lookin' at me? Turn left before I bust your chops." Kind of a *Sopranos* thing.

Or what about a breathy Marilyn Monroe voice. "Happy Birthday, Mr. President. Oh, it's not your birthday and you're not a president? Well, turn left anyway."

I guess any other voice would do. Just not the one I have. I swear mine gives me a big disgusted sigh and sarcastically chides me with, "Recalculating. Recalculating."

As a person who has an internal system which says, "You are here. Now what?" I clearly need help.

Perhaps I just need a new navigational device. One with a better attitude. One who wants to be my friend and not so darn bossy all the time. Yeah, I am thinking that if I can just get her some relationship counseling, we might be able to work this thing out. But I don't think I will ever give a rip about where North is.

Airport Security Angst

"Put your arms straight to the side and spread 'em. Stand still. Sit down. Put your legs out straight and hold them up". That's what I hear each time I fly. That's what I hear as they wand me over. Beep, beep, beep goes the chain around my neck. Beep, beep, beep goes my underwire. Beep, beep, beep go my artificial knees.

I admit I set off the beeper each time I go through security because my knees are both made of titanium. The knee doc gave me a card to carry through airport security. I don't bother. I tried it once and they nearly laughed in my face. Now I no longer carry it. It's worthless. They put me through their paces anyway.

I joked once when they were running the wand all over me. "Do I look like a terrorist?" I made some other witty remark. I thought it was witty. They clearly did not. I no longer joke around. I know it could land me in some interrogation room behind closed doors. And I am pretty sure they wouldn't hold my flight.

I flew to Arizona a couple of weeks ago. As the lady wanded me, (Is that a verb? It's gotta be a new one.) she gave me some warning advice. "The next time you fly be prepared for a *real* pat-down." I gulped and thought she was joking, though she did not look or act like a jokester.

"The new security measures are going into effect and we will be doing hands on pat-downs. I'm just warning you."

I didn't think about it again until I read in the newspaper this week that pat-downs have become reality for airline travelers.

What does this mean? The security folks can now pat-down your breasts and genitals. That's what it means. Is this necessary, I wonder? Really? Really? Come on. Say it ain't so.

I don't think I like this. But then I remember the underpants bomber who tried to blow up a plane full of people one Christmas. I swear, those goofballs ruin it for everyone.

First they stuck bombs in their shoes. Now we all have to take our shoes off to go through security. Okay, we can live with that. But now we are pushed to a new limit of endurance and one that really touches on our personal boundaries and modesty.

We are guaranteed that we will be groped, I mean searched, by guards of our same gender. Oh, that makes me feel a bit better, but not much. What it sounds like, what it reads like, what sense it makes – none of those compare to the way we feel when someone actually gropes us. One traveler said, "It is unnerving to have someone touching you in private places in full public view." I am pretty sure they are right.

What's next? Will there be canines waiting to sniff our parts to be sure we don't have weapons stuck between our cheeks – and I don't mean facial?

Wasn't it Nancy Reagan who promoted the Just Say No philosophy? I wonder if that would work as we go through security. No, thank you, I'd rather not. No, but I appreciate your asking. No way. No how. Did you hear me? I said NO. I don't want to. Not today. Not tomorrow. Not ever. Perhaps I'll take a train instead.

TSA spokesman Nicholas Kimball says, "We look to ensure people's privacy while ensuring the skies are safe." Well, we do want safe skies.

TSA goes on. "Passengers should continue to expect an unpredictable mix of security layers that include explosives trace detection, advanced imaging technology, canine teams, among others."

So I guess my joke about dogs sniffing our buttocks isn't that much of a joke. My friend, Rob, laughed, "Soon we will be going to the airport in boxers and flip flops to save time."

Well, folks, be prepared. Here comes more of the new normal. I haven't had a pat-down yet at the airport, but I can see it in my future. Those darn titanium knees just won't be silenced. Beep. Beep. Beep.

Me thinks the holiday is about to be taken out of holiday travel.

A Lesson From The Greeks

So, we are driving in silence on our way to a Tigers baseball game. We are in a bit of a snit. (Oh, puleese, don't pretend you have never had one of those.) We are listening to the news on National Public Radio. They are talking about the financial and political problems in Greece. They discuss the angry protesters and how they … I swear - they really said this. The protesters were so angry they "pummeled the politicians with yogurt."

We looked at each other and began to laugh like fools. I said, "Did they just say that they pummeled them with yogurt?"

"Yep," my husband replied. This was not good for our snit because by the time we got done laughing, we couldn't remember why we were "snitting". I know that isn't a word but it should be.

Pummeling politicians with yogurt - those Greeks, what will they think of next! First tragedy, then olives, then feta cheese. I gotta say, they're a creative bunch.

Of course, I am sure the protesters used Greek yogurt. It has a lot more substance (let alone all the extra protein) and would certainly allow one to hit a target more easily. And after all, they were in Greece. You know the old line, when in Greece do what the Greeks do – or something like that.

Remember when Rupert Murdoch got hit with a whipped cream pie as he sat in an English court? An angry woman just couldn't take it anymore. Those Brits! They try, but they are just not quite as creative as those Greeks.

Americans – we are just plain uncreative. When we think in terms of weaponry we go for guns and stuff. We never even consider the very viable option of food.

As I think back to TV shows and movies, I remember there has been some throwing of food and drink. In *Glee* someone throws a big red slushie on a girl. In *Smash* a woman tosses a drink on her ex-husband every time she sees him in a bar. In a movie, Dolly Parton and Queen Latifah get into a big food fight about the Lord or something. Does anyone remember the big food fight in *Animal House*?

Once, when we were newlyweds, we had a minor Jello fight. It was more like a very minor Jello toss. But, I gotta say, it was fun and made for a lasting memory. Have you had any food fights? Is it on your bucket list? Grocery list?

Thinking about using food as weapons makes me consider which foods would work best. Personally, I don't think yogurt is a good weapon. I think celery or a big ole carrot would be better, especially if you were close enough to whack 'em. A nice Spanish onion would make a good thing to whap someone with from afar. And, it might make them cry.

There is a real playfulness that comes to mind when you think of pummeling someone with yogurt. Playful protesting, who'd a thunk?

When one is pummeled with yogurt or hit with a cream pie, is it okay to lick yourself? I'm just wondering. I mean, who writes the etiquette for this stuff.

I also wonder how much yogurt would one need to pummel a group of people? How much would it take to get your point across or to have others even notice?

How would you get all this yogurt to the protest site? Do you need a gigantic spoon or something to whip it, whip it real good? Wouldn't you be just a little tempted to just sit down and eat it?

I also think that just the actual word pummel is a funny word. I mean, how often do you use it, let alone do it? When we think of the word pummel, taking for granted that you do this in your spare thought time, we think of it differently. We think of pummeling with rocks or stones. We think of being pummeled with hail in a storm. Never ever, not even once, have I thought of being pummeled with yogurt. Yesiree, that is really way too much for me to stomach.

What Would Yours Say?

There is a phrase I say often. My husband says it will likely be on my tombstone. "Dang, I didn't realize it was this late."

I use this phrase on Sundays when it is time to go to church. That is why we are usually one of the last people to get to Mass. It is never my husband's fault. It is always my fault. I always try to do one more thing. That is one of my big downfalls, however I do have many others.

I also use this phrase whenever I am due to go or do almost anything. It seems my days are just never long enough. I always need a bit more time, just a few more minutes. Is that too much to ask?

Lately, though, my husband says I have a new phrase that may rival the above one for my tombstone epitaph. "Boy, I sure am tired." If I am honest, I have to admit I usually don't lead these remarks with dang or boy. It's a bit stronger. Whatever.

My Grandma, Anne Empey, always joked that her tombstone would say, "I was going to start dieting tomorrow."

Have you given any thought to what yours might say? Perhaps you haven't, but maybe you are like me and others have done it for you.

Most of us have heard about the actual tombstone in Georgia which reads, "I told you I was sick."

I read some other funny ones. "Ima Goner." "This will be you one day." "I may be dead, but you're ugly."

Attorney John Goemble, 1867 – 1946, had "The defense rests" on his tombstone.

A dentist's is reported to read, "John Brown is filling his last cavity."

Another read, "He called Bill Smith a liar."

Auctioneer, Jed Goodwin, 1828 to 1976, lies under the reading, "Going! Going!! Gone!!!"

Carol read an obituary that said, "Missed by his wife, children, lover and friends". She thought it might have been a politician. Not one we know, of course, but one of those guys we hear about on the news.

Don said he wants to put "no loitering" on his tombstone. Jim said his sister always said she wanted a picnic table placed over her grave and her tombstone to read, "Have lunch on me." How cute is that?

Judy told me a friend said hers should read, "Don't hold her place in line. She ain't never been on time."

Pam, a former Ionia prison warden, saw this one. "Half the lies told by my opponents were not true." That brings to mind election ads, eh?

Pastor Jerry said he'd heard of one which read, "Waiting here for further instructions." He also reiterated one which said, "Here lies Lester Moore. Two shots from a .44. No Les . . . No Moore."

My very dear friend, Nelda Cushman, died a couple years ago. She always had the best sense of humor. Her son, Brent, wrote me that when she was nearing death, she suggested a few ideas for her tombstone. "Step back. You're on my hair." "My biggest regret was that my credit card wasn't maxed out." "Since you're reading this, you're off my ____ list!" "I had twice as many friends and half as many lovers as I deserved." "Thanks for visiting. Now go home and do something!" No wonder I still really, really miss her.

This is a motley mess but, hopefully, it amused you and gave you some good ideas. What would yours say?

A Little Silliness Along The Way

I hear a lot. I read a lot. I get some funny things that way. They don't always fit with a theme, but they do if the theme is fun. So, today I am just going to share some of the random unrelated fun things I have collected in the last couple of months.

My friend, Gary, once was talking to a young woman he worked with. He was mentioning Gene Autry. The gal gave him a confused look and asked, "Who's she?"

Gary's wife told me that when they visit his Mom, a super cool 91 year old, she always tells people, "The kids are coming." The kids are close to seventy. It's all about perspective.

My friend, Sharon, and I were with friends at lunch. We were discussing finances. She said, "When my husband goes, I'm just writing checks. When the money's gone, it's gone." We had a good laugh over that.

My grandsons keep making us laugh. The other day I had Nina Camp. They call me Nina and we have camp here every summer. I took the 4 year olds hand as we crossed the street. He said, "Why do we have to always hold hands? I'm so tired of it!"

The boys spent the night recently at their Aunt Donnas. Danny is six and he said, "Auntie Donna, I came tonight because I really love you." His brother, Louie, who is four, said, "I came because I go wherever he goes." Louie also says things are "usgusting". I will miss it when he learns to say it right. That will be disgusting to me.

My friend, Maureen, told me her Emma, who is five, was making a wish because she got an eyelash on her finger and got to wish as she blew it off. Emma said, "I wish everything could be my way." Don't we all, Emma? Don't we all?

I can't remember who told me their little one is in the process of putting it all together and asked, "Mommy, what mean language?" She couldn't figure out what the word meant. Kids are so precious.

A young Grand Rapids teacher recently shared that parenting wasn't what she had expected. "I didn't think I would have to tell them, 'Don't lick the table.' 'Don't highlight your teeth.', 'Don't put permanent marker on your eye lids.' "

Another teacher in Grand Rapids has a second grader. When she asked her how second grade was going, the little girl replied, "Good. There are a lot of hot guys."

Louie, my grandson, is in kindergarten and got his first homework assignment. It asked, "What do you want to learn in Kindergarten?" His brother had written "to read" when he had this assignment. Lou wrote, "To fly." God speed, Louie, God speed. Lesson to be learned – you don't always get what you want.

Julie was telling me the other day that her big lab, Reggie, is gifted. She didn't actually say gifted, but that is my observation after her tale. She and Don had eaten some of a pizza. When done, they put it in the box in their oven and closed the door. They left home for a while. When they returned they took note that the oven door was closed and thought Reggie had been a good boy. However, when they got into the living room, there was the pizza box torn up and the pizza all eaten. Reggie had stood up, opened the oven, took out the pizza and then closed the door to cover his tracks. She said he can also open the microwave and would turn it on with a quick lesson. There must be a reality show waiting for Reggie to show up.

Of course, my fun list wouldn't be complete without one from David Letterman. When Obama was having trouble with General McChrystal, Letterman quipped. "Obama is having trouble with his generals. But, remember, Clinton always had trouble with his privates."

I recently read a quote by Groucho Marx. He was having surgery and asked, "Will I be able to play the piano after surgery?" They told him, "Yes." He relied with glee, 'Great, cuz I can't play now."

I also read a quote from Harry Truman. Now, this may offend you, but remember, it was said by the President of the United States. I am just the conduit. Don't blame me. However, there is a good lesson in it for all of us, especially in extremely hot days. He said, "Never kick a fresh turd on a hot day." I have to agree with his wisdom. You would be wise to also.

I have a scrap of paper on which I wrote another bit of wisdom. I forgot to write down who said it to me, but I remember them well, kind of. I might later. I might not. But, their quote is so wise. "Nobody said this life should be serious." And on that, I will end. Keep laughing, folks. It's so good for you.

I'm Just Wonderin'

Some weeks are profound. Some weeks are clearly not. At least that is the way my mind sees them. In the past week, I have been wondering about a few things. Yes, they don't seem to follow any normal pattern, but normal has never been my strong suit.

I went away last week and my husband stayed home with the gifted dog. My husband told me when I returned that the week had gone well. The dog ate on time. The dog went out on time. The bed got made on time. Yadayada. Routine is not my strong suit either, so this was clearly a new day dawning at our house.

I left lots of food for my husband. I wanted to make sure he was taken care of when I was gone. I baked cookies. I bought and had at the ready all kinds of quick meats to eat, macaroni salad, soup, etc. Basically, all he had to do was open fridge and open mouth. Oh, he could use the microwave if he wanted, but life was pretty slick for him, not to mind, tasty.

As I drove across the state on my trip, I wondered about men vs. women. I pondered how different we are and why. My husband has gone to Machu Picchu, Peru, for 2 weeks and left me home alone. Of course, the gifted dog was with me but he doesn't talk much. This time and every time my husband has left me for any extended period of time, he has gotten all his stuff together for his trip. He has taken care of all other obligations that might arise when he is gone. What he has never done, not even once, is wonder if I would eat or not. He has never said, "Now, dear wife, what will you eat while I am gone?" No, never. Frankly, I don't even think it crossed his mind. He just drives or flies off and I am left to fend for myself in the eating department. He also never calls home and asks what I have eaten or if I have eaten. I do this every time I am gone.

So, ya gotta wonder, what's up with that? Do women do all the food stuff for their man out of guilt that they are leaving or out of habit or out of just plain craziness???

I have to admit that if my husband left food for me to eat or wondered and asked if I was eating or what I was eating while he was gone, I wouldn't like it. But, then again, who knows, as I can't even imagine this reality. I guess I will chalk it up to that old adage, "Men and women are sure different!" Okay, maybe you have never heard of that adage before, but it should be one, don't you think?

There are a few other crazy things I wondered about lately. As I drove East on M57, I saw a sign for Crapo road. Really? Really? Now, that is the truth, but hard to believe. How did that come about? Did someone say, "Let's make a housing development and to sell it, let's call it Crapo road." Do people keep a straight face when they have to give their address? Are they tired of saying, "No, not capo, crapo, c r a p o?" Life sure can be hard, in oh so many ways.

This reminded me of the sign I saw recently while sailing through Ionia. It made me laugh. It said, "Free Fair. $10 parking." Okay, I know there is no admission fee, but the sign still looked silly.

Yesterday I heard a couple funny things too. A guy was asked what year his birthday was. He replied, "Every year." I was alone in the car, but I laughed out loud.

Another person asked what people were doing before Facebook. They really were doing something with all that time. What was it? What took up their time before Facebook arrived and made privacy uncool?

So much to wonder about. I will end with a couple little kid things that just happened.

My nephew began Kindergarten. He was very tired with the new full schedule so his mom told him they were going to stop going to Tae Kwon Do for a while. She said, "We will just take a break from it." He said, "Yeah, I need to take a break from Kindergarten too!!" Good luck with that one, little guy.

My grandson came home from first grade and exclaimed, "I can spell now. I can spell can, r a n."

Another little first grader said, "I can add now. 2 + 2 is 3." When you think of how much we have to learn to get to our brilliant adult selves, it is a wonder we ever get there.

Life each day gives us stuff to wonder about and laugh at. We might as well take it all in.

The Clean Car Club

I can divide my friends into two groups – those with clean cars and those with cars like mine. You know who you are and which group you fall into. It is always harder for me to relate to the members of the clean car club. However, I can always relate to members of the clean plate club, but I know that totally doesn't relate to this column.

My car used to be a lot cleaner. Perhaps that is just a figment of my memory - whatever.

One problem in my car is all the bags. You know what I'm talking about – all those cloth bags we use at the grocery store. I guess I should say, all those bags we want to use at the grocery store. More often than not, I leave mine in the car and end up with the weak ones the stores provide. I am always tempted to ask the long line behind me if they mind if I run out to the parking lot and get my bags. I have never quite had the courage to do that. I am very aware that this takes longer than it sounds, as likely when I get outside, I will wonder that age old question. Where'd I park my car?? We have two cars and sometimes I look for ages for the one I didn't drive. I tell ya, life is really not easy for some of us.

Another problem in my car is all the dog stuff. There is the great big dog seat for the little tiny dog. He has to have a seat so he can see out. Life is no fun if you ride around all the time and can't see where you're going. Then there are the dog treats and the dog water and the dog dish. Oh, and the bag to sneak him in to the movie or wherever else he might need to go.

I don't really eat a lot in my car so I am saved from that kind of mess. However, I do drink lattes in the car and that has proven to be pretty tricky.

First of all, I never want a lid on my latte. Oh, no. Those lids irritate me. They are so confining. I hate those small little openings that make the latte drip down my face and onto whatever I'm wearing. And, on top of the leaking drips, the holes are just not big enough to get a good ole slurp. They also don't allow you the fun of all that fabulous foam.

Recently I realized I had a problem with lattes getting all over my car. My daughter asked to see my car manual. As I hauled it out, I noticed it had latte all over it and many of the pages had gone from white to tan.

Then I noticed the dash with hints of latte spray here and there. That happens when I have a full latte and the dog bumps me or I hit a bump or anything else happens.

When I was just starting to read the book, "The Girl with the Dragon Tattoo", I spilled latte all over it as it laid on my car seat. I had to cut edges to the pages out in order to not have it all stick together. It ended up looking like it had been caught in some wild kind of machine that ate it up in the most awful way. I suppose I could have bought a new copy but the text was fine. Later my daughter wanted to borrow it and I gave it to her. She returned it the next time I saw her and said it was so disgusting that she couldn't read it and had to buy her own copy. Some people are so picky.

I have dropped whole lattes in parking lots. I have dropped at least two all over my car seats and floor. The worst drop, however, was into my friend, Bev Geyer's, purse. Her purse was sitting on the floor and was wide open. The latte fell completely inside. Everything in her purse was wet and sticky.

She was so kind. She kept saying, "No problem. Don't worry." A couple years later she 'fessed up. She had had to replace almost everything in the purse as well as the purse itself. She even had to wash the money. She is quite a lady, though. She still meets me for lattes and never flinches.

As far as my car goes, don't judge me! We can't all be members of the clean car club.

A New Kind Of Column

Yeah, that's it. I'm gonna change things. I'm gonna change my whole approach – to my column, that is. No more fun little things. No more information. No more words of wisdom or neat quotes. Uh, uh, no way. No more of that, baby.

I am changing my focus. I am going to make a difference. Hear me roar.

I am going with the masses. The masses are what????

My new direction will be political. I am going to become one of those beloved political pundits. I intend to, from here on out, write a weekly column blasting everyone and everything. No more Ms. Nice Gal. I am letting it fly. I am sure everyone wants to hear my opinion, right?

For years now I have done this column and I have walked a fine line. You may have guessed my political feelings, but I have tried hard to veil them. I have tried to not cross lines or make others feel uncomfortable. No more of that. I am letting it fly from here on out. RRRRRRR.

I know everyone loves all the political mail you have been getting. I know everyone loves the nasty political calls which tell you all kinds of icky things about other political people. I know you will feel a big loss now that those calls and that mail won't be coming. I will try hard to make my column fill that loss. I will say all kinds of icky things about everyone in office.

And then there are all the Television ads that have stopped. I know it will be a stretch but I hope my new kind of hatchet attacks will ease that loss for you too.

Isn't this a good idea? Can't you feel the excitement? Are you as pumped about this as I am?

I intend to not worry about truth. Who needs it? I think blasting others is what it's all about. I am also not going to be bothered with how my words will affect the people I attack. That really is beside the point. And so what if it damages their families or their reputations? HELLO. This is for the greater good, folks. I am quite sure if I can attack enough and be dirty enough, it will truly help America be great again. Whoopee.

I also realize there are just not enough people yakking about politics in the media. I hope to round out that number. I want to do my part to make this a better country and state. I care. I really do. And, I am sure these kinds of tactics will certainly help right the wrongs we are facing. Don't you agree?

To close this column, I am going to share a couple political quotes. One is by Dwight D. Eisenhower, the first U.S. President that I remember being in office. He said, "Things have never been more like the way they are today in history."

What???

The other quote I want to leave you with is by that great politician, Johnny Carson. "In 1932, lame duck President Herbert Hoover was so desperate to remain in the White House that he dressed up as Eleanor Roosevelt. When FDR discovered the hoax in 1936, the two men decided to stay together for the sake of the children."

What???

So, get ready folks. I know you can't wait for next week to see the new direction my column will be taking. I know you are as anxious as can be to read all the offensive vicious stuff I will have to say about everyone. It is going to be wonderful. I just have one more thing to add. JUST KIDDING!

I Swear To God

Ethel Barrymore said, "You grow up the day you have the first real laugh at yourself." Well, I am for sure grown up then. I might as well laugh. Feeling shame can only go so far.

Over the holidays I bought several jars of cinnamon candies. I was going to make up a bunch of applesauce with them. I did one batch and we didn't like it, so I decided to return the bunch of jars I had just bought.

I never could find the receipt. I knew I had bought it at Meijers and I keep all my receipts but lo and behold, no receipt for cinnamon candies could be found. I looked, looked and looked again. This went on for a couple of weeks.

I asked my husband if he had the receipt - no luck there. Then one night in bed a light bulb came on in my brain. Looking back, it was a dim bulb but at the time I thought it was more like a bright vision. What I realized was that I had actually bought the candies at Jorgensen's not at Meijer as I had thought. Oh, yes, I could remember it well.

So, eventually I got around to taking the stuff back to the store to return it. I went to the clerk at Jorgensen's with the candies but with no receipt. I knew full well that I was goin' to have to do some splainin' to accomplish this task.

I said to the clerk in a loud strong voice that was full of conviction and what I truly believed was honesty. "I would like to return these and I swear to God that I bought them here." I am not proud of this but I really did say the 'swear to God' part with gusto. If you don't believe me, you can ask Ryan who was next to me in line. He heard the whole thing. He even heard the part where the nice lady immediately looked at me, holding one of the jars in her hand, and said, "Oh, really. I don't think so. They say Meijer."

At this point, I was stunned into silence. I know that is hard to believe. I looked at them. Yep, they each had a sticker on that clearly said, "Meijer". Now how come I never saw that before?

I looked at Ryan who was laughing way too hard over this. I said to him, "You're gonna tell on me, aren't you?"

He said, "I have to. It's way too good to let it go."

The clerk handed me back the items and tried to make me feel better by saying, "Maybe you can get a column out of this." She was serious too, because recently I saw her in the store and she said, "Where's the column?" Hmmm.

To make a long story longer, I came home and a miracle happened. I quickly found the Meijer receipt right where I had looked several times. There was a happy ending after all, except for the shame. That will linger quite awhile and I am sure whenever I see Ryan he will bring it up. Dang.

I guess I will end this with something that doesn't relate to anything here but I think it's funny. Recently a friend sent it to me.

"There's a fine line between fishing and drinking a beer with a stick in your hand."

I hate fishing and I hate beer but I think that is a cute one. And perhaps it will be so amusing to you that you will forget the rest of this column, a.k.a. confession.

My Random Mind

My mind seems to be filled with random thoughts – some silly, some worthwhile, some you decide. I thought I'd share a few with you today. Remember I said they were random.

Relax and play some games this summer, but beware. I heard someone say that the worst time to have a heart attack was during a game of charades with a bunch of bad guessers.

Go for a pleasure drive, but be careful. My husband saw a guy texting while driving. When the driver looked up and saw my husband watching him, the driver gave him the finger. My husband said, "I call that multi-tasking."

I have some questions, but no one to ask. Where does the energy come from when I hear someone is stopping over and I run, like a mad woman, around the house cleaning it up? In this same line of thinking, it is amazing how much I can carry in from the car to avoid a second trip. I'm almost a super hero. There may be a movie about me soon. I am thinking this power comes from my titanium knees . . . you probably don't want to mess with me.

Why is white zinfandel wine pink? Were they color blind?

How come my driving skills are still razor sharp and my mate's put me on my last nerve? When we go to get in the car we have to make a decision. One of us drives and the other complains – call it.

How did it happen that farm equipment is now as big as my first house and costs way way more? How did it happen that I can stick more technology than I can imagine in my teeny phone?

Why am I able to down a giant latte and then nap instantly during the day, but if I have even a bit of tea or coffee at night, I am awake for hours?

Where did some things go? You know what I mean. Remember all that macramé stuff from the seventies? Remember phone booths? Remember when gas stations had an attendant and not just someone taking your money?

Do you ever still feel amazed that the Gores got divorced and the Clintons are still married?

Did you know that more dogs are told, "I love you" during their lives, on average, than human beings are told the same three words throughout their lifetimes? I didn't make this up. It came from research by Janet Rothe. I have no idea who she is.

Jean Webster said, "It isn't the great big pleasures that count the most; it's making a great deal out of the little ones." So, eat lunch in a park, visit a farmer's market, have a margarita with a friend.

One more thing. My daughter-in-law just made a fab "sun-dried tomato" veggie dip. She's a super cook and this is a quick dip with great flavor. I've already made it twice. Try it. The recipe is in the back of the book.

To close, think about this. How many people do you see in life and on reality T.V. that make you say to yourself, 'A lot of problems in this world could be solved if we just put a tax on crazy'? I'm hoping you don't add my name to that list. I told you this would be random.

And The Award Goes To . . .

My friend, Tom, told me he liked my column last week, but. Whenever there's a "but, you know that's not going to be good. His but was, "You are too nice. You gotta get an edge. Start complaining." So here goes.

Everyone knows it is awards season on T.V. You know it because the award shows continue to, week after week, pre-empt our favorite T.V. shows. How many awards do these people need anyway? Either a movie, song or T.V. show is good or it isn't. Do they need to battle it out with who is number one in several different arenas? Maybe we should come up with our own awards.

I'd begin with the SAG awards which were on this week. I think I could have won one of those because, sad as it is to say this, I gotta a lotta stuff saggin' these days. In fact, I'm kinda saggin' from head to toe. I could win in a variety of categories.

I could also win a Grammy. I mean, I think I'm a cool Grammy. I think my grandsons would vote for me. Most of the time.

I could maybe win a Director's Guild award for bossing my dog around. "Go out. Come in. Don't jump." You know the drill. You can win one too!

Many of us could win an Independent Spirit award for not always wearing what the fashion experts tell us to, especially all those get ups we already wore in a previous life.

I don't want to just win awards, though, I'd like to give awards too.

I could give a Critic's Choice award to the people who wait until I am up to my elbows in work and knock on my door unannounced. They then ask if they can save my soul or if I have a church or if I like the way the government is running. Maybe I should get an award for not saying what I want to when I reply to them. I feel a little hot about this right now as it just happened and I still feel the flush of irritation. I am sure they wanted to save my soul, but I am pretty sure it worked just the opposite.

I'd like to give another to the people who make all the packaging of products I buy. You know all the stuff you can't open without a saw or a blow torch. One day I may just nick myself to death trying to open stuff. I find it especially hard to open medicine bottles when I don't have a little kid around to help me.

The other day a person told me they had moved into a retirement complex in Florida. (Wasn't it Seinfeld who said we all have to do that at a certain age?) Anyway, I digress. When they moved in, there was a flier under the door advertising computer set up and help. Of course, they needed it desperately so they called right away. When the person arrived, it was a 9 year old boy. Really, this is the truth. He promptly set up their computer, answered all their questions and left with a nice wad of cash in his pocket. I'd like to give a People's Choice award to all the little ones who lead us where we fear to go on our own, or if we are honest, are just plain clueless how to get there.

So, realistically, random awards for weird things we think of just aren't gonna happen. That is probably alright. As I said in the beginning, enough with the award shows. I want my old T.V. shows back.

Hey, Wait A Minute

Life throws us curve balls, unexpected things that make us say, "*Hey, wait a minute.*" Sometimes that is in delight, sometimes in dismay.

My friend, Hilda, shared something with me lately that made me laugh out loud and say, "*Hey, wait a minute.*" It completely took me by surprise and delighted me. Here it is.

"You have to work hard to offend Christians. By nature, they are the most forgiving, understanding, and thoughtful group of people I have ever dealt with. They never assume the worst. They appreciate the importance of having different perspectives. They're slow to anger, quick to forgive and almost never make rash judgments or act in anything less than a spirit of love . . . No, wait . . . I'm thinking of Golden Retrievers!" *Hey, wait a minute.* Is that cute or what? And, it's true, too.

I had a couple "*Hey, wait a minute*" moments yesterday. I am guessing you have been having some of your own lately.

I had a pain in the left side of my chest. It began in the morning and continued throughout the day. I thought of it often as it hurt. I thought it wasn't a problem, probably a kink or some gas. I was sure it would go away. As the day went on, I kept noticing it and then would think to myself, 'At least it's not my heart, because my heart is on my right side.' I am not proud of that thought. I really knew better, somewhere within me, but at that moment I went happily on with my day and my ignorant thought.

As the day continued, my husband and I visited our grandsons and had a delightful time talking about their first day of school. I left and was driving home. I thought about that darn pain, which continued to nag at me. *Hey, wait a minute.* A thought hit me like lightning. 'My heart isn't on my right side. It's on my left side. I know that for a fact. Maybe I should be more concerned with this pain.'

I called my husband who was in his car driving behind me. I asked, "Is my heart on my left side?" He kindly humored me with, "Yes". I went on and told him that I had a pain there all day. He told me to go directly to the emergency room and he would follow me.

It is not that I didn't believe him, but I sure didn't want to make a big deal out of nothing. So, I called my friend, Al Schoolcraft, who knows about heart issues and the hospital. I explained my situation to him and he added to my husband's directions, but also added, "You shouldn't even be driving!" Hmmm.

I got to the emergency room and told them I had been having chest pains all day, but that I felt fine. I went to give them my insurance card. They always have to have that before they do anything, but they didn't even want it. Someone else instantly came with a wheel chair and whisked me away. Before I knew it I had two nurses doing all kinds of things to me.

Bottom line, about six hours later, and after many, many tests, they came in with a big smile and said, "It doesn't look like it's a heart problem. It looks like you do have a very big Hiatal hernia." This sounded like really good news. They seemed happy. My husband and I felt happy. The pain was still going on, but I had dodged the old heart bullet.

I must say here that I got the very best care at the hospital. Everyone who did a test, drew blood, etc., was just wonderful and friendly. They called me "Honey", and though I don't usually enjoy that from strangers, I found it very comforting and dear.

It really makes one proud to go to your local hospital and get such excellent treatment from everyone you deal with. I teach customer service seminars and am always grading places, in my head, on their customer service. I gave them all an A. Not only were they super and professional to me, they were that way to everyone else and to each other. It was obvious they all liked their work.

So, after the ordeal, as I was leaving the hospital with information for my personal doctor, I said to my husband, "You know the pain is still there, but I am so glad that they found something and that I'm not crazy."

He came right back with, "Ohhhh, just because they found something wrong, don't confuse that with you're not being crazy. You're still crazy." *Hey, wait a minute.*

Which reminds me that one of the great secrets of a happy life is to keep laughing. *Hey, wait a minute.* Is life really that simple? Yup, I think it is. I know you've got your own crazy *hey-wait-a-minute* stories. Enjoy them.

Fans And Foolishness

Okay, I'm not all that into sports. The only time I really care is when a team I like is on a winning streak or staging a huge comeback. That kinda stuff I love. As Paul Clisura said (whoever he is),"When I feel athletic, I go to a sports bar." I don't like bars all that much so I prefer going to a movie.

I realize I am the odd man out. It seems most people I know care deeply about sports. They watch. They cheer. They discuss. They want their team to win. As I observe them, I think they are pretty weird. Here's what I've found.

Many can't actually watch the games. It's just too much for them. Watching is way too painful, especially if their team isn't winning. They walk around, go outside, do chores, dilly dally around the house or yard. Then they occasionally take a peek at the game. My husband calls it, "just getting a score".

According to Jim, Thorne Brown, former captain of the U of M basketball team, would attend U of M football games, leave his seat just before kickoff and walk around the stadium the entire game. Did any of you see the movie, Moneyball, where Brad Pitt as Oakland A's general manager avoided watching his own team play? Perhaps my husband isn't so weird after all. Then again.

When I met him he was a successful coach. Ever since, he doesn't like to watch games. When he does, he moves all over like they are in the room and actually hitting him. His body jerks, though I wouldn't call him one, and his face is all twitched and full of angst. Of course, when he actually does watch a game, he has it on mute. The sound would be way too much, over the top.

Me, I can't understand this stuff. I want sound with my T.V. That just seems normal, doesn't it? Terry leaves the sound on for the game but mutes all the commercials and all the chit chat, unless it is her two favorite announcers. Everyone else drives her crazy.

Pastor Joel yells loudly, "BOOM!" whenever his team scores. Most of the time this totally scares the heck out of his family. Being a pastor, perhaps that is his real goal.

My friend, Bob, knits while watching games. If it is a long, boring baseball game, he can do a whole sweater!

Many yell at the players and coaches. Even the ones who have never played sports in their lives seem to have all the answers. Loud swearing seems to be the mode of choice for yelling advice to the T.V.

Jack watches/listens to multiple games on TV and radio, switching from station to station when either a commercial or his mood strikes. He amazes his wife by keeping it all straight. Who's on first?

Sad to say, these odd behaviors are contagious and many women I know have also gotten weird as they watch. Denny told my husband that his wife has to iron through the games. I know that is one weird behavior I won't catch. Jodie shuts out the world when she watches any sport: no phone calls, no interruptions, no bathroom breaks. No bathroom breaks? Really?

Marty says her husband watches sports with the concentration of an owl. Kathy Jo says "Jim can watch the game through the back of his eyelids, fast forward perfectly from hit to hit or shot to shot – all the while snoring loudly." Martha's husband can't multi task except for sports. Then he can watch a game on TV, listen to one on the radio and read the sports page all at the same time. He might be gifted.

Several watch TV on mute while listening to their favorite announcers on the radio. Phil just plain listens to big games on the radio because he likes the passionate play by play.

My daughter-in-law wins all the awards, though. She comes from a sports family. On game day, her dad would wake them up by singing the Chicago Bears fight song. In fact, they sang the Chicago fight song every day. She then sang me a few bars, something about bear down…

They always referred to the two teams as the good guys and the bad guys. When the national anthem was sung, they would always stand up and put their hands over their hearts.

Their whole day would be lived around the game. She remembers her mom asking over and over, "How much time? How much time?", so she could put dinner on immediately when halftime started. They also had special pre-game and post-game food. Her father would make game day platters of special sausages and other game day delicacies.

Her story got weirder. If you came into the room and the team began to win, you couldn't leave. If you came in and they began to lose, you had to get out.

If you wore certain clothes and they won, you had to wear them to the next game. Didn't I hear that Jim Leyland never changed his underwear during a Tigers' twelve game winning streak?

Yeah, there are a lot of weird watchers of sports. All that weirdness makes for some fun camaraderie. As Walter Chrysler said, "The real secret of success is enthusiasm."

Being a Michigan State grad, I couldn't resist sharing this. A man dressed in green, and white and carrying a small dog, walked into an Ann Arbor sports bar. He asked the bartender. "Hey, can I leave my dog with you while I go to the Michigan State – University of Michigan game?"

The bartender replied, "No dogs allowed."

"But he's a special dog. He will watch the game on TV and when MSU scores, he will walk up and down the bar on his hind legs. When Michigan scores, he will walk up and down on his front legs. When Michigan State wins, he'll do back flips all the way down the bar and back."

"Wow, what will he do when Michigan wins?"

"Hey, I don't have a clue. He's only four years old."

Making Money In Modern Times

Okay, so these are hard times. People need money. That means people need work. Or do they? Is that an old concept? Are there more current ways to make ends meet? Let's see. Ladies first.

A few years ago I was told I needed to watch *Jon and Kate Plus 8*, the reality show about the Gosselins and their brood. When I did watch the show, I loved the children but was stunned by how rudely Kate treated her spouse. Later Kate said this was the way they got along and it worked for them.

Sidebar: I remember 3 friends who treated their spouses like that. The guys all took it, just like Jon Gosselin. Until one day they all ended up in D.C. And I don't mean the capital. I mean divorce court.

So Kate and Jon split. She got a reality show on her own and then showed up on *Dancing with the Stars*. As I have said before, I don't watch reality T.V., but I do have eyes that open so I saw this stuff wherever I looked - newspapers, magazines, news shows, etc.

Another way to make coin might be the Octomom route. Begin with having more kids than you think you can – all at one time is best. The Octomom had her home foreclosed and was offered a solution. A porn company offered to pay all her bills. She could make movies by day and be home with the kids at night. Hmmm. Decisions. Decisions.

You might not want to have a slew of kids at once. How about having a load of plastic surgeries? Heidi Montag, in her early twenties, had ten or more and was then all over the media. Ka-ching. You have to feel sorry for her, though. She was so fragile after all her "work" that she couldn't even hug. Sigh. But she did make lotsa money with her "celebrity".

Another idea - you could go into politics. Rod Blah-Blah-Blagojevich, the corrupt Illinois governor who the feds removed from office, made buckos on *Celebrity Apprentice* with Donald Trump. Before he was allowed to do this, he had his wife go on the *Survivor* reality show. Personally I think he should have sold some of his hair. Mine is thin and I might have considered buying some if I could have figured out a way to make it work for me.

Eliot Spitzer was the New York governor who liked call girls, especially one, Ashley Dupre, a Playboy nude model. Doesn't call girl sound nicer than prostitute? Ashley said Ka-ching when she blogged, "I just did the governor." She was then hired by the New York Post to be an advice columnist. Now there's a column you don't want to miss.

More political job opportunities: Rielle Hunter, the one who had John Edward's last child and helped take his career and marriage down, did a GQ photo shoot dressed in a man's shirt and nothing else you could see, laying seductively on a bed with stuffed animals and her little girl. My first thought was, "Yuck." She complained later that she thought GQ would do it "classy". She cried and cried . . . all the way to the bank. I think that was after she screamed to the media, "I want my sex tape back" and right before she wrote her tell all book.

If I haven't given you enough ideas for getting some money, here are a couple more.

Tiger Wood's long line of mistakes included occupations like club hostesses (that would be men's clubs, of course); cocktail waitresses; totally trashy lingerie models; trailer park waitresses; failed models; former porn stars; current porn stars (if you are in porn films are you automatically a porn star?); hookers; cougar mistresses, and on and on*. When did cougar become more than a big animal?

Sidebar: *I did not make up those descriptions but got them directly from the news.

And, of course, one more money making idea would be to have sex with a famous movie star's husband. Be sure she is one everyone loves and it is even better if she has just won the academy award before you hit the media with your news flash. This one also works best if you are a porn star, stripper and tattoo model to begin with.

And I haven't even mentioned the South Carolina governor, Mark Sanford, who found his soul mate on the Appalachian Trail or Argentina, or wait, who cares.

In summary, if you are in need of more money, you could use one of the above examples to guide you, especially if you want to be rude, lewd or a dude. If, however, you lean more toward integrity, honor, loyalty and self respect, you may just want to give Michigan Works a call.

Married With Children

Blah, Blah, Love

Maureen & Don Burns

Driving with my husband the other day, I realized there are two kinds of people - those who look up phone numbers and those who guesstimate and keep punching numbers in until they get lucky or give up. This made me think of how vital it is to look for what is really important when you choose a mate.

Recently we have been to several weddings. They were all lovely but one thing I noticed. All the pastors talked about the same thing - blah, blah, blah, blah, love. My husband and I discussed this and agreed that the blah, blah, love wasn't really what was going to make your marriage last. We can give seasoned advice now because we have celebrated 45 years of perfecto marital bliss, or at least we are still married, depends on your point of view.

It is important to figure out what is really important when two people spend the rest of their long, long lives together. Here are some things we think are vital, yet never ever, not even once, mentioned at the blah, blah, love ceremonies.

There are the bed makers and the not bed makers. Personally, I think the one who cares if the bed is made should always be the one who gets to make it. That just makes good sense. Don't you agree? Luckily my husband does too, so he makes the bed.

Everyone knows that how people squeeze the toothpaste is another essential ingredient to wedded bliss. It seems there is a universal law. No married couple ever does it the same way. This can lead to unbelievable irritation. The wisest people end up buying two tubes and going on with other important things in life. The rest just seethe for years.

And, don't forget the toilet paper. When you decide to get hitched, it will be very important to know if your future partner rolls it over the top or if they roll it out the bottom. And then there are the low lifes that never bother to put the paper on the roller. Do I dare admit that I am that kind of person? Will you think less of me? I like to give my mate the joy of doing it. It means a lot to him.

These things may seem mundane, silly even, but they can make or break a marriage. Trust me.

My husband suggested I should mention the dishes. Oh, sure. Let me state that when he proposed, he never once even hinted that the dishes were important to the deal. It was years before this surfaced as being, oh so important to him. Everyone has their personal cycles. My personal rhythm is I like to do the dishes in the morning. That worked for me until my mate retired. Then he had to get all into my business. Now he does a lot of the dishes stuff and I am loving him even more for it. He has become my hero, so to speak. The only thing I hate is that he tries to wash the dish while I am still eating off of it.

Oh, one more thing is going to church on time. My mate thinks it is good to go early and meditate prayerfully. I think there is a lot I could get done in those few minutes.

Marriage is not for the faint of heart. It is full of challenges, irritations, compromises - and, did I say, irritations? Oh, I did. Sometimes you just gotta say to yourself, "Houston, we've got a problem!" Other times you just have to bend . . . and I don't mean over!

As I said, we have only been married 45 years, but we are beginning to see promise and have hope. We are inspired by that Laverne and Shirley T.V. song, *We're gonna make it after all!*

We have learned. We have grown. We have bent. At times I have told him to get bent. And he has said, 'Right back at ya!" It is clear now, at last, that he prefers the dishes done and the bed made and we get along just fine. Each of us has our chores and roles and quirks, lotsa quirks.

If we are lucky, things balance out in life. Each person brings qualities to the marriage that the other may lack, need or want. They become the yin to each other's yang.

Last week we saw a friend who is getting married soon. He said he was beginning to think it may be the worst financial move of his life. He said his bride-to-be left his house the other day carrying a bunch of his clothes. When he asked her where she was taking them, she replied, "Garage sale." He asked, "Will I see money from that?" She replied, "Probably not." Yep, he's in the beginning stages, all right. Blah, blah, love.

I look back at our 45 years. He never jumped on a yellow sofa and told a national audience how much he loved me. He didn't take me to the Eiffel Tower to propose. We didn't get hitched in an Irish castle. He hasn't given me lovely gifts every day like Tom Cruise gave Katie Holmes. Tom would say, "This is for my lovely wife." Yeah, Don never did that, but I wrote Tom's quote on a piece of paper. I put it in the medicine cabinet. I figure if I ever swallow poison, I can read it quickly and throw up.

Don's done great in other ways. He's a wonderful partner in every way and so reliable. I can always count on him to tell me how to drive. I can count on him to tell me I made too much food when we entertain. I can count on him to say no when I ask him to play games, except one, that is.

Yes, after all these years, we have learned how to manage the stuff that drives you crazy. We kinda sum it up with "whatever".

Living The Leftover Life

Calvin Trillin once said, "The most remarkable thing about my mother is that for thirty years she served the family nothing but leftovers. The original meal has never been found."

Some historians have led us to believe that bread is the staff of life, manna. But, we know better. The real manna is leftovers. Yessireebob.

You may not know this about me, but I am a queen. Ah ha, I didn't think you knew. Yes, I hold the crown and have done so for a long time - the Queen of Leftovers. Just ask my kids.

Of course, you can't believe kids, especially when they start telling ugly stuff . . . like the truth. Truth is just someone's perspective and I am sure theirs is skewed when it comes to me and my leftovers. My husband would be a better source. He will eat anything.

Once I did my usual. Cleaned out the fridge, threw it all in a dish, put cheese on top of it and baked it. Presto – dinner. My husband arrived at the table first and dug in with his usual positive gusto. My daughter was home visiting that night. She took one bite, pushed the plate away and rudely said, "This is rotten." Some people are so critical.

My husband and I – we don't have such high standards. We eat stuff that has been around for awhile, quite awhile. We even take pride in the fact that nothing around here goes to waste. Is that something to be proud of?

I think you can clear mold off cheese and eat it. Right? Most other things that grow mold get tossed. Most, that is.

If you don't think life is about leftovers, why do you think God made those square Styrofoam containers? Huh? Yeah, there you go. That was life planning at its best.

A common comment around our house is, "Why did you cook so much?" And you can guess who says that. I will give you a clue. There are only three of us who live here and the dog finds it hard to use his words. Grrrr seems to be the best he can do.

I cook so much because I am a long range planner. I see it coming – all those nights in the future when I won't want to cook or won't have time to cook. And then, what a delight it is to pull out some frozen leftovers. It is like finding a quarter under your pillow after you left a tooth. Ohhh Boy!

When you cook something it involves lots of buying, cleaning, chopping, and on and on and on. Why not just cook a bigger portion and not have to go through this ordeal so often? I told you I was Queen. Now you know why.

I find my creativity sings when I cook with leftovers. It is amazing the concoctions one can make if they let their mind soar, or wander . . . whatever. I admit, I have made a few nasty mistakes but we don't focus on those. Oh, no. We focus on the delectable delights.

There are many cookbooks on leftovers. You don't need them. Google lists over 2,500,000 leftover recipes. I won't live long enough to try all of those. You don't need those either. Just follow my simple system.

First of all, make huge batches whenever you cook. Let them set around until they are almost spoiled. Then freeze them. Some nasty night when you are exhausted, haul the suckers out. Thaw. Reheat and eat.

Secondly, bring food home from wherever you go. Save for a long time. When you see the slightest possibility, toss it into other food you are making. Or eat them alone. Either way, you have something you don't have to cook from scratch. And how nice is that?

Third, clean the fridge and haul out anything that is still alive. Oops, I mean not dead. Mix all together. Add mayo if you want. That is always a nice touch. I like to scrounge the fridge door for all that stuff you buy and never use. Toss in a little of this and a little of that. Mix. Bake or I usually microwave this stuff. Oh, and don't forget the crowning glory, cheese, lots and lots of cheese. It doesn't matter what kind it is. Bring to the table and serve to spouse or whomever. Don't take a bite until they have survived about 20 minutes. Enjoy. Now you can be a Queen too.

Marriage - Not What It Used To Be

Marriage isn't what it used to be. Have you noticed?

If not, just take a gander at the Sunday Grand Rapids Press, the section with photos of the engagements and anniversaries. Is it me or is the anniversary section much larger than the engagement section – week after week? When did this happen? Oh, and did I mention, the couples in the anniversary section look so young these days? I wonder why that is?

Marriages do not seem to be following the old standards of commitment that they once were. A cartoon I have has a guy in a jewelry store asking the jeweler, "Got anything that says, 'Let's give it a shot for a couple of years'?"

Starter marriage is a familiar label. We all know lots of folks who have had them. And I'm not making judgments here, just looking at the signs of the times.

Another cartoon I have shows two guys at a bar. One says to the other, "I've got a trophy wife, but she isn't what you'd call first place."

Author Amy Bloom said, "Love at first sight is easy to understand; it's when two people have been looking at each other for a lifetime that it becomes a miracle." Amen to that.

Recently I had breakfast with a dear friend. She was widowed last year and was talking about how much she missed her husband. She talked emotionally about him. She was grieving still. As she talked she said, "I never ever ever considered divorce . . . however, I did consider strangulation a few times." And with that we had a good teary eyed laugh.

I read somewhere that the greatest engineering feat in all history is the bridge built between a man and a woman called marriage.

My friend just celebrated her fiftieth wedding anniversary. She was listening to a radio talk show and they were having folks call in to discuss their numerous marriages. Some had four, one had seven. She called in and talked at length on air. She discussed how she and her mate had never considered divorce an option. She said that they just worked through things rather than having calling it quits as an option. The radio announcer kept her on the line and seemed to enjoy picking at her wisdom. She has lots.

Yes, marriage is not what it used to be. Or is it? Some things have changed but some have stayed the same. Some have even improved.

One husband read a book, "You can be the man of your house". He then announced to his wife, "From now on you need to know that I am the head of the house and this is what I want. I want you to prepare me a gourmet meal tonight. Then I want you to prepare me a bath so I can relax. Then wash my back, bring me a towel and my robe. Then massage my feet. Then come to bed with me. Then tomorrow, guess who is going to care for me?"

His wife looked at him and replied, "I don't know but I am guessing it will be the funeral director."

There are many funny things that have been said to sum up marriage. Woody Allen said, "My parents stayed together for forty years, but that was out of spite."
Susan Vass said, "I've been married so long I'm on my third bottle of Tabasco sauce." Personally, I'm only on my second.

But not everyone wants to stay married. Lewis Grizzard said, "Instead of getting married again, I'm going to find a woman I don't like and give her a house."

Everyone's got their perspective. Love and marriage, love and marriage, goes together like a horse and carriage. Sometimes, that is.

Take A Hike

Don Burns

We get shocked by things like this every year, usually several times. This was how I felt during one of those times.

I wouldn't say I am really political. I keep up, though, somewhat. At least I keep up on all the political scandals, of which there are aplenty. It actually seems like a gourmet bounty of scandals filling the political arena these days. It takes due diligence to keep up on it all. I try, though. I really do. I am a good American after all, a patriot, some would say.

The seemingly endless array of scandals is almost better than the summer TV offerings. Though many would not believe it, I think I'm somewhat naive. I mean, I thought John Edwards was all that and a bag of chips. I loved him and Elizabeth and their working man values. He let her down, for sure, and he let me down too.

I always liked Arnold and his movies. I thought it was cool that Maria was a pure Democrat and he was a pure Republican and they had a happy marriage. To find out he was boppin' the maid is another big let down. I have now removed him from my list of favorite movie stars. I'm sure he doesn't care that he is now on the list with Mel Gibson.

And then there's the latest hot dog scandal – that's my code for weinergate – which has also been unreal. Oh, yes, there have been so many let downs and political scandals, where do we stop with it all? Which leads me to my point. Yes, I do have one, as feeble as it may be.

Last fall my husband and daughter hiked the Inca Trail into Machu Picchu. Now they are going to hike into and out of the Grand Canyon in September. But when he told me he is going off to hike the Appalachian Trail to prepare for the Grand Canyon trip, my astute political razor sharp memory flew to the South Carolina Republican Governor, Mark Sanford. Didn't Sanford say, "Honey, I'm not home. I'm hiking the Appalachian Trail. You can't reach me for a few days"???? Didn't he instead book to Argentina where he saw his mistress, or as he called her, his soul mate? Whatever. He was such a jerk. His wife ended up taking the real hike and divorcing the lying lout.

But now, here I am, Miss Naivety, and my husband is saying, "Honey, I'll be on the Appalachian Trail." He and I have joked about playing "Where's Waldo", I mean Donaldo, when he's hiking. Yes, we've had some good laughs over this. But after all the media mess over Sanford, it does give a wife pause.

I know my husband is going on this hike with our two daughters. I also know I am going along – not to hike, just to be along for the family fun and camaraderie. And perhaps to see if there really is an Appalachian Trail or if it is just another political apparition. You know what Robert Byrne said, "Never trust anyone over-dirty." What?????

I Swear - I Didn't Mean To Do It

It is a sad day when you realize you have screwed your kids over. Even if you didn't mean to do it. Even if everyone else did the same thing. It still makes you feel all low. And it helps you understand why your kids aren't all perfect.

My day of realization began when I attended a baby shower recently. As the cute mommy-to-be opened gift after gift, she might as well have hit me with a hammer while saying, "See, you did this wrong. You did that wrong. Your poor kids never had a chance."

Where do I begin? There are so many ways we failed. First, we wiped our kids bottoms with cold wash cloths. We didn't have "wipe warmers" so each time we shocked our babes with cold gotchas. That may be our biggest failing.

Colleen & Dan Burns & friends

When we took them to Meijers, we just stuck them in the cart. We never even considered having padded cart liners to keep them from the germs left by previous urchins. Nah, we just shoved them in, let them teethe and suck on the cart bar and didn't pay any attention to how this would affect them in the long run. As long as they were quiet, we were happy.

We put them to bed on their bellies. Yup! I know - how low could we go? We shoved pacifiers into their cute mouths and said, "Nitey, nite." We covered them with blankets.

It just gets worse and worse, doesn't it? And then we left them like that and went and watched T.V. What's a baby to do?

We had lame car seats. We had lame high chairs. We stuck them in play pens and were thrilled to have corralled them. Heck, I would throw two kids in at a time along with a dog. They loved it and I was free to do my busy. My friend said she had seven in her playpen once and one was definitely too old to be in there as he was in school already.

We had no baby monitors. When we left them alone in a room, they were on their own. If they needed us, they had to yell loudly. Sometimes we even let them cry themselves to sleep because a guy named Dr. Spock told us that was good for them.

They teethed on cribs and toys with lead paint. They got sunscreen, if they were lucky. It was like #5. They drank from the wrong kind of cups and ate off plastic that was microwaved.

We threw them into pools with wingies on their arms. They slouched in sitting positions on the floor and got no boppies to surround and brace them.

We let them sit in the front seat with Mommy. We held infants during car rides.

We stuck rough cloth diapers on their bottoms held together with giant sharp diaper pins. Is there a grown child out there who wasn't stuck with one of those pins? Sorry! I didn't, but many smoked and let the baby sit there in a cloud of grey. We drank while we were pregnant. When they teethed, we rubbed whiskey on their gums. We wanted to rub it on ours.

Life was different then. It was even more different in other places. When we lived in Spain, I gave birth to my second child, Colleen. They gave me gas for anesthetic. I didn't prefer that but that was what they gave - period, so I decided to go with it, being a big chicken and all. Also I remembered the first labor. I'm not as dumb as I look.

So, after the babe was out and next to me - still all gucky, I was still all gassed up and goofy - the doc brought my husband in and, as he rolled up his sleeves, said to my mate, "Hey, wanna beer?" He opened a nearby fridge and popped open two beers for them. Windows were open. I swear - if it was today, I would have sat up and screamed, "Really?"

Sadly, there's a lot more to this story of how I ruined my kids and I'll complete this sad tale next week. In the meantime, don't judge me. Many of you were right there with me. It's a wonder our kids turned out at all.

****

Well, well, I got tons of comments about how I screwed up my kids. It seems like there are lots of parents who could identify with all my wrong doings.

Sometimes the comments I get afterwards are the best part. Here's a couple. A very upstanding lady in the community shared that some of her worst hang overs were while she was pregnant. She said one of her kids still blames some of his on-going problems on her "behavior" while she was pregnant. Kids can be so judgmental!

Another said she used to take her kids from Greenville to Lansing, all the day down I96 with the kids loose in the back of a pick up. Another friend added, "We were safety conscious, though. We told them they could only do that if they sat down!"

We used to spray them with bug spray that probably could have killed a horse. When they were born, we let them go bare headed in the hospital. Who knew they needed knit hats?

When the kids were not babies anymore and you took them "loose" in the car, they'd be all over the back seat fooling around. You had to keep one hand on the wheel while swinging the other arm through the back seat area, trying to smack whomever you could reach. Some parents excelled at this. My arms were always a bit too short to do much good. A friend reminded me of the famous line, "Don't make me stop this car!" My husband said he was never loose in the backseat. His parents had 11 kids so they were so wedged in, they couldn't move, which was probably a good thing.

Discipline was sometimes a swat or a spanking - nothing brutal, just a little something to get the point across and help them remember not to bash their sibling with a hammer. Usually time outs were something the parents craved for themselves.

Once, on the way home from church, my brother-in-law promised his kids a "surprise" when they got home. They had been naughty during mass and it was not going to be a happy surprise. The littlest begged to get it first so he gave it to her, but good.

A big form of explaining discipline was, "Because I said so." That seemed to suffice. At least they bought it.

As they got in to school and into group sports, they suffered losing over and over and found out early that they weren't always going to be the winner. No parents were helicoptering in to assure them they were number one. If they didn't win, they didn't get an award. We were just plain cruel.

Dinners were downers. No choices - that is if you don't count the limited choice of "take it or leave it". Mine always took it. We had no allergies or intolerances to deal with. We fed them peanut butter early and lotsa sugar. We tossed in whole milk.

They went to school without phones. OMG.

When it was time for mine to come home from running loose playing in the neighborhood, I would ring a cow bell and they would come running for dinner.

Even though we meant well, we were insensitive. We drove our kids all over the country without videos to watch. The other day I saw my friend at the coffee shop. His kids were out in the mini van watching a movie they'd seen 57 times already. We told our kids "sit and look out the window - and don't bother your sister, either! I'll be back in awhile."

We thought we were the parents of the year when we drove them clear out to Colorado seeing all the sights along the way. Of course, we had no seat belts on them. We let the little one sit right between us in the front seat. She rode that way all the way out west and all the way back home. She never could see anything out of the window because she was too little. This never entered our minds until years later - poor little girl.

We let them ride their bikes and roller skates without helmets. We were just happy to have peace and quiet when they were outside. Breaking their heads open like melons really never entered our minds.

They were sad little creatures with no computer or video games to play and no organized play dates. Oh, they played with toys and they had friends come to play, but it was pretty loosey goosey, no real organization there. We mostly had coffees with friends. If they brought kids, all the better. We had more time to talk as the kids wouldn't bug us so much.

My baby sitter was 9 years old. I thought she was smart enough to entrust my yahoos with her. She was 11 before she spoke to me on her own. Now I am wondering if the behavior of my kids just stunned her into silence. And you know who you are, Mary Ann.

Few kids had braces. Now my grandson is wearing pre-braces braces. He had to pick out the different colors he wanted them to be. Say what?

Our poor kids had to get up and turn the T.V. channel manually. My teenage son used to call his little sister, who was two floors up, and ask her to come down and change the channel while he laid lazily on the sofa in front of the T.V. Sadly, she would do it.

Well, it seems like I could go on forever. Wait, I already have. It is hard to find an end to our bad parenting. I am thinking, though, that we did one thing right. We gave them love . . . and lots of it. Maybe that is what they mean by the phrase "saving grace".

Embarrassing Our Kids

What kid hasn't been embarrassed by their parents? What parent hasn't been embarrassed by their kid? Clarence Darrow said, "The first half of our lives is ruined by our parents and the second half by our children." Perhaps not ruined, but definitely traumatized at times. Think of Woody Allen who said, "My parents put a live teddy bear in my crib."

I asked people what memories they had of embarrassing their children or being embarrassed by their parents. I got so many responses I can't print them all. Some made me laugh out loud. All of them made me identify. It seems these are universal experiences.

I remember driving around town with the windows down singing at the top of my lungs . . . my kids rolled up the windows as fast as they could while slinking down so no one could see them.

I also remember taking our kids on a tour of a cave out west. We walked further and further into the dark dank cave. My husband gets claustrophobic. I have a huge fear of snakes. We began to go kinda crazy. My panicking husband asked loudly, "Where can we get out?" I whined loudly, "Do you ever have snakes down here?" Our kids were humiliated yet rose to a higher level. They stood up front, backs to us, and totally acted like they didn't know us at all. And they really were wishing they didn't.

Now think about it. What memories do you have like this?

Don Burns

Not long ago, my husband and I went to take our adult daughter on a bike ride around Baldwin Lake. We each had our ugly helmets on. I also had on big black knee braces. And, okay, our bikes aren't cool either and we ride slow. Oh, and then there is the basket on my bike with a black furry dog in it. So the three of us are ready to go on our wonderful bike ride, when our daughter looks at us, gets off her bike and heads for the house. "Where are you going?" She replies, "I am single and I just can't afford to ride in public with you both looking so goofy."

Diana's children refused to go to church with her unless she quit singing. And her mother embarrassed her when she was a child by falling asleep in church . . . and snoring.

Poor Stacy. Her folks drove her to the movies in their beater car. She was so humiliated that she had them drop her off blocks away and walked. They followed her and waited till she met her friends and then drove slowly by honking and waving at her.

Ruth Ann's family got tickets for the whole family to go to the MSU football game. None of the kids wanted to sit with Mom because she would do that horrible thing – she would talk to strangers.

Darci said she loved to kiss and hug her girls in public. They would hate it and she would tell them, "It's my job as a parent to give you a reason to go into therapy."

Rae's poor children - Erica remembers her yelling out her name in a store. Her sister, Carter, had it worse. She remembers her mom telling a 5th grade sex-ed class about the importance of wearing cotton underwear.

Julie has paged her kids in stores. Say it ain't so.

Carrie took her kids to see the Whitecaps play. The mascot tried to liven up the evening by doing the Macarena. Carrie jumped up and joined in to the horror of her kids. Hey, Macarena!

Lynne was embarrassed when her folks would come to her school choir and sit in the front row and record her on their reel to reel tape recorder. Imagine - just the thought of it.

Anne was totally embarrassed by her conservative parents. Her kids were totally embarrassed by their hippie rebel parents. When their kids were teens, Gary and Anne got a harp and a dulcimer and learned to play. When they first played in public, still not very professional, their humiliated daughter said, "Why would old people want to learn to play new instruments and make complete fools of themselves in public?"

These children also didn't like their parents to drop them off at school. They preferred to be dropped off blocks away. They wanted their parents to turn off their old music on the car radio so no one could hear it. They also wanted Anne to dye her hair, not wear her reading glasses and would often ask, "Are you really going to wear that?"

Bette Davis said, "If you have never been hated by your child, you have never been a parent." Margaret Smith said, "My parents have been visiting me for a few days. I just dropped them off at the airport. They leave tomorrow."

When my son went to Kindergarten he said he was NOT supposed to wear his Halloween costume on the bus. I told him he had to be wrong, that no sane teacher would put costumes on 25 kids. Wrong! I made him wear his costume on the bus and he sat there, the only one. I am quite sure it still traumatizes him when he thinks of it. Some people just hold on to resentment!

Connie would yell at her daughter as she ran school races, "Go Boo Boo Bear." Her friend would yell to her daughter, "Go Chicken Butt."

Janine is one of the endangered species – women who iron clothes. She would iron her boys' gym clothes. They begged her to stop. It was too humiliating to look neat.

Each St. Patrick's Day Pat would dress her son like a leprechaun and send him to school. He told her years later that he would always get beat up for it.

Patty said, "I still embarrass my kids all the time. Examples: Nicknames like Chubby-

Bubby; volunteering them for things like singing in church; trying to fix friendships for them; my behavior ('Mom, you are not a teenager, you shouldn't dress like one.'); buying matching shirts only in different colors for my daughter and me; anytime I wouldn't take no for an answer or would ask a question in a restaurant or store ('Are you sure you added that up right?' or 'Couldn't you just make a small salad to go with that?'); giving them too much affection; using baby talk; and the list goes on and on and on."

Dixie's daughter would sit several rows away from her at the movie theatre. She also hated riding in the same elevator as her mom because Dixie would start a conversation with anyone in the elevator whether she knew them or not. "Like you don't even know those people, Mom."

When Norm's daughter was in 3rd grade, the school had a luau. He went dressed in Hawaiian print shorts, shark type necklaces and beads, bare feet and bare chest – wait, I'm not done yet – and a machete. He performed a Hawaiian war dance for the kids, jumping around, swinging the machete. You are right - this wouldn't be allowed in schools today. He almost took the head off of one of her classmates, which happened to be her boyfriend. Marissa has still not recovered. Counseling can only go so far.

Dale took their kids to U of M to see the beautiful campus. The whole time they were pointing out places, the kids were ducking so they couldn't be seen in the car. Seems they looked a lot like the Clark Griswald family in the film, Vacation. They were driving a Chevy wagon with wood on the sides, luggage on top and had just lost a hubcap. Uwwwww!

He further permanently damaged one of his son's when he took him to a 7th grade party at a classmate's home. Dale got out of the car and went in insisting on meeting the parents. His son survived, but just barely.

Holly got embarrassed by her kids when she was shopping. She put a bottle of wine in her cart – one bottle, mind you – and the kids began to scream loudly, "No, Mom, don't buy wine. We don't want you to be an alcoholic." She didn't buy it, but really wanted a glass after that.

My niece wrote me about the next one. A few hours later, her Dad wrote me about the same thing – not knowing his daughter had already "told" on him. The next morning one of his other daughter's wrote me about it.

He would drop his kids off at school and make them give him a kiss. If they didn't, he would walk them to their locker and kiss them there. My niece said she didn't "think it ever got that far, but he was so crazy they believed he would actually do it." He would also watch them walk into the building and lay on the horn when they got close to the door. If they didn't turn around and wave, he wouldn't stop blowing the horn. It doesn't make this story any better to say he was an elementary principal.

Julie had it bad as a kid. Her mom had to come to the high school office and sign a slip. Julie had to wait there for her to do it. Her mom came waltzing in wearing her robe, slippers and rollers in her hair. At least she left her cigarette in the car.

Only one beats these. As the extended family gathered, my niece had an aunt say, loud enough for everyone to hear, "Oh, when did you get your boobies?" She was all excited. My niece, not so much. For the record, I wasn't that aunt.

I guess the good news was said by Quentin Crewe. "Children despise their parents until the age of forty, when they suddenly become just like them, thus preserving the system." Seems there is justice after all.

When A Child Leaves

Today my friend told me a little one had asked her, "Did your baby come out of your stomach or on a plane?" It really doesn't matter how they come. They come. They brighten our lives. They enrich us. They become our purpose and our focus. They keep us busy. Oh, how busy.

For most of us, this parenting thing is a joy – an all consuming joy. Our lives pretty much take on a new dimension when we begin parenting. Everything comes second after taking care of the kids. Going to their sports and activities, being involved in whatever they are involved with, taking care of them, feeding them, doing laundry – the list goes on.

Sometimes we are too tired to enjoy it all or to get it done the way we want. Sometimes we say or do the wrong thing. We try so hard to be the parents we feel God wants us to be. It is a tall order.

As our babies grow to toddlers and school-age kids and teens, the joys and frustrations grow too. Dangers become greater as peers replace some of our parental influence. We have to have faith. We have to pray.

As parents, we give. We give help and caring. We give rides, advice, discipline, faith, money. We give love.

And then, one day, children leave the nest. Some are going to kindergarten. Some are going to college. Some are just moving out. The time is here. We knew this day was coming. Yet it feels like BOOM.

When my first child got on the school bus for kindergarten, I stood waving and crying. I wasn't sure I would live. I'm such a baby that way. He never looked back. He was a big boy and he was so excited.

Me? Not so much. I needed to mourn, to wallow in my memories, to focus on all the experiences of raising this child. I was overcome with sadness, emotion and reflection.

When we took our children to college, each time I felt like I was giving birth to them for the second time. We packed them up. We unloaded them. We helped them settle in. We made optimistic small talk, both for their sake and for ours. And then we left them.

We are happy for our children when they get old enough to go to school or leave for college or go off on their own. It is what we want for them, after all. But it comes so soon.

We wonder. Was I a good enough parent?

Did I tell them how much I love them?

I remembered all the parents who had told us through the years, "Enjoy those kids. They grow way too fast." How true those words were.

Can one ever really prepare for children leaving? Can we prepare for the day they won't really need us in the same ways anymore?

With those we love we are vulnerable, with our children, the most. We don't hold back. We love them with inseparable bonds that deepen through years and years of caring.

As we return to our lives after our child leaves, we have new questions. Can I begin to exercise now that I'll have more time? Can I finally have time to renew myself spiritually? Can I still get my groove back? There will be time now - time to reflect; time to grow; time to clean; time to do. Yes, to everything there is a season.

Home is never the same after a child leaves. There is an empty bed and closet. There is one less plate at the table. There is much more silence.

I have never liked change. I wish I did. I teach how change is good for us. I believe it. I just don't like it. It never feels good to me as it is happening.

But, what I do believe and what does feel good is my faith - faith that God will continue to envelope my child with caring and love, even when I am not physically there to do it and faith that God will comfort and guide me with what to do in my new role.

I know my child and I will both be okay. Even though we are not together as we had been, God is still holding on to us both. The circle remains unbroken.

My Best Parenting Skill

Don & Danny Burns

September is looming. Back to school is looming. Stores and ads are calling us to come buy, buy, buy. Parents are getting kids set to go to preschool, regular school, college, move away from home for the first time or last time. Other parents are feeling nostalgic at this time of year. My father-in-law raised 11 children. After they grew up and left home, fall was always a bittersweet time for him. Those passing school busses reminded him of days that were gone, yet so dear in his heart.

Parenting is not for the faint of heart. I remember being pregnant for my first child and worrying if I would know how to parent and what to do - if I was woman enough for the job that comes with a lifetime contract. Somehow, truly through the grace of God, we rise to the occasion. We become mother and/or father. This, like marriage, is for better or for worse.

Hope brightens our days as we begin this lifetime of parenting. We hope our child will have a happy life. We hope they will always be healthy. We hope they will have faith to guide them. We hope they never have any pain. Hope doesn't necessarily have reality in it.

Hope is a mixture of expectation and desire. Added to that are dreams, wishes, and even, ambition.

One of my heroes was Robert F. Kennedy. He said, "Each time a person stands up for an ideal, or acts to improve the lot of others, or strikes out against injustice, he sends forth a tiny ripple of hope." This sort of sums up parenting.

There were many times when I had angst over my children. I guess, to be honest, I still do, even though they are all seasoned adults.

I remember sitting with teachers, principals, counselors and coaches. Each memory is filled with concern and worry over something going on with one of my children. I remember a male teacher who had tears run down his cheek as he told us he didn't know what to do. Neither did we.

There were times when I was full of discouragement, my hope was dimmed. Others lifted the veil and helped me to see light. They gave me hope with their words and encouragement. They had belief when mine was ebbing. They gave me hope in the unseen.

I look back and all the things I worried about worked out okay. Life is never a smooth path. There are always bumps, valleys to climb out of and peaks to climb up. We believe in our children. We encourage them. We do what we can to make their journey easier.

Hope is wishing something would happen. Faith is believing something will happen. Courage is making something happen. These aren't always easy to do.

No matter the age of our children, we are their best encourager. Albius Tibullus said, "Hope ever urges us on, and tells us tomorrow will be better." That sums up a big part of our job as a parent. When their minds say, 'give up', hope whispers, 'one more try'. We can be the hope whisperer.

Often there are things we can do, actions we can take to help our children. But, sometimes, there is nothing we can do. These are the times when we get to do our most important parenting task, prayer.

I pray a lot for my children. I pray over and over and over. Sometimes I wonder why God isn't answering when I think he should. Sometimes I wonder why he isn't answering the way I think he should. Then I remember that it is not my place to question God. It is my place to pray to him and have hope that he will answer in my time frame and with the answer I want. I also realize that that is just a wish. I have to have faith that God knows best and will do whatever he does in his own timing. When I am at my best, I pray for God's will. I am often not at my best and I pray for what I want when I want it. I have hope God understands me. My life itself is a sign of hope, after all.

When I had these children, I thought they were in my hands. Little did I know that before I knew it, those hands would become bent with arthritis, covered with wrinkled skin and empty of those daily parenting tasks. Those hands now have another job.

Now those hands do my parenting tasks with phone calls, emails, Facebook, touching, hugging, writing notes. Those hands play games with them and hold their hands when the opportunity arises. Those hands cook for them, do for them and reach out to them.

The greatest power, though, is when I put my hands together and lift them up to God, with hope and faith. Prayer has turned out to be one of my very best parenting skills. And I am reminded of the parenting trio - faith, hope and love, which is also known as, mother/father/God.

Hurrah For The New Kind Of Fathers

There is a new phenomenon out there. Have you noticed?

Recently at a wedding, I watched two families in front of me. One was Steve and his 17 year old son. Steve sat with his arm around his son and rubbed his back at times. They were both very comfortable with this. On the other side was Joe. His seven year old son, Joey, cuddled up into his lap.

Don & Danny Burns

I have watched my son father his two young boys. They are crazy about him. He plays with them all the time, on their level. He treats them with lots of love and respect. He listens carefully. He discusses their feelings with them. He teaches them about everything and together they absorb the world.

As I examine this new generation of fathers, I realize my son isn't unique. Many, many fathers are like him.

Carl, a former college football player, insisted he give their babies their first baths. He was comfortable doing it and talked softly to the babies as he bathed them. He relished this as his first bonding time with each of his five children.

For many of us, when our children were born, the fathers weren't even allowed in the delivery rooms. It was like a stork really did deliver babies behind closed doors. My mate was allowed in as our last child was delivered caesarean. They took her out of me and laid her directly into his arms – talk about bonding.

I do have to laugh as I write this, though, because not all cultures behave as we do. When my second child was born in Spain, my husband was brought in as soon as the baby popped out. The Doctor immediately offered my mate a beer and they stood over me, still on gas and a mess, and celebrated in the delivery room together - certainly not the American way.

Women working outside of the home have been monumental in helping Dads become part of the critical parenting team.

Doug has two young daughters. He adjusts his schedule to have them at daycare as little as possible. He makes meals so they can eat as a family when his wife returns from her out of town job. He is hands-on in every aspect of parenting.

Doug and my son follow the philosophy of working to live, not living to work. My son recently shared with me that he could do more things but that he really prefers to keep the children as his priority now. He and Doug spend as much time with their kids as they can. They agree with Tom, who shared with me yesterday, "I want to make my sons a priority in my life right now. They will grow up quickly and I don't want to look back and have missed an opportunity with them. I try to make every day count as a father."

Peter is a typical hands-on new dad. He stays home from his teaching position two days a month to care for his baby boy and avoid day care. Peter's brother-in-law will sometimes take his baby to work with him to give his wife, who also works outside the home, a much appreciated break. I think you call this a win-win situation.

Linda called her son, Bob, who was home with his baby. She said, "Oh, you're babysitting today." Bob was upset with her comment and she apologized. She said, "I told him he was right. I would never have said such a comment to his wife. Even though my husband was very involved with our children, I still had that attitude." Old habits die hard. Old thoughts die hard. Old roles die hard, for all of us.

Yesterday I chatted with Eric. He is a graduate of Cornell University and has a master's from Columbia University. He is also a happy stay–at-home Dad. He was in the middle of making homemade spaghetti and meat balls and, like many young fathers I observe, is a terrific cook.

Eric has three sons, ages 7 to 14. He doesn't really know other men in his situation and is kind of the local lone ranger in this role. He said, "Men and women do things differently. It can be a tricky adjustment, but one needs to ask, 'what is the best way to parent our children at this time in our lives?'

A Grand Rapids Dad shared, "I try to have an open comfortable line of communication with my kids, the oldest a teenage son. A significant example is being open about sex and healthy relationships rather than leaving it a mystery. I think talking to them about condoms, birth control and healthy relationships may prevent a lot of grief for my children in the future. It may even prevent teen pregnancy."

Char said, "I think the new kind of fathers is actually a reinvention of the old kind of fathers. The examples set by a father set the stage for the next generation. My son and son-in-laws had great examples. My grandsons will surely be the best fathers ever!"

That is a wonderful thing but doesn't ring true for everyone. Some fathers who shared with me said they chose deliberately to not father like their father had. They had examples of what not to do and be. They could relate more with Steven Pearl who quipped, "I phoned my dad to tell him I had stopped smoking. He called me a quitter."

There is a five generation rule: how a parent raises their child, the love they give, the values they teach, the emotional environment they offer, the education they provide – will influence not only their child but the four generations to follow. This will work both positively and negatively.

I want to applaud all the new kind of fathers. We thank God for you. The world has never needed you more. Generations will be better people because you father the way you do. You give a wonderful gift to our children, our grandchildren and our great grand children. You are making the world a better place.

The Way We Talk

Creative Answers For The Unwanted Call

Ringy ding ding, chimes, music, or whatever your phone does to ring. My husband's is the most obnoxious. Jivey music comes on with a deep voice that says, "Hello Moto". Spare me! Our daughter put it on his phone when he first got it, as a joke. He would have changed it, if he only knew how.

Anyway, what do you do when you get all those wonderful courtesy, political, sales and money begging calls??? I asked around and got some great ideas.

There are a few (very few) odd folks who are polite. They answer kindly, listen and give respect to the caller. Then there are the rest of us.

Some just hang up. I'm sure you'll think less of me, but that's my style. Don't judge me.

My niece, Sarah, lets her two year old son answer. He babbles nonsense and asks them if they are his grandma. Very cute.

Gerry yells, "Hello", and keeps yelling it as if he's deaf. His wife, Patty, tells them, "They don't live here." Someone else says, "We're in crisis here," or "We're eating dinner."

Terry asks for their phone number so he can call them back.

Laurel adds to the dinner idea. She tells them she is in the middle of dinner and asks them what time their family dinner is so she can call them and interrupt theirs. Laurel always has fun ideas. She's the one who named our book club - The Happy Bookers.

When there is a 4 second delay before the caller starts, she waits 4 seconds each time before she replies to them.

She also got a call from a company wanting to sell her windows. She let them go on with their entire sales pitch and then said she was interested. She asked about their long range payment plan, told them she was renting, but was sure her landlord would approve. She added that she could only afford five dollars a month. They hung up on her and didn't call back. Bingo.

Diana replies, "I have to step away from the phone for a second." She puts it down, puts it on speaker and never returns until she hears the dial tone. Susan tells them, "I have someone on the other line trying to sell me something, can you hold?"

One couple acts like they are having a big fight and keep yelling at each other about stupid things. They ask the caller to help settle it. Aren't people creative?

Ryan gave me some great ones that he's heard. "Sorry, I can't talk right now. My neighbor's house is on fire."

"Hello? Hello? I can't hear you very . . . hello? Must be a bad connection." Hang up. If they call back, repeat above.

"Please leave a message after the tone." Then hang up.

Ryan had a friend who got a call while doing a word puzzle. As soon as they started their spiel, he broke in with questions about how to spell a word or what this word meant, etc. Clever!

Alvina asks political callers things like: "Do you agree with that policy; are you going to vote for that candidate". They get off the line quickly.

Beth informs them that if they call her one more time before the election, she will be sure to vote for the other candidate.

Sue tells them sad things that happened in her life.

Barb says stuff like, "Now is not a good time." "I just can't focus." If they ask for the lady of the house, she tells them she's out.

Elmer said he tells them, "I'm not here." Evelyn's brother tells them, "He died last week."

Hilda has a brother who says on his answering machine, "Hi, I'm making changes in my life. If I don't talk with you or call you back, you're one of my changes."

Candy knows someone who begins chatting with them. "Where are you calling from? Do you do much fishing there? I got a nice trout today. What's your weather like? It's beginning to rain here." Silence from the caller as they've hung up.

Stephen is a really nice guy. He gives them all respect and kindness and thanks them and says he's not interested. When they continue, he calmly apologizes for their hearing problem and hangs up.

Marta tries to sell them something. "Would you like a whole year's worth of …."

Another answers, "I'm the housekeeper. No speak-a-da English." They are saying this all in English, by the way.

Andy heard this one. They pretend the caller has phoned in the middle of a homicide investigation. They pretend to be the detective and start asking questions. "What's your full name? Your location? How did you know the deceased? What type of dealings have you had with them in the past? When you last saw them …." I love this one.

But the best is one my husband heard. The guy listens to the caller go on and on and is silent for quite awhile and then in a slow creepy voice says, "What are you wearing?" Yewwww. Hang up.

What's A Guy Supposed To Do?

The other day our friends shared this story. Dale stopped at Dunkin Donuts. He asked Mary if she wanted a donut. She said, "No". He went in and came out with two donuts. She said, "What did you get?" He said, "I got myself two donuts. You said you didn't want one." She retorted angrily, "Well, you could have surprised me!" He looked at us and shrugged his shoulders, "What's a guy to do?"

Ah ha. That is very typical of the clear, or should I say unclear, communication problems with men and women. They just find it hard to understand each other.

Dave said, "My wife is a gorgeous, kind, thoughtful, holy woman whom I adore." I get the feeling he is covering his bases with this intro. He goes on. "However, she has one flaw. She lies like a rug when it comes to saying, 'I'm just going into the store for a minute'. Her minute is more like hours but I don't dare say it. Now, after twenty years of marriage, I drop her off at the store for her minute. Then I can go home, use the bathroom, make a sandwich, watch ESPN and relax in the chair with the dog in my lap. In about an hour I return to get her. She comes out and smiles, 'See, that wasn't too long, was it'?"

He goes on. "She will also spend almost every minute for months obsessing over every single detail of a child's upcoming wedding . . . but if I ask, 'What's for supper?', she looks at me absently and replies, 'I don't know. I haven't thought about it."

While driving in busy Boston traffic, Jim was having a horrible time merging. He asked his wife, Harriet, how it looked on her side. "Fair," she said. "Fair doesn't help," Jim came back. She replied, "Well, that's what it looked like to me."

Brent is amazed that a woman can save money by buying something. He also says he can't imagine why anybody would be against gay marriage, because at least two people of the same sex have something in common.

Another thing that stymies Brent is when a woman complains about her mate's drinking beer and watching football all day. When asked where she met him, she replies, "A sports bar."

Al sums it up. "Men are always willing to take a break from TV to talk with their spouse. However, most women seem to use a lot of words and details to describe a situation or they pose a long, drawn out question. I have learned to shorten the discussion with, 'Huh' or 'What?'. Then I can get back to the ball game."

Chuck says his hearing has gotten worse, or so his wife says. She says, "You're a tease", to which he replies, "You want me to cut the cheese?" He has tried to simplify his life by just answering, "Yes, dear."

My friend, Ron, shared about a couple who was watching TV. The guy was drinking martinis. All of a sudden he says, "I love you." His wife responds, "Yes, but is that you talking or the third martini?"

He says, "It is me talking to the third martini."

A friend shares how he doesn't understand women. "They ask for opinions on all sorts of patterns, fabrics, wallpapers, clothes. He thinks his response is never valued and he has learned to look at the selection and ask which one she likes best. Then he agrees. He has learned how to play the game. He also said he doesn't understand how women shop for clothes and shop for clothes and shop some more. "Men," he said, "walk into a store and say I need a suit." They show him three and he picks one. When asked by his wife, "Don't you want to look around?" He answers, "No, I just needed a suit." He said learning the secrets to shopping have made his marriage of fifty years pure bliss.

Male and female communication differences extend to moms and sons too. Jim was walking his dog with his mother. The dog tried to stop to urinate. Jim pulled him along. His mother said, "He has to mark his territory." Jim said, "He doesn't have any territory." To which his mom retorted, "Of course, he doesn't, you won't let him mark it." Mothers get the last word!

Pete sums up this age old dilemma with a joke. You may have heard it, but it sure nails this topic.

A guy comes upon a genie who tells him he will grant him any wish he wants. The guy asks for a bridge from California to Hawaii so he won't have to fly. The genie says that is impossible because there is not enough steel and concrete to do it. He asks if the man has another wish. The guy says, "Can you explain how women think?" The genie slumps and asks, "Do you want two lanes or four?"

The Color Of White Lies

My friend was out to dinner with his 14 year old granddaughter. They talked about how the food wasn't very good and they'd give it about a C minus. Right then the waitress came by and asked how their food was. My friend said, "Oh, good, thanks." When the waitress left, his granddaughter looked at him and said sweetly, "It's okay, Grandpa, I lie sometimes too."

I pride myself in being a very honest person and honesty is very important to me. However, don't we all lie just a little bit? Oh, you don't think you ever do? Let's see about that.

Here are some questions we may lie about, just a little, just a teeny bit. You may even call it fudge. I mean, it's not really an out and out lie. Is it?

"Have you ever smoked?" That's a good one. I was with someone recently when they were asked that by the doctor. They answered, "No." Later, I asked them about it as I knew that they sometimes smoked. "Oh," they said, "that doesn't count. That's not what the doctor meant." Oh, really. Someone else told me they always answer no to that question because if they say yes, their insurance rates will go up. Dang, that's motivation.

"Do you exercise?" "Sure, regularly. Well, does talking on the phone count? Cooking? Eating? Using the remote? I am pretty faithful about all of those."

"How much do you drink?" "Oh, not much."

"How many glasses of wine do you have a day?" You wonder - how big a glass?

The worst lie bait is this one. "How much do you weigh?" What woman doesn't hate that question? When I am at the doctor and the nurse hauls me over to the scale, often pulling me by my hair to get me there, I cringe with fright. "Can I strip buck naked? Can I come back after I fast for a few days? Can I write it in the chart myself?"

I think the only time we are really, really honest about how much we weigh, is when we are about to go up in a small plane and they ask. When the plane will likely crash if you don't tell the truth, it is time to be honest. Throw caution to the wind, bite the bullet and just fess up.

Have you ever lied about money or purchases? "Is that new?" "Oh, no, I got it ages ago." "Yes, but I got it on a huge sale." What you really mean is you got it "for" sale. "How much did you spend on that?" "Ahhhh, I can't remember." Complaining about your poor memory is always a good one to use here.

Adlai Stevenson said, "A lie is an abomination unto the Lord and a very present help in time of trouble." He was a man who understood these things. We lie to be kind. We lie to be polite. We lie when we don't want to hurt someone.

Someone cooks for you. "Do you like it?" "Oh, yes, it is delicious. I'm just full. I had a big lunch." Once I had a dinner party and a good friend didn't eat much of the main dish. I asked her if she liked it and she replied, "Well, it's not as good as other things I've had here." Nicely put. She obviously didn't want to lie. I kinda wish she had.

There is a Yugoslavian proverb that says, "Tell the truth and run." That can be mighty good advice.

"How do you like my hair?" "How do you like my outfit?" My friend, Maggie, always smiles sweetly and says, "If you feel good ...."

Here are some other hard ones. "Do I look as old as them?" "Am I as big as them?" "Do I have that many wrinkles?" "Can you tell I lost five pounds?" "Oh, you haven't changed a bit!" "Did you miss me a lot?"

I asked around to see what other people were lying about. People lie about their kids. Just like with money, you can round up or round down. With talking about our kids, we usually round up. I don't think that's really lying. That's probably just good parenting.

I was told that people lie about who is related to them. "Are they related to you?" "Ahhhhhh, not so much . . . maybe distantly. . . I don't really know. Who, again?"

How about when asked, "Who did that?" "Not me, nope, not me, for sure, not me."

Sometimes people are afraid to tell the truth. Samuel Goldwyn said, "I don't want any yes-men around me. I want everybody to tell me the truth even if it costs them their jobs."

I've seen people lie so much that they get all mixed up in the lies. Keeping it all straight can be quite a task. Bette Midler said, "I never know how much of what I say is true."

Marriages and close relationships are filled with these kinds of dilemmas. We were getting dressed recently to go to a big gathering. I said to my husband, "Do I look too chubby in this?" He looked at me and said, "Do you really think I'm dumb enough to answer that question?" We had some good laughs over that, but I never did get an answer. He didn't want to lie, I guess.

A Lot Of Blah

We often laugh with our friends, David and Patti, about his Aunt Dot from England. She visited and went to the local post office. When she returned she was all excited and told them, "The postmaster said he was gonna knock me up."

They didn't know how to respond and were kind of shell shocked. Until they figured out that in England, knock me up means call me. Okay then.

When you think of it, it is quite amazing, miraculous even, that we all communicate so well.

Not that it is that well actually, but it is what it is. I recently asked folks for examples of marital communication. I expected funny ones. I got normal ones that we all could relate to but not necessarily funny ones. I got the idea for this column when my friend, Sally, said she came home and her husband said, "Your cousin called and somebody died." I think this is the opposite of TMI. This is clearly NEI – not enough information.

My friend, Don, said, "After 43 years of wedded bliss, I must say that communication skills between spouses deteriorate rapidly year after year. My dear wife, on more than one occasion, says that talking to me is like 'talking to a manatee'. Whaddya suppose she means by that?" Hmmm, I'm not sure. I looked up manatee because I wasn't sure what it was – a large aquatic plant eating mammal. Doesn't sound like a compliment, Don.

Of course, men and women are just different. We think differently. We talk differently. Trisha reminded me that in the movie, *The Break Up*, with Jennifer Aniston and Vince Vaughn, they fight about doing the dishes. She asks him to do the dishes. He prefers lying on the couch and playing video games. They fight. She wants him to help. He wants to be left alone. Finally, he turns off the video game and stomps into the kitchen to help her.

She then is mad that he is not happy to do it. She says, "I want you to WANT to do the dishes." He responds, "Why would I WANT to do the dishes?" This sounds way too familiar to many of us.

My friend, Alison, emails her husband as efficiently as possible giving only the information he needs, trying not to bother him. She will include several questions to which he responds with one word, "Yes". She is beginning to sense he may not be reading her emails very well.

There are communication snags within families. Folks just don't always understand what you mean. Patty wrote me that a guy was having prostate surgery. His wife asked their daughter to stop and get him some Posies, which are undergarments. The girl brought flowers, but, of course.

Gary had a male student get a text message from his mom. It told the student that his grandma had died and his mom signed it LOL. The boy was stunned that his mom would be so blasé about poor Grandma. Later he realized she meant lots of love, not laugh out loud.

Rae told me she leaned over and said to her mate, in a loving frame of mind, "Thank You for sharing your life with me." He said, "You want to borrow my knife?"

Our cousin, Maureen, said that to get her husband's attention, she will ask, "Where would you like to be buried?" He has more than once responded with, "Who's getting married?"

We are about to wrap up our first year of my husband's retirement and it has gone very nicely. Except for one day he followed me into the bedroom and told me, "You know if you put water in a dish, it will clean easier later." All I could do was glare. I have only been doing dishes since I was tall enough to reach the sink. It isn't that I don't know this stuff. Some days I just don't care. I'm sure he doesn't understand me.

Communication seems like a lot of blah, blah, blah. That reminds of when my brother in law, Gerry, died. The people gathered to say a rosary. His son had his fiancé there. She wasn't Catholic but was a good sport and knelt quietly. Later she said to me, "I kind of zoned out and when I came too I could swear they were saying the same thing over and over." Welcome to the family, sweetheart.

Communication does seem like a lot of blah, blah, blah. It does seem like we say the same things over and over. It does seem like we don't always listen well, or read emails clearly enough. It does seem like we don't really understand what the other person means.

So often talk is cheap, until you hire a lawyer.

To Swear Or Not To Swear

To swear or not to swear, that is the question. Well, it may not be the question you had on your mind, but it is the question I have been pondering.

It seems swearing has new legitimacy. Time magazine said that cursing can ease your pain. Hot Darn! I have substituted darn there for something else, but I am guessing you knew that.

Time says, "Shouting a four letter word when you stub your toe or hammer your thumb may ease the pain. In a British study, researchers had volunteers immerse their hands in ice water and repeatedly shout either a curse word or a neutral word like table. Those who cursed withstood the pain longer and reported that it hurt less." And to that I say, "Duh." I also say, "Who pays for these studies?"

Who would ever yell, "Table" when you hit yourself with a hammer? Come on. Sometimes even "Darn" doesn't quite do the medicinal effect that stronger words do.

Time magazine goes on, "Curse words raise your heart rate and prepare you emotionally for battle."

Hmmm. I just heard some soldiers in Afghanistan being interviewed on NPR and they sure used a lot of curse words. Perhaps they always talk that way so they are ready for battle whenever it arrives. As they were quoted there were actually more "bleeps" than words. You could barely figure out what they were saying. It was mostly bleeps and ands.

So I did some major research. I mentioned at the Coffee House that I was considering doing a column on swearing. Boy that got their attention. They instantly became a chattering group of cursers. Not cursers really but pretend cursers. They came up with all kinds of things people say that are close to cursing but not cursing. It makes you wonder, of course, when people use pretend curse words, who is the pretending for? Are they fooling themselves? Are they fooling others? Are they fooling God? Are they better people because they don't really curse but pretend curse? Even if they are better, I bet they hurt more.

Here are some of the things they came up with. "Dang Nabbitt." "Son of a biscuit." "Ding Dang."

I am telling you, they got pretty wild as they continued and absolutely everyone was in on the game. "Fudge." "Freaken." "Shoot." "Shugar." I decided to spell it like that seeing it is replacing another S H word.

"H. E. Double Hockey Sticks". At this they laughed and laughed. I hadn't heard of this one before but they bent over chuckling with that one as they all had used it.

One I couldn't figure out but they all had heard in their families was, "Cheese and

Rice." That made no sense to me but they told me it substitutes the Lord's name. Whew. Who'd a guessed? Not me. Say it fast and you can figure it out.

Using the Lord's name in vain is something I don't like. In our home you can't do that and you can't say, "Shut up", which I have always considered swearing. Those are both big no-no's. Once my daughter said about someone, "Mom, they swore." She was shocked. What they had said was, "Shut up." I taught her well.

The coffee house pretend cursing committee kept on. "Caca." "Cripes." "Sugar Jets." "Judas Priest." "Jimminy Christmas." "Fiddle Sticks."

Later, I asked a couple of very religious folks I know what they say when they pretend swear. They pretended they never do, but they had heard others who do. They came up with "Gol Darnit". "Oh, fudge." "Gee Whiz." "Oh, my gosh." "Oh, my gol." They also said "Holy Cow". But one of them had said that in India and found out it was a very bad thing to say there. He said it was worse than any swear words he could have said. Whew. Having never been to India nor ever even thought of swearing in India, I am not so worried about that one.

One friend said her father always vehemently said, "Son of a basket of peaches." After that he would immediately go into true Italian curse words.

I have a friend in Greenville who is German. She often swears in German while playing Mah Jongg and none of us really know what she is saying. But we get her gist.

I got a couple more from folks. "Frack." "Why the face?" "Horse feathers." "Oh, sheep on a shingle." And a couple that make no sense to me at all - "Peter, Paul and Mary," and "Shut the front door."

I gotta say it has been fun research going around asking folks what they say when they pretend swear. This morning I asked a man I didn't know and when he looked at me, his face lit up like and he immediately came up with, "That's a bunch of Schmidt."

Who knew there was so much pretend swearing going on in the world? And I know I have just touched the iceberg here.

But now we have a dilemma. The next time we bash ourselves in the head with a sledge hammer or drop a thirty pound frozen turkey on our toe, what do we do? Do we do as Time would suggest and let 'er rip? Or do we revert to our creative side and bring out our pretend swearing but then hurt more. Ah, decisions, decisions. Isn't life hard?

That Means What???

Communication is hard. During a security check at the airport I heard a guy asked if he had any pornographic material. He looked stunned and replied, "I don't even have a pornograph."

Okay, I didn't really hear that but I love it and think it's funny. Communication is hard, though, and I have had some interesting communication glitches come up in the last couple of years.

Words change. We grow up and learn them and then some of them go and change their meaning on us. For example, the word gay used to mean happy. Now it has a whole new meaning. When one says, "He's so gay." They usually aren't talking about their happiness level.

My husband reminded me. "Long hair music used to mean classical music. Now it means sixties or grunge or who knows, but not necessarily classical."

I am guessing the word hoe used to mean a gardening tool. Now it has a much different meaning. I will let you guess the common definition of that one.

I had an interesting thing happen to me a couple of years ago. I met a young man who was moving to Dallas. I told him my daughter's friend was living in Dallas. Both guys were the same age, from western Michigan, engineers working for big Texas companies. I got the email and phone information from both of them so they could connect. They seemed to be excited to have a home boy to get to know while they were living in the south. At the end of this information giving, I said to the young man I had just met, "There, now you two can hook up." He paused rather awkwardly and then said, "You do know I'm not gay, don't you?"

And that is how I found out that hook up has a new meaning. It used to mean getting together. Now it means getting together in a very intimate way. All I know is they never "hooked up" or contacted each other. I think I scared them both off. Hmmm. And they could have had such a nice time sharing a beer together and visiting. Life is so complicated.

I am guessing that years ago if one said a person was high, they meant they were in a highly elevated place. Now that means they are most likely on a chemical substance or alcohol.

In 2000 I read that having tea was a new phenomenon that was catching on across the country. I decided to get into tea parties. In January 2000 I had my first inaugural tea party. That meant it was my first one. I got lovely invitations and put on, what I thought, was a fancy special tea party. I served hot teas and teeny goodies. It was very la-dee-dah in a nice way. I invited eight of my favorite women. That began years of my hosting tea parties. I even started a tea party group in Grand Rapids. I have had tea parties solely for the sake of tea drinking and friendship. I had one for my friend who was dying of cancer. I have had special birthday tea parties. I have had lots of kinds of tea parties for many different reasons.

Fast forward to this year. A lady I know a little in Grand Rapids called me about a common friend we have who was having some trouble. She called me about four times. The last time she said, "I have to go. I have a tea party."

I was elated. I said, "Oh, I'm into tea parties too. In fact, I have the most delicious lavender cookie recipe." Silence, and a bit of disgust seemed to come from her and she then said, "I mean a political tea party."

I was silent and shocked. This was not what I expected and I didn't know how to respond. "Okay, I gotta go," I said. I was not only shocked that we were talking about such different things, but, heck, she didn't even ask for my lavender cookie recipe. Hello!

So now I am sad that tea party has a different meaning. It is even on the news, for heaven's sake. Do I have to put a P.S. on my next tea party invitations? "P.S. This is not a political affair." How unfun is that? Why didn't they call that group something else? Why did it have to take over the fun, innocent tea party name? I mean, really, politics aside, there are a lot of different things they could have called themselves.

So, words change or at least their meanings do. I am now careful when I talk about hooking people up. I never confuse being gay with being happy. Not that gay people are not happy, I know many who are.

When people say someone is high, I usually don't think they are in an elevated location. When someone discusses their new hoe I am quite sure they have a new gardening utensil. But then there are some people . . .

It is hard to keep up in this world. Sometimes I think it is impossible.

I was discussing words like this with my doctor today. He said, "Making love used to mean kissing." I was surprised. But then I remembered seeing some old movies where they sang about that and I thought, "Whoa, Bessie, I can't believe they said that way back then." Now it makes sense. They were talking about kissing.

So what do we do with all these words that change as we go along in life? I don't know, but if you want to ponder it while you eat lavender cookies, the recipe is in the back of the book.

Growing Old Or Growing Up?

Stanley Ross had a great quote about communication. "Open your mouth only to change feet."

Have you ever said something and wished you hadn't said it that way? Has anything you ever said come across differently than you meant it? Has anyone ever said anything to you that hurt or upset you? I am guessing these are pretty universal human experiences. Do you agree?

When babies are born, they have a soft spot on the top of their head. People have to be careful until it firms up. It is delicate, fragile. I think we all have soft spots, emotional ones, and they remain sensitive into adulthood. We get hurt when someone says something that hits our soft spot or spots. Other things can be said to us that don't bother us, but things that hit our soft spot, well, they hurt. They can really make us angry.

My daughter and I realized this concept once and, since then, I have used it in many talks. It is appropriate in all communication, whether in the workplace or with friends and family.

Today I was discussing it with a good friend. I had said something awhile ago that hit his soft spot. Of course, I hadn't meant it and would never have said it that way had I realized his sensitivity. I do have to say, this is not the first time this has happened to me. I have been on both ends of this ordeal.

My friend told me how he felt as a child when other kids said mean things to him. Those certain words really developed his soft spot. Of course, this tenderness does not harden as we grow up. We remain sensitive in these areas.

My soft spot was also developed when I was a child and was caused by repeated negative things that were said to me. To this day, if anyone says anything to me in that realm, oops, off I go into my tender area.

I remember a few years ago, someone said something to me that upset me for days. I discussed it with my friend several times. After a bit, she calmly said to me, "Maureen, I think you have overreacted and I think you did so because of how you were treated as a child. It brought all that up again." I immediately knew she was right. Putting it in that framework allowed me to understand and let it go.

Why do I bring this up? I bring it up because I think it happens often as we all communicate with each other. When we take the time to think about our personal soft spots, it can help us to handle our reactions better.

Everyone has different soft spots. What are yours? When I ask people, it is amazing that after a couple minutes, they can come up with what really bugs them, their main sensitivities.

For some, it is feeling dumb. They don't want anyone to make them feel dumb. For others, it is being told what to do. They don't want anyone to tell them what to do. For some, it is being made to feel lesser than. There are many, many soft spots. I believe they come from early life experiences that seemed negative to us. It is like we got bruised in our egos and those bruises did not heal. The skin on them can be rubbed off easily with words that reactivate our old wounds.

I can take a lot of things that are said to me. But when something really upsets me, and I continue to be upset for awhile, I have to stop and think. Did this affect me like this because it hit my old soft spot? For me, it is almost always what has happened.

The next time you get angry over something someone said to you, ask yourself. "What does this trigger inside? Why does this make me feel so upset? What really makes me mad here?" The answers will likely bare your soft spot to you. Usually these kinds of incidents point to the same inner feelings over and over . . . and that is what we call our soft spots.

Communication is not easy, but understanding things like this about ourselves and others, can make it easier. Life is a journey. We grow old. We don't necessarily grow up. But if we keep learning, we can become better at this thing called living – both to ourselves and to others.

The Times They Are
A Changing

Dumb And Dumber

Do you remember the movie, *Dumb and Dumber*? Well, we are living with that on a daily basis. Oh, it isn't us. Oh, no. It's our cell phones. His is "dumb" and mine is "dumber".

Our kids and the rest of the world, have "smart" phones.

The other day we talked about our history of phones. What's yours? You didn't always have smart phones. Remember?

Our first phone memories are of great big black phones hanging on the walls. My husband remembers having to crank it to make a call. As he is much, much older than me (okay, so it's only four years, still . . .) I don't remember cranking phones.

Everyone had their own individual rings. His was two long and one short. Ours was three short and one long. These were called party lines, though I don't remember going to any parties. When it was your personal ding-a-ling, you picked up the phone. This made it easy for neighbors to pick up when you were talking and listen in on your conversation.

My husband has a fun memory of his grandpa talking on the phone. The other person said, "Is there a noise on the phone?"

Grandpa replied, "Yeah, that's Billy Bob (the name has been changed to protect the guilty). He listens in on our conversations."

At that point, a third voice pipes in, "No, no, tain't me!" and hangs up.

Operators would come on the line and plug you in on a switchboard connecting you to the person you wanted to talk to.

Next came big clunky dial phones. Following that were smaller ones called princess phones. They were oval shaped with push buttons and they came in colors.

And then the word mobile, which used to describe gas or homes, began to be used for phones. This turned into cells.

The first mobiles were great big clunky things, nearly the size of a back pack with huge antenna sticking out of them.

A couple years ago, I would see people going for walks and talking to themselves.

At first I felt sorry for them and thought they needed drugs, pronto. Then I realized they had an earpiece you couldn't see and a phone somewhere in their clothes. Who would have ever believed this stuff?

It doesn't seem that long ago that we went to hear a futurist speak. He described how phones would be in a few years. I remember he said this incredulous thing. "Right now in Japan there are people taking pictures with their phones." No one really believed him. Who would?

Remember the first car phones with giant aerials sticking up. At the car wash everyone had to remove them. Now the phone rings and I push a button on my steering wheel to answer it.

There are also voice activated ones. My husband would just tell his to, "Call home." And it would.

Now, phones do it all. Even my "dumber" phone can take pictures. Of course, I don't. One day a photo popped up and scared the life out of me. I don't know how it got there or how it went away.

My cell has all kinds of symbols at the top of the screen. I only know what one of them means and that if it blinks, I need to charge it.

Not long ago I figured out how to text on my "dumber" phone. This isn't easy as it has no keyboard. I gotta push the g three times to get an i. Too much work, for sure. I only text when I want to be cool. Of course, that never happens either.

Connie told me her husband, Gary, has a "dumbest" phone. It doesn't even text. She said he told the clerk at the phone store that he only wanted a phone that would make and take calls. The guy said, "We don't have phones like that, sir."

A friend told me today that she hates shopping and paying full price while watching people searching their smart phones for coupons so they can pay less. She said the other day someone asked her how she made a salad she was serving. She began to list the ingredients from her memory. She couldn't remember one, but her grandson said, "Sour cream." While they were talking, he had looked up the recipe on his phone.

I love how a song plays in a store and my daughter points her phone in that direction and it tells her who is singing and the name of the song. I think she can buy it on the spot and have it sent to her Itunes library and it goes into her cloud and all her other stuff. I use the word stuff because I don't know what the heck I am talking about here. This is all beyond me, in the clouds, for sure.

Recently we got an Ipod to play our music. My friend, Stacey, said to me, "Why are you getting an Ipod? All you need is a phone. It does everything." Of course, I had just bought the Ipod, so I was stuck with it. Now I guess I gotta make the big move and get a smart phone. I can't live another minute without being able to get my email, Facebook, internet, camera, GPS, weather, church and movie schedules, menus, games - oh, my, will this sentence ever end? I could write on and on and on about what my new smart phone will be able to do.

But the question that haunts me is this. If we upgrade to smart phones, will it come to pass that we realize our phones aren't the real dumb and dumber? We are!

Change Bites

Remember that song that went, "Turn, turn, turn..."? Well, everywhere I turn lately, there is change. I don't like change very much. I like growth. Is there a difference here? Am I being too picky? Please don't email me with answers to that.

I go to my church and they have changed the wording to the entire mass. I'll be honest, I don't like it. It seems minor and not necessary. I wonder why they are bothering when there are so many more serious things we could be addressing. I wish I had been asked to be on the committee that thought up all these changes. I have a lot of thoughts I could have given them. Perhaps I missed their call.

I think back to when the entire mass changed from Latin to English. I remember all the "older" people complaining about it. Have I become one of them? Say it ain't so, please.

This morning during church, I leaned over and whispered to my husband. It probably came across more like a whine than a whisper. Okay, so I whimpered, "These changes are driving me crazy." To which he instantly replied, "How far was the drive?" What a smarty pants he is. I gotta say, he made me laugh out loud which is always a good thing. I'm thankful for him.

So there are changes at church. Then I go home and grab my Sunday paper and there are changes there too. I see that soon the Grand Rapids Press will only be delivered to my door three days a week. Apparently the other four days it will be printed but I will not receive it. I don't like this one bit. Whose idea was this? No one asked me what I thought about this either. Did I miss their call, too?

I never ever read the paper when I get it. I wait days, sometimes weeks. If I am honest, I've even waited months. One thing is sure, though. I always read it. Now my whole routine will be screwed up. You know the one. Go get the paper and let it pile up routine. Dang, so many change challenges to endure.

Yep, change bites. If change is so good for us, why does it feel so bad? Why does it irritate us so much? There is something to be said for the same ole same ole.

I went shopping for clothes not long ago. The store display windows were full of styles I, and some of you, have already worn in an earlier part of our lives. I swear I wore those outfits in the seventies. I refuse to buy them again, today. I always say I won't buy anything I wore previously in my life. I mean it, too. I write this with a perfectly straight face and a sincere heart. Yet as I sit here writing this, I'm wearing a shirt that is tie died and covered with peace signs. Okay, so some things I apparently will buy. Sometimes it is hard to even understand ourselves.

There are some changes that I do like. Really, I mean it. Let's see if I can think of some. I like the new T.V. season. There are a lot of good shows and some are really new and different concepts. You know, new concepts like revenge and terrorism. Me likey.

Another thing I really like these days is the warmer weather we've been enjoying. Bring it on! So far this warming trend feels mighty nice.

I like some of the new restaurants in the area and I like the new menus in our local Applebee's and Big Boy. I also like that they will still make some of my old favorites, even though they no longer appear on the new menus. Okay, change is good, especially when I can still hang on to the old.

Mama Don't Take . . .

In the last few years I had some odd encounters. You see, I was one of the last hold outs to switch to a digital camera. It seemed I just loved my big ole camera and my Kodachrome film.

The odd encounters would happen when I would shop for my Kodachrome. I went into a fancy hotel gift shop in Phoenix. I searched and searched but couldn't find film. Finally, I asked for it. They looked at me incredulously. "Film! We quit carrying that quite awhile ago. Nobody buys it anymore." I slunk off with my big ole camera – not only shot down but also filmless. Dang.

I went to Rite-aid and asked to buy film. The girl looked at me confused, "What?"

"Where is your film?" I repeated.

She yelled to the back of the store. "Hey, we got any film?"

"If we do, it is ...." At last they found a couple dusty yucky boxes of film on the back of a shelf. "Yeah, we don't carry that anymore." I left with film but still shot down. Yikes.

I had a couple more experiences like that, each one painful. One time in Grand Rapids, a trainee said to the clerk. "I never heard of film before. What is it?" I am not kidding you. She really said that. I thought about beaming her with my heavy camera, but my senses got the best of me . . . at the last second. Lucky for her!

A year ago my family took pity on me. I think because I was embarrassing them with my big ole camera and all my film antics. They got me a digital camera that fits into my pocket. I didn't want it. I hate change. I loved my kodachrome, after all.

"Mama, don't take my Kodachrome away. I got a Nikon camera. I love to take a photograph. So, mama, don't take my Kodachrome away." Paul Simon sang this into a hit and into my heart.

Kodachrome and Kodak are more than just film and cameras to me. I was born in Rochester, New York. Most of my male relatives worked at Kodak. In fact, when I think of my relatives – Grandpa, Uncles, cousins, even some aunts – they all worked at Kodak, many from young adult through retirement. We were a Kodak family.

Kodak was a city within a city. It was more than a household word, it was King. Everyone believed it would go on forever.

Kodak and Rochester turned out like Detroit and the car makers with similar fates. Almost everyone worked in the industry. They ruled the roosts. Then the industry tanked. Kodachrome died due to digital cameras, technology and foreign competition. Both Detroit and Rochester are now desperately trying to forge ahead, but their former glory days are likely not returning. Neither is Kodachrome.

Not long ago, the last rolls of Kodachrome were developed in the world. Yup folks, not one place left in the planet. The last rolls were developed at Dwayne's Photo in Parsons, Kansas. In fact, they processed 700 rolls a day right up until the end – and those came from all over the world. It seemed everyone loved Kodachrome with its bright colors.

Kodachrome not only inspired Paul Simon to write a hit song, it also is the only film to have a national park named after it, Kodachrome Basin State Park in Utah.

Kodachrome was a baby boom product. It began 75 years ago. It is now done, over, finis. If you find any stray rolls of Kodachrome lying around in your drawers, just toss them or save them as antiques. You won't be able to develop them. Kodachrome can't be developed on your own. It needed special chemicals that are no longer made.

I have long been a photographer wanna-be. My kids were mostly grown when I felt I could afford a good camera. I loved it. I have a whole big box full of beautiful Kodachrome photos of nature. I love them even though I don't have a clue what to do with them.

I have to change my camera attitude now. I have to forget how great the sound of that click was as I shot photos with my big ole camera. I now have to get excited about my tiny digital camera and all the greatness it can do. There are many benefits to it. I know because everyone tells me. I am not sure I am ready for it. I still have a little more grieving to do.

Ogden Nash said, "Progress might have been all right once but it has gone on too long."

A CBS news reporter said about the end of Kodachrome, "Progress is defined as an advancement or improvement, but in some ways it's hard to see how a world without Kodachrome qualifies as either."

As for me, I just keep hearing Paul Simon in my head. "When I think back on all the crap I learned in high school, it's a wonder I can think at all. And though my lack of education hasn't hurt me none, I can read the writing on the wall. Kodachrome, you give us those nice bright colors. You give us the greens of summers, makes you think all the world's a sunny day, oh yeah! I got a Nikon camera. I love to take a photograph. Mama, don't take my Kodachrome. Mama, don't take my Kodachrome. Mama, don't take my Kodachrome away…"

The Customer Is King . . . Or Maybe Not

There is a true story about the bus headquarters in England getting all kinds of calls complaining that the bus drivers would not stop to pick up the people. They would be waiting at the bus stop and the busses would drive right by.

Of course, the office knew this could not be true, but they called the bus drivers in to tell them about the complaints anyway. When they said they had been getting these absurd phone complaints, the bus drivers said, "There is no way we can pick up the people and stay on our schedule."

We are all customers in many different ways. We get customer service in many different ways.

Recently I had a new experience. I bought about six items. They sat on the checkout lane between me and the clerk. She took my money and began to walk away. I said, "Can I have a bag, please?" She reluctantly put them in a bag and said, "I can't read minds." I had been there shopping for the day with my family. Her comment was the icing on the cake in a day of bad customer service. We laughed as it got worse and worse, each place we went.

In a shoe store that day, I asked if I could try on a pair of shoes. The clerk looked at me kind of irritated and said, "Well, I was going to clean up, but I guess I could get them for you." She sighed heavily as she did this enormous favor for me.

Another day recently, my daughter and I had a mother-daughter day and spent it in another small quaint town. The customer service was excellent all day, except for the final stop and a very rude male clerk. It seemed sad to have him tarnish the day of great service.

I have a cartoon that shows a woman at a customer service counter in a bookstore. She asks for the self-help section and the clerk replies, "If I told you, that would defeat the whole purpose, wouldn't it?"

I think it is Ben and Jerry's ice cream in Vermont that has the great customer service two-part philosophy. 1. The customer is always right. 2. If you have further problems, refer back to number one.

Today in many stores, clerks are few and far between. It takes longer to find what you want and longer, still, to find someone to give your money to. My biggest customer service yank is when I need to call someone like my cable company. The people I get on the phone are in India or the Philippines. I want to give up before I even get started.

I remember when the customer was king. I find that when I get good customer service, I usually never consider going anyplace else. I don't look for lower prices. I prefer to go where I am treated well and it is worth it to me.

All of this reminds me of a funny story that happened to us years ago in Spain. We were at a German restaurant. We asked if the German chocolate cake was good. The waitress said, "It's dry." We asked about something else and got a similar kind of negative comment. We finally said, "What do you recommend?" She said in her uncheery tone, "A cigarette."

Mahatma Gandhi summed up what customer service is all about. "A customer is the most important visitor on our premises. He is not dependent on us. We are dependent on him. He is not an interruption in our work. He is the purpose of it. He is not an outsider in our business. He is part of it. We are not doing him a favor by serving him. He is doing us a favor by giving us an opportunity to do so." I think Gandhi nailed it.

That's Life

Three Perfect Things

Kids think differently than us. They just do. Over the holidays my grandson, Louie, age 6, said, "Nina, what to know my three perfect things?" Of course, I did. "God, peaches and dogs."

I am wholeheartedly with him on the God and dogs part - the peaches, not so much. I mean, I like peaches, but I never think of them as perfect. I mean they aren't the same as a soothing glass of wine or a really good chocolate truffle.

Grandson, Danny, age 8, piped up then. "Mine are God, family and books." When he said books, his face lit up like a bonfire. Whoosh. Perfect, for sure.

This got me thinking about how little, if any, thought we give to our "perfect things". We are very aware of what isn't perfect, what bugs us, what we don't like. I began to ask others, "What are your three perfect things?"

I got all kinds of retorts. "What do you mean? About me? About my life?" The best clarification I could give was, "Whatever. How about the first perfect things that come to mind?" And, off they went.

Bev said, "Holding a newborn baby, sleeping in my own bed and turtle sundaes." Faith said, "Feet that don't hurt, cocktails without calories and the actual time to play games." Carol said, "Clean, fresh smelling sheets, a page-turner book like Harry Potter, and a snowy day that says stay in and read that good book."

Laurel said, "Lord, love and laughter – and nearly everything in my life fits in to those three categories." Holly came up with, "Snuggling in flannel sheets warmed up by the electric blanket, the aroma of bread baking in my oven and hugs from the grandkids for any reason!" She then wrote me back that "the first one can quickly be ruined with a hot flash".

You may think this is just an adult question, but you would be wrong. Kyra, our beautiful 2 ½ year old grandniece, immediately came up with, "My brother, pink and red!" Her brother is 6 weeks old. Cool that she likes him and thinks he's perfect. And who else, but a youngun, pauses to appreciate pink and red.

Jordan is 4. Hers were, "Peachy, baby dolls and Barbies." Peachy is her cat. Ah, life is so simple at 4.

Tim asked his 10th grade US History students. He began with his, "Time with family and friends, rocking my children to sleep in the middle of the night when they were babies and watching the sunrise and sunset in Tully Cross, Ireland". His students said the following: "family, God and shoes"; "naps, video games and my mommy"; "sleeping in, food and more food" (he is a lean six foot seven).

Phil was the first to respond. "God, sunsets on Lake Michigan and smiles from my boys – or any child, for that matter!"

Jesus, God, Mary and faith ranked right at the top for most. But then came some others. Hilda said, "Ice cream, ice cream and ice cream." Diana said, "Merlot, merlot, merlot". Gisela said, "Snow, books and a cup of tea". Terri said, "My retirement, health and energy – and I appreciate all three every single day." Someone added, "Tax rebates". Glenda added, "Shopping ranks pretty high, too."

Jodie made me howl with hers and I know it's true, too. "God, snowflakes and my nipples." Jodie had breast cancer, both breasts removed and reconstruction surgery. My husband and I were at the local beach with our grandsons one day. Jodie pulled up in her car and jumped out yelling with joy, "I got nipples. I got nipples." We, especially my husband, didn't know what to say, but we were oh, so happy for her.

A few others were quite normal. Marty – "Loving our cottage on the lake, my caring husband and watching our kids succeed." Sally added, "Laughing with my husband at our dog, Scrabble and good books." Darci thinks, "The human body and all its fascinating systems that work together in harmony, crystal formations and smiles." Laura and her husband came up with, "the soups she makes, flying in a clear blue sky, that first day of spring and baby's smiles." But then a couple wild ones came in.

I have been asked to withhold their names and for good reason. "My friends, my friends, my friends – God knows it isn't my family!" And another one, "God, circles and deceased men." Hmmm.

So, what are yours? Ask your family and friends what are theirs. We spend so much time griping and looking at the negative. Instead we can take Louie's lead and focus on the perfect things in our lives. For me, I'm gonna go with faith, family and dogs, but why do I have to stop at three? There's so many more when we stop to think about it.

Car Talk

"And we'll have fun, fun, fun till daddy takes the T-bird away," sang the Beach Boys. There are a lot of songs about cars. Remember the Beatles singing, "Baby, you can drive my car"? Cars are more than just something to get us from here to there. They are part of our life, our personality, our history.

We all have memories of taking our driver's test and getting our driver's license.

 For those of us that are parents of kids old enough, we also remember vividly when our kids got "da keys". What teenager doesn't long for keys and wheels and freedom. They all go together, don't they?

Last weekend my youngest daughter got a new car. Okay, it is used, but it is new to her. She has had an old Jeep for the past eight years. It was very rustic and had no air conditioning. She's not into cars all that much. She mostly uses public transportation. She has, however, minded not having air conditioning on these very hot humid days as she drives between here and Chicago.

The other day she drove her Jeep here to pick up her new car which she bought from a local dealer. The temperature outside was at the top of the charts. She sat in traffic for an hour and then the drive took another four hours. By the time she arrived in Greenville, she was physically near collapse and felt ill for several hours. I think she had a kind of heat stroke thing going on. But, here's the deal, and I think it relates to all of us.

As she sat in traffic cooking herself, she got all sentimental about the Jeep and all they had been through together for the last eight years. She thought of the places she had lived, the different roommates, the different jobs, the different boyfriends, and the many experiences she had while owning and driving that old Jeep. They had been through a lot together and shared good, bad, fun, sad, and all the things eight years of life hold.

Coincidentally, her father and I had been doing the same kind of reminiscing the night before about all the houses and apartments we had lived in. Each one held separate but important memories that defined our life: the first apartment; married housing at Michigan State University where we brought home our first child; Spain where we had a baby girl; three different spots in Greenville and each one full of distinctive growth and experiences for us. Each place we lived in we loved. Each one holds a special place in our family history together. Each was full of good, bad, fun, sad and all that life holds.

Ours cars are just like the places we live. From the cool Mustang my husband had when I met him to the lemon I later bought to the wheels we drive today – they each have taken us on more than a ride. They have taken us on a journey through our lives. So have yours.

It is kind of fun to stop and think about all your cars and all the places you have lived. When we think about it with our experiences in mind, we realize how we have grown. We also realize that life isn't about the destination. It is about the trip. Hopefully, for each of you, when you stop and think of how your different cars and homes relate to your life journey, you will have some great memories and feelings of joy. Go ahead, take the mental ride. Hopefully, you will feel right at home.

Errands Of Domestic Despair

If Rodney Dangerfield were alive, he could say, "There are two things that get no respect, me and errands."

At least that is a thought I have often had. I get no respect for doing errands. Nor do I get any credit. And yet they eat up my life. If we took all the time we have spent doing errands, whew. How many years would they add up to?

Errands run the gamut from noble to nasty. At one end of the spectrum we have taking soup to a sick friend. At the other end is dropping off our pet's poo to the vet.

In a recent action film, a guy calls home to tell his wife he is "going in", insinuating he may not return. She ends the conversation with, "just bring home a gallon of milk when you come." And, he does.

One stop shopping stores make errands a bit easier. I heard a comedian in Grand Rapids once. He was in from Los Angeles and said how much he liked Meijer stores. He said, "Where else can you stop and get a pack of gum, a pizza and a tractor?" I have been waiting to use that line for about 15 years.

I asked folks for their take on errands. One said, and I won't use her name to protect her marriage, "Have you noticed that when you go with your husband to run an errand it turns into a day of errands?" Yes, we do that too - but I can't say it's the fault of my husband.

My daughters remind me that much of their childhoods were spent riding shotgun while I zoomed around town doing a few errands. I always thought it would be good bonding time for us. I am pretty sure they do not look back on it in that same light.

One person wrote me, "I am only working two days a week, yet for some reason I still don't get my errands done and end up having to do them on the weekend. What is up? I need a time management class. And, by the way, why is it my job to do all the errands? Help!!!" I won't use her name either. I'll save her good image. Her initials are P.M.

A friend wrote that she does her mom's errands but hates to buy the Depends. She uses all kinds of "strateegery", as Will Farrell would say, to be sure the clerks know the Depends are not for her.

That reminds me of watching Harrison Ford on Letterman one night. He was dating Calista Flockhart who is much younger than him. He said they stopped at a store and he ran in to get diapers for her baby. He asked the clerk where the diapers were. The clerk sent him to the Depends section. And he finished by saying, "And I'm Indiana Jones, for God's sake!"

Darlene said one thing she hates about errands is how her car goes directly where it wants and not where she meant to go. My car does that too. In December I meant to go to the AmericInn twice but found myself in the Meijer parking lot before I came to. Don't you wonder who is driving sometimes?

Tara said, "Never tell anyone you're going out to pick up something or the list will grow quickly." That is true. I often say to my husband, in my most pleading way, "While you're out . . ." My fun friend, Mary, said, "All errand spots should have drive-through windows . . . and bathrooms." She also mused that, "Errands procreate like gerbils and just when you think you've gotten rid of them, a whole new batch arrives to take their place."

Barb said, "I wish I had an errand girl." And as I checked, there are several services that will do errands for you. Umm, pretty tempting.

Harriette said, "I absolutely love errands. They treat my sense of order. I plan my car path and which is the best direction for turns. It also assuages my sense of accomplishment – get it checked off my list." I gotta say, I do this same routine and I do like gettin' them done.

What I get weary of, though, is that they come right back at ya. You take stuff to the cleaners. You gotta pick it up in a few days. You buy stuff. You gotta take it to be recycled when you're done.

I guess one of the good things about doing errands is the good people you get to know along the way. Almost every spot has a friendly face to touch base with and they brighten the chore. I could go on with this silver lining idea but I really gotta go run some errands. And run. And run.

The Glue Of Heritage

Recently I have been touched by the glue of heritage. What, you say? Let me explain.

We were at mass at St. Mary's in Carson City. The high school seniors were being honored. It was also a mass honoring the graduates from fifty years ago, 1962. The graduates were asked to stand and face the audience. Then the 1962 graduates were asked to stand. The speaker then said, "Look at them. This is what you will look like in fifty years." Everyone laughed. But then she went on, "This is your heritage."

I loved the thought of heritage. It has many different dimensions in our lives.

This weekend my family went to Rochester, New York, to celebrate my Uncle Bill turning 90. He is not just an average uncle. To me, he has been like a dear father.

My family has lots of broken parts: siblings I never grew up with; a "new" sister that has turned up; half siblings; step parents; step grandparents; blood cousins; cousins that are not blood; several fathers; and on and on. It may sound really odd but some of you can relate. Not everyone is blessed with the typical kind of family.

So, with all that said, this gathering for my uncle was full of these familial parts. As we sat around laughing, talking and sharing our common uncommon stories, no one would have doubted we were kin. Even though many of us were meeting for the first time, we shared common heritage. Just like a marriage vow, these family histories have been for better or worse, for richer or poorer, in sickness and in health. As it turned out in many of our stories, that sickness was often manifested in alcoholism.

As my uncle was being honored, I thought of how he and my dear aunt have been the glue that has held all of us together, our heritage glue. Because of them we are still a family connected with love and laughter. Because of them we are proud of our heritage. Because of them we know our family history and how our ancestors came to America and when. Because of them we know each other and celebrate each other as we celebrate him.

Heritage is where and who we came from, where we have lived, who has touched our lives. This can be made up of blood or not. It is usually family but can also be community, church, schools and neighbors. We don't live this life solo. We are part of others and they are part of us.

In my life, I think of many of my friends as family. I love them. We share history. We are there for each other. They are part of my heritage and part of the joy of my life.

We, as individuals, can consciously be the glue of heritage for others. We share the life journey together. We laugh. We encourage. We celebrate. We are there for each other when need be. We help. We grow together.

What is the work of the glue of heritage? I think it is communication. I think it is reaching out and including others with open arms. I think it is acceptance and love. I think it involves laughter, reminiscing and keeping history alive.

This weekend when my 88 year old Aunt Mary met my grandson Louie, she held his hand and looked into his vibrant six year old face and said, "Louie, I am going to love you for a long, long time." He smiled back and said excitedly, "Okay, I will love you too!" And that is what the glue of heritage is. The love is the glue. The long time is the heritage. Whether we are reminded of it at a mass for graduates or at a 90 year old birthday party, the glue of heritage is a wonderful thing and it is good to pause and reflect on the richness of it in our lives. It is also good to be thankful for it and then to consciously reach out with open accepting arms to give it to others. Oh, and remember, good glue sticks for a long, long time, if you're lucky.

Aunt Mary Empey & Louie Burns

And Now I'm Found

I was lost . . . but now I'm found. A lady called me to speak at a church in Edmore. I agreed and said I'd been there many times before. Because of that, we never discussed directions or an address.

The night before the event, my husband and I drove by the church on our way home and I said confidently, "That's where I'll be tomorrow night." Ignorance is bliss.

The night of the event I arrived a bit early. My heart sunk. My stomach began to clinch. There was not a single car in the parking lot. Oh, man, I thought, this is not good.

I looked at my notes. They said Our Savior Lutheran Church. I looked at the church sign where I was and it read Methodist church. Okay, punt Maureen.

I figured surely if I drove around Edmore, I'd see the church. How hard could that be? But, alas, that mind frame turned out to be way too optimistic.

I drove and I drove. I stopped and asked several different people for directions. Clearly none of them had a clue. This, however, did not stop them from giving me directions. I am sure I appeared desperate to them. I kind of was.

Now, folks, I have pondered this for years. What is it about humans that makes them always give directions when asked, even when they have absolutely no idea what they're talking about? Why don't they ever just say, "I don't know.", "I don't have a clue.", "If I knew, I'd tell you". Is not knowing a condition that self-esteems just can't bear? No one wants to look dumb and I understand that feeling.

Perhaps it is kindness that makes people give you directions when they don't know. They just really want to help you. Perhaps they've just been wanting to tell someone where to go all darn day and conveniently you showed up and gave them the opportunity.

There are all those jokes about men never stopping to ask for directions. Perhaps the men know they will likely not get a good answer so they just don't want to bother. Maybe men know more than women after all. Then again . . .

I am sure some of you have wondered by now, why didn't she use map quest or her Garmin. Map quest has steered me wrong many times and my Garmin doesn't like me. She only likes my husband. Plus, I didn't have an address.

Well, after way too long and driving several miles and asking several people, I still didn't have a clue. I made some phone calls but no real people answered. The answering machines just didn't have a clue either. I finally did what I had to do. I stopped at a pharmacy. It had just closed but I saw a light on and a man inside. I pounded on the door and a nice man came. He steered me in the right direction. He was like a savior to me as he steered me to Our Savior Lutheran Church. Bless him.

I don't know about you, but I don't like being lost. Who does? We're always on a time schedule and there is never time in it to be lost.

As I drove home I thought about being lost. We get lost in many ways. I remember being lost in Algebra class. I am regularly lost with my computer, my digital camera, my cell phone and even my TV remote. Sometimes we are lost in love, lost in politics, lost in a job, lost in a relationship, lost with our finances. My friend and I are both currently lost in the maze of doctors, health care dilemmas and insurance "stuff".

Being lost in any way is a curve ball and life continues to throw us curve balls. Fortunately there are always people and resources that can help us find our way, no matter how we are lost. If we persevere and keep looking for help.

So we need to keep asking directions, keep looking for the right answers. Someone can lead us along. We can find our way. We can always smile down our road of life and think, "Yes, I was lost, but now I'm found." Happy trails to you, fellow traveler, however you are lost.

Imagine This . . .

So, imagine this. You are a handsome guy. You marry a beautiful lady. You are both highly educated and you have great jobs, a lovely home and three beautiful, bright daughters. Life is good. And then it gets better. You have a baby boy. Now you have the world by the tail.

For two years you dream about things this boy will do, places he will go, sports he will play, a full life he will live. Yes, life is good – very, very good.

Then your son turns two. You notice he doesn't talk as much. You notice he has quit playing with his toys. You notice other changes. He is losing skills. He begins to jump a lot. You think this is because you have a trampoline, but inside, you begin to have an empty scared feeling. You work in education. You have seen this behavior. You have seen autism.

You mention it to your wife. She does not agree. She is in the first stage of coping with grief or change - denial. As this situation continues, she comes to realize and she is able to cope with it better than you.

I am sharing a personal story here. It is the story of my friends, Scott and Jenny. Their son is six years old and a beautiful boy. Around age two, he developed classic autism. He is now verbal but not conversational.

In 1984-85 there were 557 kids in Michigan with autism and it cost the state $4.4 million to educate them. Today – are you ready for this – in Michigan, there are more than 15,000 children on the spectrum of autism and it costs Michigan more than $100 million to educate them. The average societal cost per person is $3.7 million to care for each of them over their lifetime.

When our friend's son became autistic, they knew no one else who had an autistic child. Now, however, most of us do know someone who has autism. Why? Because autism is like a racing train hitting our society. Why is that? What is causing it? No one knows.

Today one in 110 children is on the autism spectrum. Boys are the most affected. It hits one in 70 boys. In fact 75 percent of those with autism are boys – a whopping three out of four. These statistics are chilling.

Autism affects more than just the individual. It affects the entire family. People miss that. They feel sorry for the child but forget how it permanently affects the parents, siblings, grandparents, and everyone who knows the child and cares for the family. The autistic child often doesn't know he has autism. He doesn't know that he doesn't fit in. The aspergian child knows he is different. He tends to feel unaccepted, weird. John Elder Robison describes these feelings well in his personal account, Look me in the eye. It's a must read for everyone to help us learn and understand.

Do you have children? Do you know children? Will you ever have children or grandchildren? Then you need to learn about this. We must open our minds and hearts to help us handle situations we may encounter with children and adults who are on the spectrum of autism. This can make us better people, more empathetic, caring, knowledgeable and productive. It could happen. We never know how and when our life might change and the spectrum will become a very real part of our personal world. That is, if it hasn't already.

The train of autism is barreling toward all of us. Since I have become aware, the statistics have gone from one in 1,500 to one in 1,000 to one in 70. The train is not slowing down. In fact it is speeding up and none of us knows how close to our personal lives and families it will hit.

(This column won as Associated Press award.)

To Bully Or Not To Bully - NOT!!!

Do you remember the first time you were bullied? Do you remember the last time you were bullied? It seems like bullying is something kids do, but unfortunately, it is also something adults do.

Females bully. Males bully. Kids bully. Adults bully. Teens bully. Teachers bully.

Coaches bully. Pastors bully. Parents bully. Siblings bully. Friends bully, but friends who bully turn into enemies or as I recently read - frenemies.

I asked a 41 year old male what his first memory of being bullied was. He instantly replied, "I was walking home from elementary school alone. Some older boys in school were behind me and threw snowballs at me the entire way. I just let them because there wasn't anything I could do." He added, "I'm sure I was bullied before that but that experience comes to mind first."

I think I saw the first time my grandson was bullied. He was in a room with 5 year old girls. He was barely two and he was thrilled to be playing with them. One girl said in a snotty way, "You can't play with us because you're a boy. You have to get out."

I watched his little lip quiver and his eyes pop. He didn't know how to respond. Welcome to the world, little boy. As hard as it was to watch that, I knew it was the beginning of what happens to people in life.

A couple of years ago I had a local businessman bully me. He asked me to go to an empty back room with him. As soon as he closed the door, he started in with verbal attacks. I was stunned. After several very nasty minutes of this abuse, I said, "You have no right to treat me like this." I left. It took me a long time to recover, but then I don't think we ever fully recover from the meanness bullies do.

Bullies know better than to bully in front of people who may stop them. They know they are doing something wrong. They thrive behind closed doors or where their victims are alone and unprotected or unaware.

Bullying is a form of violence. It can be mean looks, words, and actions – all meant to intimidate. No matter the intention, bullying can hurt bodies, feelings, friendships, reputations and property. Bullying stops trust.

There have been several cases in the news about teenagers or their parents bullying other teens. Sometimes these victims have committed suicide, then it makes the news. Some of these perpetrators are now being charged and it is handled as a serious crime.

What is it that makes bullies bully? An educator recently told me, "Hurt people hurt people". Ah, yes, I am sure that is true. However, it does not give anyone the right to hurt others, just because they have been hurt or are hurting. I mean, haven't we all been hurt and are hurting about something?

We each make our own choices based on how we want to be and how we want to live. I love Maya Angelou's advice, "Take the higher road." That isn't always easy, but the buck should stop with us.

We lead in three ways: by example, by example, by example. We can lead with a positive example or a negative example. These are our choices.

A positive choice never includes mean or hurtful looks, gestures, words or actions. A positive choice never includes aggression toward another. We should make positive choices. We should expect respect and encourage respect and dignity for all.

As adults, we should not tolerate bullying when we see it. We need to step in and stop it or report it. We should not let it go. When we do, we become part of it.

Almost always when we hear of events like campus and high school shootings, the shooters have been bullied. Bullying begets violence.

In a list of the continuum of violence, it begins with eye rolling, intimidating looks and goes on through many stages – name calling, threatening, stalking – to name a few. The last two listed are stabbing and shooting people. Enough said.

Yes, when I read about teens who have committed suicide because they were bullied, when I read about heinous crimes that were committed by people who had been bullied, I am saddened. Yet I do not know these people.

However, I need only think a second and I realize I do know bullies of every age, profession and sex. I know their victims too.

If we can all have the courage to stand up and confront bullying behavior whenever it arises, it will make our little corner of the world better. And that would be a higher road, indeed.

Surprise! Surprise!

Sherry andMaureen

Surprise! Oprah Winfrey made all the media markets with news of her finding out she had a surprise sister.

My girls and I watched the show. It was very emotional for us. Why? Because it was my story too, and the story of several people close to me.

My surprise sister, Sherry, lives in Illinois. She needed her baptismal certificate and when she got it, was stunned to see another man listed as her father. The man she knew as her father had recently died. She confronted her mother, who tearfully told her that she had had a fling with a man after WWII and gotten pregnant. The guy took off. The guy, of course, was my father.

My parents got divorced when I was a tot. My father took no responsibility for me or Sherry. He remarried and had 3 children. I have 4 half siblings from my mother's second marriage and 3 from my father's. Surprise Sherry added one more.

Sherry hired a private detective to find her dad. Ironically, he, also, had just died. She wrote his sister and told her story. Unbeknownst to Sherry, my aunt had Alzheimer's so never responded or told anyone. Years later my aunt died, and the letter was found.

I called Sherry as soon as I was told about her. Weird – we had the same voice. We met at a teeny restaurant in Muskegon. Everyone found out we were sisters meeting for the first time. People kept coming up very emotional, some crying. "This is so beautiful." It was not your usual night out.

Sherry and I hit it off right away. Our personalities are just alike. We have the same smile, the same sense of humor. She is shy like me. We even have the same favorite color, which was the favorite color of our grandmother, whom Sherry never met.

Since then, we have shared birthdays and holidays with gifts. We talk occasionally on the phone. We really enjoy each other and seem to fit like sisters. A great comfortableness surrounds us when we are together. We have met several times alone and with our children and spouses. Everyone feels like family and a good time is always had by all.

Sherry never knew our dad. I can tell her son how he is the spitting image of his grandpa. I can tell her how she and her son have her dad's personality and big brown eyes. I can help her put the pieces of her life together. In this process, we both have become more whole.

I thought I was unique with my wild and crazy family. Not so much, it seems. About the same time as I was getting a new sibling, so were others in my close circle of relationships.

My dear friend, Wanda, had a similar experience. Her parents divorced when she was a tot. She was raised an only child and never knew her biological dad. She knew he remarried and had kids. Wanda was very content with her life, so never pursued it.

Wanda was contacted by a friend who told her that a sister of hers, Crystal, wanted to make contact. Wanda called her.

Crystal, in Ypsilanti, was raised with 3 brothers, but no sister. However, she knew she had one someplace. Crystal then came to meet Wanda. They embraced, cried, and talked the whole day.

Next step was to meet the 3 brothers. "We now get together and have wonderful times. We have many similarities. We want to spend more time together in the future. We have had lots of photos taken of our new family. Our hearts are just so close. There is a lot to share. I feel more complete. I always wondered." She also got her medical history and found important things, like her dad had diabetes.

Marion had a similar experience. Her parents divorced when she was 4. Her dad remarried and had a baby girl, Annie. He was killed 6 weeks later in a car crash. Marion knew this girl existed, but had no contact with her.

About the same time as Wanda and I found our new siblings, Marion decided to follow up on a note about Annie that she had been given years before. She called Annie, who was shocked to hear from her.

They met and shared and are glad they did. Though one lives in Grand Rapids and the other in Florida, they visit each year. They connect for birthdays and holidays with gifts. Annie never had children and is excited to become aunt to Marion's six children and 13 grandchildren.

About this same time, Gary also got a new sister, Helen. She found Gary on-line. His sister is about 30 years older than him. When they met for the first time in Pennsylvania, where he is from and where she lives, they looked at each other and laughed and laughed and laughed. "I guess this alleviates any doubt," she said. They are mirror images of each other. I told Gary I always thought he'd look good in a dress.

"We are now best friends and communicate regularly. It has been an easy and wonderful relationship. And a further bit of irony," he adds. "I was in the same seminary in Texas with her son, my nephew, and we were classmates and acquaintances." It's a small world.

There is a quote I love. "A stranger is just a friend you haven't met yet." Between Oprah, Wanda, Marion, Gary and I, it seems a stranger may just be a sibling we haven't met yet. We never know what's around the corner in our lives. Get ready.

What Is God Up To?

We see raging fires on the nightly news. They are always someplace else. They ravage our Upper Peninsula, New Mexico, Arizona, California, and now, Colorado.

We have new neighbors. Their son and his family live on the mountain near Ft. Collins, Colorado and have two children – ages 6 and 8. They live in their dream house, a cedar chalet with a cathedral ceiling and wrap-around deck. To get off the mountain, they need a truck or SUV and 30 minutes to maneuver the winding, narrow road.

Very environmentally conscious, they own 17 acres in a canyon. They have been evacuated several times due to fires. It doesn't concern them all that much. They have been there and done that. Oh, they don't take it lightly, but they know they always get to go home and everything is always alright. Until now, that is.

On June 9, 2012, our friend's son was gone, so his wife got the automated call that the county sends out. It said they had to evacuate. She took the call seriously and grabbed the kids, the dogs, the computer housing their photos, and their box of passports and important papers. With smoke in sight, she and the kids began the long trek down the mountain. 3000 were evacuated from this fire. Picture very slow, bumper-to-bumper traffic with lots of horses in trailers and everyone anxious. Think Katrina.

As they left in a hurry, no one realized the little boy was barefoot. Luckily, he found his favorite purple Crocs in the car. They were too small, but he was happy to have them. They had no pajamas or underwear - only what they had on.

Sadly, they left behind their two cats. They have hope, though, and the Humane Society has gone up and put water out for them. Remember, cats are wise and they do have nine lives.

This family has been fortunate and able to stay with friends. Now their insurance company is trying to find them a rental.

This fire is the worst fire in Colorado history. So far it has taken 189 homes and cost 17.2 million dollars. The firefighters are proud, though. They have saved 500 homes. Their number one priority has been to save lives and they have only lost one, a woman who likely never checked her messages, the big message being from the county, "Evacuate now".

This fire was not started by man. Somehow that makes it easier to take. Colorado has a problem, the very invasive pine beetle which has destroyed fields and fields of trees. Those dead trees sit like candles waiting to be lit. Nature lit them with lightning. The lack of rain and snow has only added to the fire.

At the briefing center for evacuees, there is a board. For days and days the board showed no word, no word, no word. On this blackboard, house numbers are put up and marked yellow if your house is okay. If marked white, your house is gone.

This center holds two different briefings. One is just for the media. The other is only for home owners. When the home owner meeting is over, they are privately and caringly led out a back door away from the media.

Our friend's son called again after a few days of evacuation. "It's bad. We may have lost everything."

And then they saw the board and their house number marked with white. Their worst fears were confirmed. Now they knew. His next call wasn't a call. It was an email. "I can't really talk about it. Our house is gone."

They have not told their children yet and are being very careful about how they handle that. They have asked their parents to come. They need family now.

They have good insurance and think it will cover much of their loss. His co-workers chipped in their sick days to give him 8 ½ weeks off. They have also received many donations. The first one was from a person in Joplin, Missouri, who had survived the tornado last year and wanted to help someone else. People are good.

It will be weeks before they are allowed up on the mountain to see their property. It is just called property now. There is no home. It is important for them to return and have closure. They need to see what is left and mourn their loss.

There are so many decisions to make. They will rebuild. It will be a long time making replacement lists, remembering things they have lost – like her grandma's antique dishes. There are some things you can't ever replace. Life just goes on.

Stop reading for a minute and think about how many homes make up the number 189. Think of the homes around the nearby lakes, the nearby housing developments, the neighborhoods near you . . . I think and I count and I still am not up to 189. I keep going and keep counting, adding more developments and more neighborhoods. I am still not to 189. It is very hard to make this real in my mind.

Our neighbors have been touched by fire before. In 1992, her Mom lost her home in a Michigan house fire. His sister, brother-in-law and their three boys died in a house fire in Marquette in 1985. They told me, "Life comes in threes, so we are hoping this is our last fire".

I watch the fires on the news. They are never real to me. And then I meet a new friend. She shares that her son just lost his home in the fire. I hear her concern and pain. I look into her anxious eyes. I hear her phone ring and see her as she emotionally talks to her son. Now the news has a face. It is real. I can feel it.

As always, tragic things are not just hard for the victims, but also for the family and friends who love them. Our friend's daughter is also very upset over this and just found a quote that is lifting their family. "When you're down to nothing, God is up to something." So we all have to wonder, what is God up to?

My Personal Boycott

I'm in a rut. I have a bad attitude and I'm boycotting. Boycotting what, you say? Oh, nothing normal like football or vegetables. Though I just saw the movie, Contagion, and I probably should put more consideration into the food I eat and the hands I shake. I probably should boycott bat infested pork.

What I'm being all negative over is fall - the season, that is. Crazy, you think? Oh, come on. There must be at least one other soul out there who feels like I do. Anyone? Anyone?

Yesterday I drove home from Grand Rapids. Along the way I saw a huge tree full of red leaves, then another big tree full of yellow leaves. WHAT, I thought? Wait a minute here. Where did September go and when did summer end? I am not ready for summer to end. What do you mean it ended over a month ago? How can that be?

I still go to the Farmer's Market and ask, "Where's the corn? Where are the blueberries?" I'm not ready to embrace winter squash and gourds yet. I don't want to buy pumpkins and mums.

I still have my side of the garage loaded with lawn chairs, beach rafts, life jackets and summer remnants. I feel that putting it all away is like giving up. Summer flew by too fast, way too fast. I don't think I even realized September was upon me and now that's gone too. Is my life actually going that fast?

I probably need to get a grip, move on. I probably need to go make some chili and stew and get into the spirit of things. Nobody cares about my boycott and poor attitude. Summer and September flew on by and never gave me a thought. I have to get over it, deal.

My poor house sits here without its fall décor. My front door does not have a fall wreath. I told you I'm on a boycott. It may be ridiculous, but there you go. Sometimes we just lose our grips on reality. We just don't make sense . . . to others. I make perfectly good sense to myself.

One morning soon I will wake up and find my car all covered with frost. I will have to go search for the scraper and then, say it ain't so, scrape the windows before I can drive away. That will quickly throw me into reality. That will quickly make me clean out the garage and put all the summer fun stuff away.

For a week now, I am frozen, cold, wherever I go. I am pretty sure that is due to the fact that I have refused to put my summer clothes away and am in need of warmer things. A nice long pair of pants and a warm sweater would do me just fine. Why, oh why, am I being such a poop?

I think the crux of my negativity is what is looming ahead. I went to Meijers the other night at 11 p.m. It seemed empty. I walked along the aisle and saw mittens, snowsuits, boots, shovels. Oh, I'm a smarty. I know what all that means. It means winter is coming, soon, and with it the lack of sun, the early dark nights, the snow, the ice, the Christmas shopping. I get tired just thinking about all that. I want just a bit more summer, please. Is that too much to ask?

Maybe I just need to get myself to a football game, a fall fest, an orchard or some other fall "thang". Maybe immersion is what I need. Enough with the whining, the boycott, the negative attitude. It is time to kick myself in the rear and embrace the fall fun. It is time to go have some cider, maybe even a fall donut. Orchard, here I come, ready or not. I guess, I will have to leave my boycott at home. And before I leave, I guess I should get out some fall clothes and fall décor and on the way I should go buy some mums and pumpkins and gourds and winter squash. And look forward to frost on my car and cold, icy days. Well, maybe not. One step at a time. One step at a time.

Choosing Today

The other day I am working in my office and I see my friend, Carl, walking around the lake with his wife and daughter. Carl and Alison have done this regularly for years so that is not the surprise. The surprise is that Carl had just had brain surgery in Detroit a few days before.

I yelled out to cheer him on, even though he didn't need it, and he gave me a big smile and a thumbs up.

I went back in and thought of what an example Carl is. How many of us think we should go for a walk or should do this or that - and for all kinds of lame reasons, we never do it? We never get up off our butts to do all we can with this gift we have called life.

You see, Carl, is battling a rare form of brain cancer and because of that, his priorities are clearly in order.

Recently I heard a lady speak at Aquinas College. She was talking about how she had had a stroke and was sharing her recovery process. She said, "I looked up to God and said, 'Okay, God, you got my attention!' "

Perhaps that is the problem with the rest of us. Life is daily and we take it for granted and it hasn't gotten our attention yet.

I talked about this with my brother-in-law, Mike Devereaux, who has just reached almost four years of recovery from stage 3 Non-Hodgkin's lymphoma. Mike said, "Cancer is a taker. It takes all kinds of things from you, but it is also a giver. It gives you opportunity. I was given the opportunity to become more - more of a husband, father and friend. I choose to take those opportunities."

Today, this moment, now, is the most precious thing we will ever own. All the world's wealth can't buy it. It is a pure gift from God to each of us. We each get our own very special gift of life to be used however we choose.

In the routine of life, people often put lids on themselves. They do this by avoiding risks, being afraid, saying no to positive opportunities, staying in their comfort zones.

This gift of life is terminal. None of us get out alive. We also have no idea when our time will be up. As an old country song by Billy Dean says, "'Cause we're only here for a little while . . . " Like it or not, there is no greater truth.

I am always struck by the fact that there are no funeral hearses with U-hauls behind them. We go out alone. We leave all our "stuff". Most of us will leave to do lists undone.

Carl shared thoughts with me. "This is a time where family and friends are much more important to me. I have a strong belief in God. Living with existing illness that may lead to one's death makes me much more appreciative of the actions in life that are connected to friendships and learning. We all hope for ourselves and our family to keep moving forward in life for goodness and with kindness. We all want to move in a direction that is positive and makes a difference."

A friend added, "We all have to deal with the cards we are dealt. Being prepared helps us as we enter all the different periods we go through in life. We have to adjust to the new normals in our lives."

My friend, Amy, put it in different words. Amy is a breast cancer survivor and her beautiful little daughter is a cancer survivor, also. Maddie, her daughter, had leukemia when she was 22 months old and just celebrated her 7 year cure date. Amy's words of wisdom are, "You need to put on your big girl pants and just deal with it!" Amy's great sense of humor only adds to her wise perspective. I find I often am helped by her words.

As I watch my friends that face tough times like these, I am inspired by their positive attitudes, their strong faith in God and their clear perspective on what is important in life. They give us an opportunity to examine how we live our lives and to learn from them. They are great examples of strength and diligence.

Perhaps on a warm sunny day soon, you can go for a quiet walk with yourself and think about these things. As Mike reminds us, no matter what, we are all also given opportunity. We need to choose to take the opportunities.

I will close by one of my favorite poems by Horace Mann.

Lost Today

Somewhere between sunrise and sunset
One 24 hour, 24 carat golden day
Each hour studded with 60 diamond minutes
Each minute studded with 60 ruby seconds.

But don't bother to look for it,
Because it's gone forever
That wonderful golden day,
I lost today.

After I finished this column, I went to have dinner with a friend from Canadian Lakes. She is in the midst of chemotherapy for stage 3 cancer. What she told me just seemed to follow the above poem. She said, "I just live for today. I get up every day and think, 'what a beautiful day', and then I think of all my many blessings. I work on my relationship with God and I stay positive."

The present is where she chooses to consciously live. And, really, shouldn't we all be doing that? The past is done and the future isn't here. Living positively for today - that's the ticket.

I Went To A Garden Party

"I went to a garden party" sang Ricky Nelson. Well, this week I went to a garden party and I highly recommend it to you. Here's how it went.

My exercise gang sat in the hot tub one day last winter after exercising. The idea came up that perhaps summer would actually come someday. It was hard to believe at that moment. Someone said, "We ought to have a garden tour." And that was all it took.

Today we had our garden party. Twenty of us met and carpooled to five member's

beautiful gardens. Each had lovely music playing as we toured their spectacular gardens and each offered a light drink or a teeny tidbit. We didn't go in the homes, but stayed in the yards. It was easy as pie, at least for the garden viewers, perhaps not so easy for the gardeners. They did a lot of getting ready for the tour, I'm sure.

We ended the tours with an outdoor lunch at the last garden. It was a perfect ahhhhh kind of thing to do on a hot summer day.

So, I suggest it to you. Consider doing a garden tour with your friends, your church, your club, your neighborhood, your exercise gang, your family. It can be done as simply or as fancy as you want. It could be as easy as, "Can I come see your garden?" Nothing else needed.

People work hard in their gardens and it is obvious their efforts are labors of love.

It's nice for them to have someone want to come and look at their gardens and oooh and ahhh over them. It is also nice to have someone come and ask questions and pick their gardening knowledge. Most of these folks have tons of gardening wisdom to share and people like me need all the help we can get.

Doing a garden tour can be a simple and very delightful thing to do. Your garden tour/party can be organized with great detail or thrown together in a jiffy. It could be with wine or tea or a glass of ice water. The point is just to enjoy.

The other day, I was chatting with my friend, Julie, who is a fabulous gardener and hosted one of the gardens on our tour. I said, "You're not going to believe it, Julie, but I am really getting into gardening." She looked at me rather dismayed and said, "You're right. I don't believe it." She knows me too well, I guess.

After the tours, I sadly realized that my gardening is a bit weak. I have been considering myself a gardener now because it is after July fourth and my potted geraniums are still blooming. This is a whole new experience for me. I have watered and fertilized them several times and feel all full of my gardening self. I can open the Miracle Gro all by myself and I even wear a gardening apron. Oh, and I've got gloves too. You don't want to mess with me when I get my gear on.

I have lots of rocks in my front yard so I guess you could say I have a rock garden. In reality, though, it's really just a big buncha rocks. Here's a quote by Richard Diran, whoever he is, and I loved it. He said, "I have a rock garden. Last week three of them died." Hmmm.

Oh, The Restless Wind

"Oh, the wayward wind is a restless wind." So says the old song. This week, however, I found it really is.

I had a job last Friday in Escanaba. Being a sane person, I fretted about the snow and ice I would likely encounter as I drove. Well, isn't it just like life not to bother us with what we have worried about?

As I neared Mackinac Bridge, I was surrounded by deep fog. I am afraid of heights and crossing the bridge is always a major deal for me. I force myself to do it. I think it's good for me. This time, though, it wasn't as bad because I wasn't sure I was even on the bridge. I could only see a teeny bit in front of me and I couldn't see the lake at all. I couldn't see how high I was or how far I had to go. I inched along.

The fog continued for the two and a half hours to Escanaba. I never saw anything on my sides and I could only see one car length in front of me. I didn't have a clue where I was going. I just kept going – slowly, oh, so slowly.

When I arrived they told me, "It is never foggy like that!" How lucky was I?

Coming back on Friday, the sun was out and it was lovely. Then I noticed that every so often my car would whoosh out from under me. There was a restless, powerful wind. I had to be diligent with my attention and keep both hands tightly gripped onto the wheel. Not my usual behavior. In fact, it was so windy that I found I could hardly sip my water bottle. It seemed too dangerous to let go for even a second. Even my dog, who usually sleeps on our drives, sat rigid and alert in his car seat. He was shaking a bit, staring out the window and I think I heard him whine, "What the ????"

As I approached the bridge, a huge sign warned "High Wind Alert . . . Escorts Available". I assumed this was not the kind of escorts politicians get in trouble for. I was right. When I got to the bridge, I asked the toll lady what advice she had for me as I drove across in the strong winds. I also told her I was afraid of heights. She probably could have figured that out by the greenish hue to my face and the blinding fear in my eyes. But just in case she hadn't noticed, I told her anyway. She advised me to pull over and wait for the free escort. I gladly obeyed.

Immediately a truck pulled up and a good looking guy got out. He reminded me of my friend, Glenn, so I liked him right away. He got in and over the bridge we went. He said he had escorted nearly 30 cars so far that day.

I noticed two long lines of vans, semis and pick-ups waiting to cross. He said the wind was too strong to let them go alone. They had to be escorted by a pick-up that would lead them at 20 m.p.h. and no faster. He said if not, they sometimes blow over onto the bridge.

As soon as we crossed, a pick-up took him back so he could escort some other sissified drivers. As for me, I was feeling like I had just made one of the best decisions of my life.

Sometimes we need to hold on to the wheel. Sometimes we are better off if we let go and turn it over.

As I continued on, so did the wind. My daughter, Colleen, called to check on me. She knew it was windy and was concerned. "I hate to scare you," she said, "but I keep thinking about John and Elizabeth Edward's son. The wind just took his car and he died."

"Gee, I hadn't remembered that. Thanks so much." Sometimes we are better off without the caring of others.

A bit further, a huge pine had blown down and lay across both lanes of the expressway. My hands gripped tighter. I thought of what it must be like to go through a hurricane or tornado. It is truly unimaginable how something you can't see can be so powerful.

When I was a kid the town of Standale was destroyed by a tornado. The next day, my Dad took us to gawk. It looked like the big bad wolf had just huffed and puffed and blown it all away. You never forget sights like that.

As the hours went on, I began to think of songs about wind. I remembered Jim Croce singing, "You don't wee into the wind." I cleaned that up a little, very little. Still, it is good advice and it made me laugh in my tense situation.

A couple years ago, I was coming home. I hit ice at the top of the hill and flew towards a huge pine. I missed the tree and was able to get home safely, though shaken. I told my girls and they asked, "What did you do?" I told them I had just said, "Jesus, take the wheel." That was a popular country song at the time and they had a good laugh at me, not with me. In reality, though, I had done just that.

I arrived home safe and grateful from Escanaba. I had held on tight and I had let go and turned it over. As I unpacked, I thought of how life, like the wind, can be wayward and restless in so many ways. Hold on tight. Let go. Turn it over. Life is a balancing act.

It's Five O'clock Somewhere

I spent last night with that famous Buffet guy, not Warren, Jimmy. I felt it was an experience I needed to have in life. I was right.

Two friends and I drove to Clarkston, along with nearly 16,000 other happy folks. Everyone is happy at a Jimmy Buffett concert. The party began the minute we hit the parking lot, which opened at four, even though the concert began at eight. One described it as "a frat party mixed with a bachelor party mixed with a bachelorette party." That nailed it. I have been to university tailgates and this was no ordinary tailgate. This was a tailgate with an attitude, a margarita attitude.

Where do I begin? Should I begin with the bare-chested guy wearing a very skimpy grass skirt with cheeks showing through – and I don't mean facial? He did have a thong on. I know because I stared long enough to see it. People came dressed for the occasion. We saw Parrotheads, pirates, shark hats, coconut bras and Hawaiian shirts.

My friend leaned over and said, "I may be the oldest person here." Nah, people were all ages and all pumped. The parking lot was full of big expensive SUVs. This crowd was making it in life and Jimmy was part of their MoJo.

As we meandered, we were each given a Jello shot. Prior to this, the only Jello I'd had was full of marshmallows and fruit. We were also each given a free margarita. These came from friendly strangers that sure seemed like good folks. I mean, how much nicer could they have been?

At promptly eight o'clock, the song, *Tequila* erupted from steel drums and The Man came on stage, barefoot and smiling. My friend said, "You know if you put him in a suit in the White House, he could pass for Joe Biden." She was right, but who could get him into a suit?

Tequila was the perfect opener for this crowd. Margaritas were flowing like a raging river. We were doing our share. We wanted to be sociable, for sure. I had given my friends the word. "Don't give me another margarita - no matter what I say." Two's my limit, well, maybe three. We were in *Margaritaville*, after all.

Jimmy is as charming as they come. He has a way about him that makes you feel he came here just for you. Someone asked him, "Do you ever get tired of this?" He replied, "No, I sing for the people. I'm the soundtrack for their party." And think about it, how many parties and events have you been to where Jimmy was the soundtrack? Jimmy is in his sixties, balding and grey. No matter, he couldn't be cuter. He also is no slouch. He has authored three books and is only the sixth author* to reach No. 1 on both the New York Times fiction and nonfiction lists. He writes his songs, too. "I still call 'em records", he laughs. He's a dude in more ways than one and as beloved and American as apple pie. He scanned the place and said, "Where's the recession in Michigan?" Clearly not here on this night. As Jimmy says, "I sell escapism."

My other friend, Darci, has been coming to Jimmy Buffett concerts for over 20 years. She couldn't remember if this was her 10th or 14th concert. She loved this one as much as all the others. She, like most of the crowd, could recite every word to every song.

At the end of the evening, it was obvious that everyone had fun, but no one more than Jimmy. He loves what he does. He has made a wonderful life of following his bliss and wasn't that the advice we were all given?

To close, he brings onstage, Bret Michaels, who had recovered from a brain hemorrhage. The crowd went wild, including me, who thought it was Kid Rock. I even said, "When did Kid Rock get so cute?" Everyone standing and singing *Margaritaville*, yelling, "Salt, salt, salt". Ah, what a great way to end the evening.

Because not everyone got to see Jimmy in person, here are a couple ideas on how you can enjoy the Buffett glow. You can go to a Mexican restaurant. Sit back and enjoy a margarita. They are yummy and come in several sizes and flavors. Another option, Connie raves about 1800 Ultimate Pomegranate Margaritas in a bottle. She refers to it as, "Perfecto!" They also come in lemon, blueberry and other flavors. Delicioso!

Or, if you want to stay home and have a cheeseburger in your own paradise, I have the very best margarita recipe. It came from my friend, Bea. I made it for our couple's book club and after two margaritas, one member, a local esteemed veterinarian, quipped to everyone, "Why don't we forget about discussing the book and just have a group hug." That would sum up the Jimmy Buffett magic.

I will close with a couple of my favorite Jimmy Buffett quotes. "I just want to live happily ever after, every now and then." "Indecision may or may not be my problem." And, to wrap it all up, two more. "Wrinkles will only go where the smiles have been." And, "If life gives you limes, make margaritas."

My margarita recipe is in the back of the book. Yummm-O! My dear friend, Larry in Arizona, thinks his margarita recipe is the best - so that is listed too. Check them out and see what you think. And be sure not to drive heavy machinery after you test!

*The other five authors were Ernest Steinbeck, William Styron, Irving Wallace, Dr. Seuss, and Mitch Albom. Interesting, eh?

What's Happenin' Now

Most of the time, I don't watch the Grammys. If I do, I tend to fast-forward and watch only what I like. But, I watched and rewatched Lady Gaga doing *"Born This Way"*. I really liked her dancing, the song and the message.

I knew there was a Monster Ball coming to Van Andel Arena, but assumed it was big trucks. Wrong. It was the name of Lady Gaga's concert, which was sold out by the time I understood. When my niece called with an extra ticket, I was excited to go see what Gaga was all about.

I talked to my friend, Val, who was also going. She asked me, "What meat are you wearing?" I said, "Burger lined with salmon." She replied, "I'll be in pork with sage." We had a good laugh. We were joking about when Lady Gaga wore fresh meat to the MTV Video Award show. I think it was her way of saying, "Bite me."

Van Andel Arena was filled to the brim with 11,000 eager fans, many in Gaga fashion. I wanted to describe that for you but words come short. Unless you can get the picture of a lady in a nude leotard with bright yellow caution tape wrapped around her.

I usually fall asleep watching T.V. at 10. Gaga came on at 9:20, 50 minutes after her opening act which I didn't recognize. They began with, "If you aren't British and you aren't gay, you haven't heard of us." True dat.

I love concerts and have been to the best, but never have I heard screaming like the Gaga fans. It made me think of my poor husband who once took our daughter to see MC Hammer. He got seated in front of a speaker and still believes he has damage from it.

Gaga was more like a Broadway show than a normal concert. It was definitely an adult show and very inappropriate for children, though there were plenty there. One teacher I heard of dropped off her 8th grade daughter with a bunch of other young girls. All I can say about that is OMG. Even high school students who were there thought it was adult only material.

The music, the dancing, the costumes and sets were top notch. She writes all her own music and her voice is so good it could knock your socks off. But, who is this Lady?

Only in her twenties, Gaga is a woman in charge. She began playing the piano at age 4, composed her first piano ballad at 13, attended a private all-girls Catholic school where she was very studious and disciplined, then attended NYU.

Gaga was on the cover of *Time* Magazine's *2010 World's Most Influential People* issue. She was the top selling artist of 2010 and the first to gain over a billion views on YouTube. She has played for Queen Elizabeth II and posed on the cover of Rolling Stone Magazine wearing nothing but a few bubbles. Not baubles, bubbles.

"She isn't a pop act, she is a performance artist. She herself is the art," states Cyndi Lauper. She calls herself a designer of fame and the University of South Carolina had a full-time course called, "*Lady Gaga and the Sociology of Fame*".

She has been criticized for outrageousness. Chris Rock sums it up. "She's Lady Gaga. She's not Lady Behave Yourself."

Bullied in school, she claims emotional scars from it. Her message blasts "You arc okay. Be yourself. Be who you are." Alison, a young teacher, said after the concert, "I felt like I walked out taller because she really makes you love who you are. She is one of the most artistic people I have ever seen. I loved being there and knowing the diversity in the audience and that everyone accepted it!!! It was a very positive experience."

Yes, diversity was rampant. One gal overheard this from the guy in front of her. "This is the only time I will ever wear a boa in the men's room and be okay with it."

Val and Greg stood up for the entire concert and were about 15 feet from Gaga. They, of course, were crushed by young people who filled the floor space with them. One girl asked them baffled, "Why are you here?"

A friend said, "It was very entertaining. She's a great singer, but I think she was more demonic than Marilyn Manson was at his concert. I was really turned off by the swearing." "What did your wife think?" I asked. "She said she would rather go to a Marilyn Manson concert than to see Gaga again – and she doesn't like Marilyn Manson."

I agreed about the language. I was also turned off with the blood she had all over herself for the last half of the show and confused why that was necessary.

I was young, but I remember a young guy named Elvis Presley coming on *The Ed Sullivan Show*. He was outrageous with his sexy moves. I remember taking my kids to see Madonna in concert and worrying about her outrageous song, *Like a Virgin*. It turns out they were both talented music innovators and have stood the test of time.

Lady Gaga is the new outrageous musical act. She is what our children and grandchildren are watching and listening to. Gaga has a bra she plugs in at night to recharge it. Just like her bra, we need to stay plugged in to what's happenin' now. And make no mistake, readers. Lady Gaga is what's happenin' now.

Goin' For It

Be Not Afraid

I'm afraid. I'm scared. I don't like snakes. I don't like water. I don't like heights. I am claustrophobic. I am afraid of speaking in public. I am afraid of dying. I am afraid of the dark. I am afraid to be alone at night. These are all things we hear people say.

Let me ask you this. And be honest, okay? What are you afraid of?

A couple years ago, I saw a small green snake on my step. I screamed bloody murder and my wonderful neighbor, Doug, was instantly alerted and in help mode. I survived, but I gotta tell ya, every time I am near those steps, I am on high alert. I am afraid.

We recently put a bunch of rocks on our beach. You can imagine how happy I was when a guy I recently met saw us and told us how nice the rocks look. He also said, "You know they will harbor snakes." I could hardly respond. Fear choked me. Say it ain't so, please . . . pretty please. I would like to say I haven't thought about it since, but in reality, I have only thought about it while awake.

In a few days I am going to walk the Mackinac Bridge. At least that is my big plan. I am pretty sure I can go the distance. I may hurt doing it, but I think I can do it.

What I am not sure about is how I will manage my enormous fear of heights. My fear of heights is very physical. It feels like my body turns to Jello and my legs are not there, like I will fall. I feel woozy. I shake. My heart races.

I believe that fear grows each year. You either get a piece of it or it will lock you into a mental prison of fear forever.

I have driven the bridge several times. It is never easy or comfortable. I am afraid to go in open elevators, but I keep doing it. I need to know I can. I am afraid of open escalators. I can hardly stand to be on one. Each time, I am not sure I will survive.

I am walking the bridge with four friends and two of my daughters. My husband might even go. Julie and Gisela, who are going with me, are also afraid of heights. Why are we doing this?

We each feel this is something we have always wanted to do. My friend, Bev, is going so I figured that I might as well go with her. What better opportunity could arise?

What makes people push hard to accomplish something that is so hard for them to do? Gisela puts it this way. "I am deathly afraid of heights, but it is important to not let it paralyze you. I have climbed the Tower of Pisa, gone on a Ferris wheel, ridden in a cable car. These were very difficult for me, but I did it. It makes me feel like I have really accomplished something. My fear will not rule me."

I cannot imagine what it will be like to stand on the Mackinac Bridge. I feel physically upset when I actually imagine it as a reality. I felt physically sick as I talked to the lady at their chamber office and she described it.

Tonight a friend told me that she has walked it and you can feel the bridge sway. I will file that comment away with the one about the snakes in my rocks. I will name this file "things I don't need to know or think about".

I have thought about what I can do to make this easier on myself. Lotsa drugs? Nah, that ain't it. Lotsa booze? Nah, that ain't it either.

I am going with positive imaging. I plan to visualize in detail how easy and wonderful this walk will be and how great I will feel as I do it. Oh, yeah, and how great it will feel when it's over!

I will also be praying big time. I think I will be calling into action my "Please Pray for Me Team". My son suggested I could say the rosary as I cross. That's a great idea. I did seven entire rosaries once while having an MRI done. Yup, prayer is definitely going to be a major part of my survival action plan.

Eleanor Roosevelt said, "You gain strength, courage and confidence by every experience in which you really stop to look fear in the face. You are able to say to yourself, 'I've lived through this. I can take the next thing that comes along.' You must do the thing you think you cannot do."

Julie told me she got woozy looking at the pictures on the bridge walk website. She says she is in denial right now about her fear of heights being a factor. She is hoping to be surrounded by people so it won't feel so high. Good chance of that as they say some 17,000 people walk. She says she won't look down and will only walk on cement, no grating. I guess I won't tell her then that the chamber told me there are two parts where the bridge does its expanding thing. These areas are grated and you have to cross them. Who knows? That may be easy. Or, then again, that may be where we just stand and wet our pants. If we get that far, and I sure hope we do, I will tell you right now – wetting my pants will be on the bottom of my things I am afraid of list.

Ah, How Sweet It Is

Jackie Gleason, an old comedian, used to say, "Ah, how sweet it is!" And remember Charlie Sheen shouting, "Winning!" That is how I am feeling today. I am pretty sure my six walking partners are feeling the same. We made it. We walked the Mackinac Bridge without a hitch.

This may not be such a huge feat for the 36,000 other bridge walkers. Most just go out and get 'er done, enjoying it as they amble. I read that a 90 year old man walked it. My neighbor, Gene, just told me he and his wife, Carol, walked it and do every year. When we began the walk a guy we all knew happened to be walking right in front of us. It's a small world after all. What made our walk different was that we had to battle our huge fear of heights. Accomplishing that, though, made seeing that finish line seem all the sweeter.

The bridge was so crowded that it was hard to walk fast. The crowd set the pace. There were kids on dad's shoulders, people in wheelchairs, babes in buggies, folks on oxygen, some with a walker. Julie liked seeing the National Guard lining the middle and edge of the bridge. She was unsettled, however, when she noticed the rescue boat and hovering helicopter. Lucky for me, I never noticed them. At one point, the bridge began to sway a lot and people around us were all staggering to remain grounded. I saw the woman staggering in front of me. I was staggering myself. But somehow, in my "la-la I'm so lovin' this" state of mind, it never dawned on me that the bridge was swaying. I just thought . . . oh, wait, I am not sure I thought at that point.

I am pretty happy to have walked the bridge once and I would do it again. What I really don't want to do again is drive home on Labor Day with a gazillion people on the roads.

I got a lot of well wishes for this walk. I got a lot of prayers, encouragement and hugs. I got some really negative comments and I got some really great advice.

Mindset seemed to play a big part in it for me. I visualized it in detail. I visualized how great it would feel and look and be. And it all came true. And then there were all those people I begged to pray for me. Bless them, for sure!

As so many things are, the reality wasn't nearly as frightful as the thinking ahead of time. We had worried about the grating and looking through to the water. The big open expansion parts were covered up, so you hardly know they were there.

A friend told me to relish the beauty and the wow it would be to look out at the lakes. Another told me to think about how close I would physically be to God. My masseuse gave me a great breathing exercise to calm me – four in, hold for four, eight out. Joyce reminded me to hydrate.

My doctor told me to think of all the people that had already lived through it. I told him that was what I had done when I was in labor with my first child. My sister-in-law told me not to worry until ten people ahead of me had fallen in, then to begin to worry. Marty told me to take my happy feet and just enjoy the walk.

From our priest's sermon, I made up a mantra, "Fear, get thee behind me!" It felt quite powerful. You might want to try it when you need it.

As we set out at 7 a.m., the sun came up and a lovely rainbow appeared. I mean, really, how cool is that? Talk about a divine omen.

I had several people ask me why I was attempting this if I was afraid of heights. The answer was I had always wanted to do it and I didn't want to not do it because I was a "scardy cat". What kind of example would that be to my grandchildren? And, do we really want to let fear box us in? I think it is always good to push our limits.

I realize this quest was teeny compared with what many others are doing. Darrin ran the Boston Marathon. Rosemary and Eron just completed a dualathon. People are taking a new class, trying new things, meeting new people, moving to new places. Some are going through divorce, some are getting married. Some are joining dating services, some searching for jobs. People have physical, mental, emotional and spiritual quests. There are really more quests taking place than I could ever cover. Everyone has their own.

What are some of the things on your back burner? Is now the time to plan to do them? What is holding you back? Step by step, dreams and desires become reality. Abe Lincoln said, "Always bear in mind that your own resolution to success is more important than any other one thing."

But if you want a little more than your own resolution to your success, let me be the first to encourage you. Ahhh, how sweet it is.

Donna, Cara & Maureen Burns, Bev Geyer
& Jose Olivieri

Gisela Peek, Maureen and Julie Momber

Six Little Letters . . . Three Teeny Words

Sometimes it isn't the big things in life that are the most important. I am talking words here. We think big words mean someone is smart. That may be true. However it was brought to my attention the other day, that six letters made into three teeny words, really say a lot and can make a person feel mighty proud.

I recently stopped in to take my friend, Jo, some soup. Jo fell not long ago and broke one wrist and sprained the other. She met me with a brace on one and a cast on the other. Jo needs her hands, as we all do, to do all that has to be done in a day. She asked me to come into her bedroom and put the pillow cases on her pillows. I did it quickly – my wrists aren't broken, so it was easy for me. She told me how she had changed the sheets by herself and then heard herself say three words she realized she was saying all the time these days – the profound wisdom of six powerful letters made into three teeny words. "I did it!"

Last week our Louie turned six. He was engrossed in putting together a puzzle. When he finished, he ran into the kitchen and yelled, "I did it!"

Yesterday a friend who hates early mornings, came to exercise early and was so proud of herself. "She did it!"

Last month my husband had knee surgery for a torn meniscus. His surgeon, a young beautiful woman, came in and chatted with us. I asked her, "What was it like to replace the first knee you ever did all on your own?" I can't imagine doing that, getting the tools, the hammers and saws and all, and then beginning. I am sure when she was done, she must have felt, "I did it!"

My friend, Laura, had a stroke this fall. She is my age. She has fought the comeback fight and now is back to driving and speaking normally. She radiates joy, beauty and a big smile. Her recovery shouts to all, "she did it".

Another friend, Lynne, has just completed several grueling sessions of chemotherapy where she had to stay in the hospital for days to get it. She has tried to do water aerobics during the last few months but could only do ten minutes or so before she was exhausted and had to stop. The other day she did 30 minutes. The next time she came, she completed the entire class. "She did it!" What a milestone!

My husband worked, like many of you, raking leaves. It's an insurmountable project that takes days and lots of hard physical work. What a smile he wore as he came in and said, "Job done for the season. I did it!"

We all have jobs, projects, things we are trying to improve on. When we get them done or achieved, the feeling of "I did it" is powerful. It propels us to do other things and is a positive example to others.

My friends, Lana and Kelly, both lost 25 to 30 pounds over last winter and have kept it off. (Unfortunately, their success did not rub off on me.) They both feel justly proud that "they did it". Why is it so much easier to just think about it?

I have several friends going through huge lifestyle changes - some through divorce, some have been widowed. It is wonderful to see the strength and pride they show as they go on with their new life roles and radiate the feelings of, "I did it. I'm doing it." Sometimes it is the things we aren't sure we can do that make us the proudest when we "do them".

Here we are at the holidays. I don't know about you, but the season and all the work it entails – decorating, shopping, cards, etc. – wears me out just thinking about it. Due to some early holiday entertaining, I had to get my house decorated early. Now I am so grateful and happy that "I did it". Kelly has had all her decorating, shopping, and wrapping done for a while. She loves to tell everyone that "she did it" and is just relaxed and enjoying the season.

For years, I have wanted to bake French bread like my friends, Linda and Karen, do. Theirs is always perfect. I bought the special pans a few years ago. They gave me the recipe. What I lacked was the courage. Although I love to cook and bake, I just didn't have the feeling that I could actually make French bread and have it turn out. Well, at last, "I did it"! And, it was easy. Too bad I let those years go by being stuck in my fear of failure. Yes, it is just bread, but isn't it just like all the other things in life that we try or want to try?

A funny thing, as I was finishing this, I was at the Blodget Hospital Coffee Shop, waiting for someone in surgery. I asked the volunteer cashier to add a tip to my credit card payment. She couldn't and called for help. When she completed it, she pumped her arms high and yelled, "I did it." And she didn't even know about this column.

So, think back on all the things you can say that about – "you did it". There is still time to tackle a few more things on your list. You could check it twice and then jump right in. When the new year arrives, you can have an even bigger list that at the top says, "I did it"! Good luck.

If you would like the French Bread recipe, it's in the back of the book.
You can surprise your family with it and say, "I did it"!

Run Baby, Run

Run baby, run. Run for your life.

Cara Burns

Imagine four traffic lanes each packed with people running. You stand there and they run by you. They run so fast it is nearly impossible to scan through them to pick out your child who is one of them. They run and they run. There are young ones, old ones, small ones, bigger ones. There are some who run slowly, others who go so fast it nearly takes your breath away. There are many racers in this race. They each have their own gait. Some make it look easy. Some you wonder how they can keep going. Some look like they are having the time of their lives. Some look like they may die before they end.

Some run in pairs. Some run in groups. Most run alone. Some are tuned into their own worlds, earphones plugged in to turn off the distractions. Others are open and looking around to acknowledge the world. One guy is running barefoot, the new phenomenon. We saw him three times and each time he asked us, "You got shoes?" He was clearly having fun with his situation.

There are 25,000 who run this fine day. Our daughter, Cara, is one of them. It is the Chicago Half Marathon. The sun is out. A lovely breeze refreshes. The world is good. Everyone cheers the runners on.

"You can do it." "You're awesome." "You're looking good." "Yeah, looking strong." "Good job." And on and on. Lots of encouragement. There are no jeers, only cheers. As I watch this, I think it is a metaphor for our lives.

We burst into life and our race begins. No matter whom we love and know our race is unique, individual and solitary. We each live our personal journey, our personal race of life.

If we are lucky, we have cheers along the way. People encourage us. We encourage others. Do we cheer others enough? Do we get cheered enough? Unlike the marathon, it is almost impossible to get through our race of life without jeers. People all too quickly put others down, discourage, demean. Do we do more cheering than jeering? Do we allow ourselves to get jeered when we shouldn't put up with it? Do we think cheers but not say them?

"You can do it." "You're awesome." "You're looking good." "Yeah, looking strong." "Good job." We can't get enough in our run of life. It's fuel for our tank.

Mark Twain said, "I could live two years on a good compliment." They keep us going. They lift us up. They warm us and embolden us.

Just like a marathon, in our race of life we get discouraged, tired. Things hurt. We fall. Ambulances are at the ready.

We also run it with excitement, pumped. We run with purpose.

Melissa Etheridge, breast cancer survivor, sings, *I run for life*. We run for life, too. We run for our life as this is the only one we get. Where are we in our race? The first quarter? Half way? Heading towards home? Looking at the finish line? Almost there? Every part of our race of life has its own markers, its own goals, its own hardships and excitements.

As with a running race, our races of life are different lengths. Some get to run the marathon of life. Some only get a sprint. Mostly our choices are in how we run our race, not how long it will be.

As in a race, there is a monitor to check how we did, how we performed in our life race. It captures our movements and sums it up at the end. We each have our own individual accounting. We can hope and wish for certain results, but our performance will be told by our chip.

When some run a race, they just want to finish. Others want to be fast. Others do it for fun. Some want to prove something to themselves or others.

Just like in a race, in our life journey some want to see what happens to them. Others want to make things happen. Some go for the gusto. Some are lackadaisical. (What a fun word to use. I don't think I've ever written that before.) But I get distracted. And so do we in our run of life. There are lots of distractions vying for our attention, keeping us from our true purpose, keeping us too busy with things we don't really care about.

The similarities of races and life are many. As I thought about all of this, as thousands of runners ran by me the other day, I remembered my brother-in-law dying. I was struck by his son, who sat on the edge of his bed and for hours kept cheering him on. "You can do it, buddy. It's okay. You can do it."

My friend is dying right now. She may very well be gone before this goes to press. She told another friend, "Don't feel bad for me. I had a wonderful life."

She ran her race. She is about to cross her finish line. Her chip shows a life well lived.

I love the saying, 'On the day you were born, the people around you laughed with joy.

Live your life so that on the day you die, the people around you will cry with sorrow.'

For each of us, it is always time to reevaluate. How am I doing on my race of life? Do I need to speed up, slow down, change my gait? Am I cheering others? What's my purpose?

You're awesome. You're looking good. You can do it. Good job. Run baby, run. Run for your life. It's the only one you get.

On Living A Better Life

I Quit

"I quit the family!" That was announced by my four year old grandson as he gave a dismissive wave and walked out of the room on his scrawny little legs. Something hadn't gone his way.

We have had many good laughs over that, but it also gives one thoughts to ponder. Who hasn't wanted to quit the family at some point? Or quit the church? Or quit the job or the class or the group? Or the marriage?

I remember a friend who, years ago, left home. She felt she needed to just quit it all for a bit. She went to a motel in Lansing and got herself back on track with some serious reflection and solitude. She didn't really quit the family. She just took a much needed break.

Sometimes we quit relationships. There are several reasons to do that. People change. Friends change. We change. Relationships sometimes need to be adjusted. Relationships sometimes have to go. We can wish them well and then drastically change our relationship with them.

On the other hand, life isn't just about the good times. We shouldn't necessarily quit the family, job, church, etc., just because things may not be going the way we want. However, I think it's probably normal for us to have the thought of quitting run through our mind on occasion. Other people can be such a pain, right? It's never us.

I have a cartoon I love. A lady goes to the complaint department and says, "What have you got on fixing other people?"

I also love the one where a woman goes to the complaint department at a major store. She says to the person at the desk, "My husband is rude."

All that reminds me of a guy I know in Grand Rapids. He likes to tell people, "I'm quitting my subscription to you. I'm sick of your issues."

There is a great motto. " This too shall pass." That is the good news. Life has its ups and downs. We can take that to the bank. It is a given, a sure thing.

Art Spander said, "The longer you stay in one place, the greater your chances of disillusionment."

Remember the old song that went, "I beg your pardon. I never promised you a rose garden."

Life is full of joy and happiness. It is also full of rough times.

Twice I was fortunate to hear the poet artist Gwen Frostic speak. I remember her saying, "The winds of change will break the hearts and the backs of those who can't bend." We need to be able to bend and flow with the ups and downs of life. Quitting may not be the best response for us.

In my first book, *Run with your Dreams*, I quoted Calvin Coolidge.

"Nothing in the world can take the place of persistence.
Talent will not, nothing is more common than unsuccessful men with talent.
Genius will not; unrewarded genius is almost a proverb.
Education will not, the world is full of educated derelicts.
Persistence and determination alone are omnipotent.
The slogan "PRESS ON" has solved and always will solve
the problems of the human race."

Pressing on, working through things, waiting things out – all of these may be the best option we have in challenging situations.

My grandson quickly forgot that he had quit the family. In a short while, he was hugging and happy.

If we feel we want to quit things, but we press on, we may find things better than before. Life is a buffet of experiences and feelings. Life doesn't come with a guaranteed safety net.

Nothing is completely safe. When we risk trying, loving, or living fully, we are still always putting ourselves at risk.

I shouldn't end on something so silly, but I just read it and it made me laugh out loud. What did I just say? Nothing is completely safe. So, here is the silly quote I just saw. It is by Bob Rubin. "Condoms aren't completely safe. A friend of mine was wearing one and got hit by a bus."

Knock, Knock - Who's There?

Open. Close. Open. Close. We open and close things all the time.

When you close the door, you can snuggle into your home. When you close a box, drawer or cupboard, you can keep things safe. When you close your eyes, you can get a much needed rest.

There have been lots of songs about closing. The Beatles sang, "Close your eyes and I'll kiss you." Lyle Lovett sings one of my favorites, *Closing Time.*

We are all aware of other closings. Plant closings lead to unemployment. Classes fill so enrollments close. At a certain point, reservations for events close. Some meetings are closed. Some coffins are closed.

People close their ears and won't listen. People close themselves off from other people and end up alone. People close their hearts and become hardened.

Perhaps the worst closing of all is a mind. When we close our mind, we close our life experiences. We close our opportunities. Along with closing one's mind comes closed thinking which leads nowhere.

When we close our minds we quit growing. Closed minds say that there is nothing new or worthwhile to learn, there are no new people to meet and there are no new thoughts and ideas to explore.

When we close our minds we are saying we don't need anyone else. We know it all and we are all that is important or valued. But, no man is an island. No one knows it all. We must stay open to live a positive life. Success comes because someone is open.

Being closed is like being shut off. Utilities get shut off and leave us cold and in the dark, so with closing our minds. A respirator is shut off and someone dies, just like one who quits growing and being open to life.

As I wrote this, I was thinking of the many new things I have experienced recently because I was open. I learned new music when I went to see Lady Gaga. I learned about Hurricane Katrina this week when a friend took us all over New Orleans and showed us her Katrina reality.

I met a new friend whom I just loved and felt like I had known forever. I ate a new food – grilled oysters. I had never even had an oyster before, let alone grilled. Unless oyster crackers count, which they don't.

I had a new drink at a Mexican Restaurant – a sangrita. It is a combination of a margarita and sangria and all I can say about it is, "Yummo".

I tried a new exercise class and experienced Zumba. I learned some new moves for water aerobics.

I read a new book, *Sarah's Key,* and learned about a part of history I had not known about. I highly, highly recommend this book. It's excellent.

I heard a great new joke, but I won't put it in, just in case you aren't open-minded.

I learned several new words and what they meant. Unfortunately, I can't remember them, but when I see them again, I swear I'll know them.

I learned new ways of doing some things. I had my old ways but someone showed me new and better ways. Presto!

I learned some new, and profound to me, insights into my life. This came from a new group I am in.

Not long ago I learned a new game, mah-jongg. Through that I met new people.

The list goes on and on and on. It seems like if we are open, newness just comes at us from every angle. Through that our lives become richer.

Knock, knock. Who's there? It doesn't matter. Just open the door and yourself and let newness in.

Oversize Load

So, yesterday I was driving to Grand Rapids for my friend's funeral. The sun was out and it was a beautiful day. I always am happy when the weather co-operates and is nice for a funeral. It just seems to make things a bit better.

As I went down the road, there was an enormous tractor/trailer/thingy ahead of me. Across its behind it had a bright yellow banner which read, "Oversize Load". And I thought to myself, 'yup, there are many days I should wear one of those across my behind'. Well maybe not there, maybe it should go across my chest like a Miss America banner. But the location of the banner isn't the important part – the message is. Can you relate? I bet you can.

Physically I have carried around an oversize load. Some would say I still do. I don't like those people. But I am well aware of the many burdens of carrying around a physical load. Of course, I am thinking in terms of pounds, but there are many other physical burdens that are "Oversize Loads". No matter how it manifests itself, carrying burdens around a is a hard thing to live with. It takes extra work, energy, patience and high doses of positive thinking.

I have lived with oversize loads of work: deadlines; sales quotas; travel demands;

energy levels; and on and on . . . I could sum it up with work, work and more work or with "Oversize Load". Our body warns us when we are overloaded. When my eye starts twitching, it is my body warning. It never lies. What are your signs? How does your body caution you? We may pay attention or not, but the signs are there. They might as well be blaring from a megaphone, "'Oversize Load', beware Bucko!"

Emotionally, I have lived with and through "Oversize Loads". So have most of you. Sometimes these pass in a short while. Sometimes they hang on for a long time. Sometimes they stay with us but dim here and there. I remember a counselor once referred to the "walking wounded". Sometimes emotional wounds are definitely "Oversize Loads".

As I passed the huge vehicle on the East Beltline, I wondered. If one looked up "Oversize Load" in the dictionary, would my picture be there? Of course, that's ridiculous. It might be yours.

This is not always in our hands. Life just plain throws stuff at us and we have to react, cope and go on and on and on. Talking to a friend yesterday, she was in a fog of emotional overload. Her father is dying and she said that was just one of several major things happening. Her stress was palpable over the phone. I could hear her audio banner – "Oversize Load". I thought of the phrase, "This too shall pass." It does, but it is still a lot to finagle through. (I have never written the word finagle before. I didn't even know how to spell it. It's a fun word, though. To write, that is.)

These things aren't always negative. Positive things can cause lots of good excitement. The problem is our body doesn't know the difference between positive excitement and negative excitement. It treats them equally and gives us stress to cope with both. For example, if I climb to the top of the Sears Tower (which has a new name now that I can't remember), and walk out on that see through platform over Chicago, I will feel major stress. When something absolutely joyous happens to me, I will also feel major stress. The fact that my body treats both experiences the same is totally wacko. And then again, that is a ridiculous example, because I would never, never, never ever walk out on a platform like that. Height is not my friend.

Moving can be an "Oversize Load", as well as trying to sell a house, looking for a job, taking a class, caring for kids or caring for someone ill. Actually, almost anything can become a burden.

It is good to get a bit of perspective by realizing that everything we are and do can turn into an "Oversize Load" at times. When that happens, having and using good stress tools is a must. Listening to others as they warn us, care about us and push us to do things can also help ease our load.

When we see an "Oversize Load" driving down the highway, there are usually vehicles in front and behind it. They all drive slower. They are cautious, as are those around them, passing them and waiting for them. This situation seems to be a good example for us as we meander and finagle (now I've used it twice) through our individual roads of life.

Yes, just like the machinery on the highway, we all carry "Oversize Loads" at times. They can be physical, emotional, spiritual, financial, work-related, etc. It is good, then, to put on our mental banner and accept that we are carrying a giant burden right then. It is a good thing to let others help guide us forward and cover our back. It is a good thing to go slowly and with caution.

I'll close with a cartoon caption I saw once. Perhaps you can relate to it as you haul around your current "Oversize Load". "I've tried relaxing, but I don't know, I feel more comfortable tense."

Love Makes The World Go Round

"Love, Love, Love" sang the Beatles. "Love is all we need."

At Easter, Christians celebrate love. God loved man so much that he gave his son for us. In turn, people love God back – a right back at ya kinda thing.

Love comes in a variety of tones.

Brotherly love, familial love, parental love – these are all a special kind of love - deep, forgiving, unconditional. That is, of course, the norm or the way people hope it will be. There is a Polish proverb that states, "The greatest love is a mother's, then a dog's, then a sweetheart's." In many instances, that may be true.

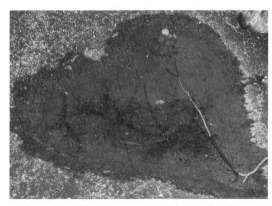
A heart formed in the pavement of Maureen's driveway.

First love is tender. Some first loves last a lifetime. Most flicker out and move on to other loves. H.L. Mencken said, "A man always remembers his first love with special tenderness, but after that he begins to bunch them."

New love is exciting, full of awe and wonder. New can last, but it changes as time passes. It can even be more beautiful as it ages and ripens. Or, put another way, Dr. Karl Bowman said, "Love is an obsessive delusion that is cured by marriage."

Love birds are part of that new and first love thingy. You know - when two people forget that the world is around and only have eyes and time for each other.

Love at first sight is probably rare, maybe non-existent. I remember the thoughts I had as I first laid eyes on my mate. I don't know if it was love at first sight, but it sure did make a solid impression that never lessened. Perhaps love at first sight is actually major attraction at first sight. But then, major attraction at first sight can certainly happen without love ever entering the picture. This is all really complicated.

True love is a beautiful thing. It is even more beautiful if both people feel the same way.

Love is blind. We have all seen that to be true. It can be hard to see the faults of others when we love them. I once read, "Love is blind, and marriage is a real eye-opener."

"Love you" seems to be the modern way for many people to end telephone conversations. I hear it wherever I go and it is coming from men, women and children. I think it is a good thing for the world.

Self-love is a very important part of loving others. It is the bridge that allows us to love others. I also think it is not a given. Many of us have to work hard to attain it.

We love our friends, our pets, our work, our home, our things. Love truly makes our worlds go 'round.

This is just a sampling of how love comes in a variety of forms and names. Nelson Rockefeller said to Henry Kissinger, "Never forget that the most powerful force on earth is love." And so it is. May your life and heart be filled with love in a variety of forms.

Assuming We Have Assumptions

Last spring a sweet little girl, eleven years old, came by to sell me magazines for her school fundraiser. As I sat pouring over her catalog, she saw I had my church directory lying on my desk. She said, "That's Christian." Then she screwed up her face and said, "No, that's Catholic."

I said to her, "You know Catholics are Christian. We all believe in the same God."

She went on, and remember I said she was only eleven years old, "But Catholics worship Mary."

I explained to her that, "We do not worship Mary. We honor Mary. We worship Jesus Christ as our God just like all Christians do."

She is quite a precocious and delightful young lady and we went on to discuss other things.

Later, our encounter got me thinking about how we, as humans, assume many things, whether they are correct or not. And we assume about everything.

Stephen R. Covey said, "We simply assume that the way we see things is the way they really are or the way they should be. And our attitudes and behaviors grow out of these assumptions."

Not long ago we were on a local car lot looking for a car. Almost as soon as we got onto the lot, the salesman, a seemingly very nice man, told us a horribly racist joke. He assumed we would think it was funny. We did not and later I saw his boss about the matter. The salesman called and apologized. This experience reminded me of a quote by Marshall McLuhan, "Most of our assumptions have outlived their uselessness."

We, as humans, make assumptions about everything. We also believe our assumptions to be truth. All of these are in our emotional bag of coping skills and we treat others and what they say and do accordingly. If we are able, we need to question the validity of our assumptions. Paul Broca said, "The least questioned assumptions are often the most questionable."

I have had times when someone close to me assumes I did, said or thought something for a certain reason. I am always shocked, as I think they know me so well, that they would know better than that. Apparently, assuming is sometimes more powerful than knowing.

I often assume things that aren't true. I assume what someone is thinking or why they did something. I am often wrong. I assume you all do this too.

Before I was married I had a very beautiful roommate, Rita. I remember how people would assume she was not friendly and that she was stuck up. Do people still say stuck up? I think they assumed this because of her beauty. However, they assumed wrong. She was just very shy. Henry Winkler said, "Assumptions are the termites of relationships."

Recently I assumed something about someone that wasn't true. We had a nice chat afterwards about how people often assume that about her. Her outgoing personality leads them to assume she is a way she is not. It was another good lesson on assumptions not being truth.

We are all full of assumptions. We will continue to make assumptions. We are all human. We are all vulnerable.

However, my recent encounters have reminded me to stop and think about all the assumptions I make and have. Which ones are correct? Which ones harm me, harm others, and harm the world? Which ones would free me if I let go of them?
As parents, we teach our assumptions to our children. They grow up and teach them to our grandchildren. Everyone assumes they are truth.

Alan Alda said, "Begin challenging your own assumptions. They are your windows on the world. Scrub them off every once in a while or the light won't come in."
I assume we all need to challenge our assumptions. Many of them have outlived their usefulness. Many of them hold us back and hold our world back.

I am going to assume you agree with me.

Thanks For Showing Up

The other day a woman said something to me that really surprised me. I was in Livonia about to speak to 350 people. She had hired me. Just before we went up front, she said, "I want to thank you." I thought, okay, that's nice, then she went on with the part I found so interesting. "I want to really thank you for showing up. You just never know if people will show up."

I was kind of stunned. Of course I would show up. Who wouldn't? It was a job. It was a commitment. It was the professional thing to do. I couldn't even imagine not showing up. But she got me thinking . . . showing up . . . an interesting concept and perhaps one not to be taken for granted.

People die and hope folks show up at their funerals. People graduate and hope others show up at their open houses. Groups host events and expect people to show up.

Now that it's good weather, families hold garage sales and hope buyers show up. Churches hold services and hope the faithful show up. Businesses open based on the dream that clients and customers will show up.

I met my husband at a party at my apartment. He showed up . . . and I'm so glad he did. I have been sick or laid-up and friends have shown up with food and caring. I'm so glad they did.

And then there are the times when we wait and wait and wait for someone to show up: the nurse telling you that you can finally see the doctor now; the cable guy that you have waited six hours for when you should have been at work; the police when you are in an accident; your graduate to receive their diploma when 240 others already have; the firemen when you forget to close the flue on the fireplace and fill the house with smoke. (Am I the only one who has waited for that?) It's a given that much of our life is filled with waiting for someone to show up.

And then there are the times when they don't show up: the friend who forgets your event and never shows up; the loved one who misses a plane and doesn't show up for the holiday; the friend who doesn't show up at the wedding. Sometimes people let us down. They just aren't there for us. They don't show up in a variety of ways.

As I think about showing up, I wonder. If governments wanted to go to war and no one showed up, what would happen? Wouldn't it be a different world if bullies quit showing up in schools and family events and work settings?

Yes, the lady who hired me made me think. We show up for work. We show up for events. We show up for our lives. Sometimes we show up when we don't know what else to do, we just show up. Sometimes that is more than enough.

Woody Allen said, "Eighty per cent of success is showing up." I think he's right. When we show up we participate, we get involved, we grow, we help, and we touch others.

As we look at how our life is going right now, we might ask ourselves, am I showing up? Am I showing up for myself? Am I showing up for those I care about? Am I showing up for my career, my community, my life? And if you think you are, you might look at yourself in the mirror and say, "I want to thank you, really thank you for showing up. Not everyone does, you know."

Reflecting On The Quality

I have a sign on my refrigerator that says, "Meditating while multi-tasking". Unfortunately, that sums me up! And those of you who know me can testify that is true. Many of us are traveling at the speed of life and it is too fast, way too fast.

My friend, Martha, recently had a new grand baby. We were talking about what a special time that is. When a baby is born, the world stops for a bit. Life goes on, but we step out of the busy into our own special place. We savor every bit of the experience.

While playing Scrabble recently, we got talking about savoring things. One said, "Savoring is highly underestimated."

Connie shared how her mother-in-law said that a visit from her family would last her for months. She would relish every minute of it by going over and over it in her mind, savoring it slowly.

I often think of that with surprise parties or events. When I have had a surprise happen to me, I am always in a fog while it is going on. I am in shock, really, and I can hardly enjoy it or take it in. I actually appreciate it more when I know about it ahead of time. When you have time to look forward to something special, it is a joy to savor the expectations. Then when the event happens, you can enjoy it more, and when it is over, you get to relish it again in your memory.

Marcus Aurelius said, "Very little is needed to make a happy life." I think that is quite true. This week we said good-by to our dear aunt, Julie Burns. She was mentally with it until the end. She would have turned 90 in a few days. As she faced her life ending, it was truly a time to savor the people and good times she had had. She even savored her faith as she told us not to worry for a second about her, that she was going to a better place and that she was ready to go. We had some very special time with her sharing all we meant to each other. What a blessing to have time to do that while the world stops for a bit.

There are many things to savor every day - a cold, crisp winter day, the smell of fresh cut grass or a sheet hung out to dry. How about a beautiful snowy day where the world is blanketed in white? What about a beautiful sunny spring day with tulips and daffodils perking and everyone feeling renewed?

We can savor a sunset on the beach or while driving in the car. We can savor a good book and snuggle in to devour it as we let the world go by.

I think music is a good thing to savor. I never hear Pachelbel's *Canon* without letting out a deep breath and taking in the lovely music to soothe my soul. Any music you love can be savored. We just need to take time to do it. Clarence Clemons playing his wonderful sax in the Lady Gaga song, *The Edge of Glory*, Adele's fabulous voice singing some of your favorites, *Bring Him Home from Les Miserables* - the list is enormous.

Friends and family can be savored, rather than being taken for granted. To stop and really listen to them, to stop and really look at their face, appreciate their smile, their eyes, to hug deeply as you think about how much they mean to you – there are so many ways to savor them.

Life rushes by pretty fast. A friend once told me, "There are no rewinds in life, only pauses and fast forwards." How true he is.

May I suggest taking time to pause more, to savor more, to slow down and enjoy more. Seneca reminded us, "The wise will always reflect on the quality, not the quantity of life." That Seneca, he was such a smarty pants!

Certainly smarter than the guy who was told by his doctor that he had three weeks to live. He excitedly said to the doc, "Okay, then I'll take the last two weeks of July and the week between Christmas and New Years."

A Gift We Give Ourselves

Recently I have spoken at several volunteer appreciation events. It is amazing to me how many people volunteer. It is equally amazing to me how many people don't.

I can't remember when my husband and I began volunteering. I think it has just been a normal part of our life together. It feels good.

Yesterday a woman who volunteers at a hospital said to me, "My husband asks me why I don't quit working here. I don't get paid. It takes up so much of my time. He doesn't understand. It seems to him like I give and give. To me it seems like I get and get. I get new friends. I get to make a difference. I grow. I get to be with people. I get way more than I give. I wish he could understand."

I realize there are many who do not volunteer. I would like to encourage everyone to try it. You could begin with a baby step. Think of something that is easy for you, something you really enjoy and are good at, perhaps something you did as a career or hobby. Look and listen to find a place that could use your skill and expertise.

Then try volunteering for just an hour a week or an hour a month. See how you like it.

Life is about choices. We can choose to watch more T.V. We can choose to putter around. We can choose to go out and make the world a better place by doing something to help make that happen. We each get to make our own choices.

Here are some ideas. People who taught or worked in schools might tutor, be an aide or on a school board. People who love sports might help at the many sport programs in schools and the community. Churches need volunteers. Hospitals need volunteers. You could join an organization. The Lions, The Rotary, Women's Clubs come to mind. The groups you can join are endless.

If you worked with money or numbers, you might want to count money at church, help a group with taxes or accounting. If you were a nurse, doctor or dentist, there are numerous programs and clinics that could use your skills for those in need.

People who like to drive can drive people places. You can drive sick children to hospitals. Car dealers need cars driven from here to there. If you fly, you can fly sick people for treatment. If you love to garden or do yard work, you can come to my house. Just kidding. Well, email me, we'll talk.

Political groups need help. Soup kitchens and food pantries need help. Habitat for Humanity needs help. If you are an engineer, accountant, electrician, builder, manager, baker or candlestick maker – someone can use your skills.

You can work with people. You can work on your own. You can work any time of day or night. You can work with sick or well or dying people. You can work with babies, children, teens, adults or seniors.

If you sing or play a musical instrument, someone needs you. Your chamber of commerce needs you. I could go on and on. Wait, I already have.

Jim is a local banker. He serves on the library board with me. "Volunteering has been a priority for me. I mentored teens for several years – boys at risk of not graduating. I loved it. I probably got as much out of it as they did. I also did job shadowing at the bank. I felt one boy and I really connected. He seemed to feel my passion for banking. The next day he was quoted on the front page of the newspaper about his shadowing experience and said, 'After spending the day shadowing Jim at the bank, I have decided on a career as a mortician.'"

Jim and I had a good laugh over that and he added, "It didn't stop me from continuing to volunteer." Jim has a very busy family and career life. He commutes 70 miles round trip to work. He still finds time to volunteer with passion.

Bo is committed to volunteering in his daughter's third grade class and is the faithful Friday morning math guy. Elementary boys need strong male role models. Bo is a professional plumber and a great example of the many ways we can volunteer. You don't see many dads in the classrooms.

Dan said, "There are plenty of opportunities for volunteerism that will make a significant impact in the lives of people - everything from one-on-one mentoring to helping clean up camps, to handing out boxes of food. You don't need to go very far to find a need." Roger Coles, an avid volunteer, sent me a couple good quotes. Einstein tells us, "It is every person's obligation to put back into the world at least the equivalent of what he/she takes out of it." Gandhi put it this way. "Service to others is the rent you pay for your room here on earth." All I can add is amen!

Einstein tells us, "It is every person's obligation to put back into the world at least the equivalent of what he/she takes out of it." Gandhi put it this way. "Service to others is the rent you pay for your room here on earth." All I can add is amen!

Tiptoe Through The Tulips

Remember that old adage – "when life gives you lemons, make lemonade"? Holland, Michigan, put that into action in the real world. And, good for them! Their adage is "when life takes your tulips, celebrate the stems". Their tulips bloomed early due to weird warm weather, thus, leaving only stems for the famous Holland Tulip Festival.

We are told to look for the silver lining. We are told to be positive. We are told to not cry about spilt milk. Putting these grand ideas into action is not an easy task. It is easier for some folks than others.

Recently a lady was chatting with me after a talk. She said, "My husband is so negative. He always sees the cup half full. I always look on the bright side and it is really getting hard to be surrounded by his negativity every day." This is a problem I have heard often from people. It is extremely difficult – not to mention what a daily downer it is – to live or be surrounded by negative people.

In a perfect world, we could follow the advice of nay, nay, stay away. But sometimes they are our spouses. Sometimes they are our parents. Sometimes they work in the spot next to us. Sometimes they live next door. You get the dim picture.

Attitude is a choice we make daily, sometimes hourly. Though I consider myself a very positive person, there have been times I have had to give myself a big talking to. I have had to consciously flush the negativity out of my mind. Sometimes it has even become absorbed into my body language and my tone.

The great comedian, Flip Wilson, made famous the line, "What you see is what you get." That is so true. What we focus on is what our life becomes.

We never go to the store naked. We always remember to put our clothes on. But some days we need to stop and put on our attitude as well. Sometimes it is not there automatically. It must be a conscious decision. This decision can change our day. This decision can help change our life.

Attitudes are contagious. We must beware of negative people as they are very powerful. One negative person can bring down ten positive people just like that. We can't afford to hang out with negative people. They will sink our ship. They will ruin our day. They will make our life sour and bitter.

No one ever asks me to come speak to a group on negative thinking. "Please come. Our group is just too positive. Can you help them be more negative?" No, that never happens. Those calls never come. Instead, I have had years of requests to help people be more positive.

But, really, looking at the bright side is an inside job. It is a personal view point. Robert Schuler said, "Our attitude is always in our hands." That is true. No matter how much someone wants to ruin our positive attitude, they can only achieve that if we let them. We hold the power.

Do you wake up saying, "Good morning, God"? Or do you wake up saying, "Good God, it's morning"? That is your first wake up call to how your day is going to go.

A guy was fishing on a dock. He saw a bucket of crabs and noticed that they stayed in the bucket. He was aware that crabs can crawl out of a bucket so he studied them. What he saw was if one crab tried to crawl out, the others pulled him back in. The moral is – don't let the crabs in life get you down. Don't let the crabs keep you in the negative bucket of life. Negative people want you to stay in the misery with them. They don't want you to escape and be happy or successful. Beware. Remember that you have the power to crawl out and go on your positive way.

I think it is helpful to make a list of what you are grateful for each day. You can write it down or just think it through. I also try to think of three positive things about myself. This is not always easy. The negative is always at the ready to pop into my mind quickly. It is amazing how simple things like this can keep us thinking positively.

Edith Armstrong put it nicely. "I keep the telephone of my mind open to peace, harmony, health, love and abundance. Then, whenever doubt, anxiety or fear try to call me, they keep getting a busy signal – and soon they'll forget my number."

Wisdom, Nuggets, Advice And Tidbits

Here it is, that time of year again. Open houses fill the social calendar. Graduation gifts to buy. Caps and gowns. Joy and tears. Memories and anticipations. I like to get some wisdom or at least some interesting thoughts from commencement speeches recently given.

Arnold Schwarzenegger received an honorary law degree from Emory University. He quipped, "This is my first law degree. Finally, the Kennedys will think I'm a success." He ended his commencement speech by saying, "Be sure to stay hungry for helping others. Look beyond the mirror." Terrific advice for everyone. Most models for life success will list helping others at the top of the list. How are we doing in that area of our lives?

Julianna Margulies, from The Good Wife, spoke at her alma mater, Sarah Lawrence College. She said, "an important thing in my life has been the phrase, 'Learn more, not earn more.' Stay true to who you are and you will be more likely to find happiness, even though it may take a little longer." She added, "Don't be disillusioned by the current state of the world. Simply work to make it better." No wonder she's such a good wife dishing out that kind of wisdom.

Author, John Grisham, spoke at University of North Carolina at Chapel Hill. "Each of you is an original. Each of you has a distinctive voice." He urged grads to tell their stories. Glenn Beck at Liberty University said, "Faith can help put a faltering nation back on track." I would say amen to that.

My favorite of the commencement messages I heard and read this year was Oprah Winfrey at Duke University. "You are responsible for the energy that you bring." How true is that? We see negative folks coming and they are in a fog of negative energy that spreads. This works in reverse with positive energy. What are we spreading?

Oprah went on, "We ask ourselves, Who am I really? Will I do the right thing or the popular thing? Each of us has to stand in our own shoes. Will you stand in them with integrity and courage? You know what is right. Follow your gut. When you have to ask others, get still, listen until you know the answer from within." She also said, "You never know what kindness you might offer to someone that will last their lifetime." She said, like all of us, that she continues to learn and struggle with life's lessons on a daily basis.

I guess I will add my own to the above messages. I would encourage grads to live life with a lot of L words.

Love - The more the better. Love people, animals, life. Oh, yeah, and yourself.

Laugh - Laughter is the glue that bonds coping and life. We all need as much of it as we can get.

Learn - Commencement is the beginning of lifelong learning as we become the teacher and student combined. Never stop learning. As soon as you do, the world leaves you behind and never looks back.

Look and listen - Barack Obama encouraged grads at the University of Michigan to look at both sides. If you are a conservative, watch some liberal stuff once in awhile. If you are a liberal, watch some conservative stuff once in awhile. He said it much better than I just did, but the message is right on. In other words, be open-minded as you look and listen.

I will close with a nugget of brilliance I found yesterday on a notepad in Grand Haven. It's from E. B. White and I can really identify with it. "I arise in the morning torn between a desire to improve the world and a desire to enjoy the world. This makes it hard to plan the day." And there you go - wisdom, nuggets, advice and tidbits - all for the good of the graduates and us.

Riding The Roller Coaster Of Life

So many reflections go into a week. So many experiences. Some are fun. Some are not. Life is a mixture of all the parts. Here is a couple I had this past week.

One came from my grandson, Danny, who is in Kindergarten. We were at a local bazaar and it was lunchtime. I asked him if he would like to eat. He asked what they were serving. I answered, "Sloppy Joes".

He screwed up his face in sincere shock and yelped, "Uwwwwwwww. Yuck. What's that?"

I explained what sloppy joes are and he said, "Sounds like a disgusting diner to me." Hmmmm. Never thought of it that way. A new perspective, for sure.

On a tender note, last week was the dedication of the new Habitat for Humanity home. I have been part of a wonderful team working with the family getting this home.

People think of Habitat and they think of nails. But hammers and nails are only one facet of working with Habitat. There are so many more roles: gardening and landscape; financial and parenting classes; counseling on a variety of things; constructing the home; and much more.

About 75 attended this dedication. A prayer was said blessing the home. Then several people spoke. The greatest part of it all was watching the wonderful, grateful and totally overwhelmed mother and her four daughters. To see the love, gratitude and admiration they had in their eyes as they experienced this event was a sight to behold.

When the Mom first told her oldest daughter that they had been chosen to get a new home, the girl said, "I don't understand. What does that actually mean?"

Her Mom replied, "It means that if you ever in your life need a place to come home to, you'll have a home." I still can't repeat that to others without crying.

T.S. Eliot said, "Home is where one starts from." This family has been blessed with a fresh start. For all who worked on their home, in any way, they have each been blessed by being a part of this project. From *if I had a hammer* to the giving of the key, this is a gift to be grateful for from every direction.

On an anxiety note, several close friends and/or family had serious health issues last week. Some resolved now. Some pending. Days tinged with worry and prayer.

Sloppy joes. The blessing of Habitat. Health scares. A gamut of experiences. A variety of emotions and perspectives. All in the space of a few days. It turns out life is a roller coaster, after all. Hold on for the ride, folks.

Against The Wind

"It seems like yesterday, but it was long ago . . . we were young and strong . . . we were running against the wind."

Watching Bob Seger perform to 12,000 loyal fans was top of the line entertainment. Seger should be called Mr. Rock and Roll because he is just that. Nearly two years older than I am, he sports a grey mop of hair, a sweaty head band, glasses, a grey beard, and a young heart. He epitomizes the quote, "Age is just a state of mind." It seems Seger doesn't mind and neither do his fans.

We go to lots of musical events, but nowhere have we seen better musicians than Seger's Silver Bullet Band. To have just heard the sax player, Alto Reed, would have been worth the price of the ticket. He was definitely as good as it gets. I'm wondering if he made that musical name up. Come on!

Most of Seger's band has been with him for 30 or 40 years. When you can play that kind of music, why go anyplace else?

Seger, a fabulous musician himself, also writes his songs. He sings with passion and his music comes across unpretentious and uplifting. He sings for the people, his people. The music he and his group make is the best of what rock and roll can be.

Another in a long line of great musicians from Detroit, he makes Michigan proud. Detroit may have had trouble with the car industry, but they sure have achieved super limits in the music industry. As if Seger and his band weren't enough, he brought out another Detroit superstar, Kid Rock. The place went wild.

It's great to attend a rockin' event where you and your kids and their friends all want to go. Seger brings all ages together. The guy next to me, about 30 years old, kept screaming out, "I love you, Bob." Once he yelled, "I want to have your baby, Bob." Now that's a dedicated fan!

Who hasn't been moved by that *Old Time Rock and Roll*? Talk about a standard party song! I think there is a rule someplace that states you have to play that to get a party started.

It wasn't just the great music that got me as I watched Seger. I kept thinking about how we all run "against the wind". For each of us, for every age we go through, the wind is a different force. It can be time. It can be health issues. It can be career challenges. It can be family things we need to tend to. The wind is always in our face and we're running as fast as we can . . . against it.

Afterwards, my daughter reflected. "His songs meant one thing to me when I was young. Now that I'm older, they have a whole different meaning, but they are still relevant to my life." I agreed. Seger's songs came out when I began raising my family. I related to him then. Now, 43 years later, my husband has retired, I am a grandmother, and Bob still speaks to my life. Great music can do that. It is one of life's wonderful commonalities.

"The years rolled slowly past. . . I found myself seeking shelter against the wind. I've got so much more to think about – deadlines and commitments, what to leave in, what to leave out . . . against the wind. I'm still running against the wind. I'm older now, but still running against the wind."

What wind are you running into now? What is life blowing your way? Where are you seeking shelter from your wind? Do you look at your commitments and deadlines and wonder what to leave in and what to leave out?

The winds of life can blow hard. They can turn into tsunamis. They can blow softly against our face. Rarely do they stop blowing.

Our life is made up of reactions – how we react to the wind in our lives. This is our race. This is our life. "Still running . . . still running against the wind . . . against the wind."

Step By Step

I drive in my driveway. Daffodils stand all perky and springy to greet me. I am lifted by the feel and thought of spring, of life anew. Ahhh, how sweet it is.

I have just visited with my friend. His wife has breast cancer and is at her radiation treatment. She is doing well; however, they have other heartaches. Their daughter-in-law is fighting for her life with stage 4 pancreatic and liver cancer. She is only 35.

Life is so, so hard.

I also visited this morning with my friend who recently had her knee replaced. We talked about lots of things that have been difficult for her and things that have been difficult for me. We talked as good friends do, loving and supportive of each other, encouraging.

Last night I visited with my friend whose son, a young man, just had cancer surgery. We sat together with other friends. Everyone is going through their own private ground zero. Two of the ladies that sat laughing and sharing with us have battled breast cancer. One of them also had a darling little girl who has bravely fought cancer. No one said life would be easy.

Yet, we sat and laughed and talked. We hugged and shared. Some of it was trite. Some of it was serious. Some of it was silly. All of it was special.

I think we all have lives like this. We look around at the people in our world and see that many are suffering. The suffering floats. Sometimes it is this one suffering, sometimes it is that one, and sometimes it is us.

We do what we do best. We bring food, gifts, flowers. We pray. We call. We send notes and cards. We pray some more. We celebrate when things get better.

Sometimes in life we wonder, how do people get through this hard stuff?

By this time in my life, I have seen a lot. I have had friends have husbands and children die. I have had friends face their own death. Some did it bravely and some were angry till the end. I have seen people face the hardest things with faith and it lifted them, somehow. I have seen people face tough stuff without it. The list of what I have seen is varied and fills a spectrum of life's hardships.

What inspires me today is the daffodils. They push through the earth each spring and smile, like an old friend saying, "I'm back." That could also translate as, "Life is good." Or, "Life goes on."

Alcoholic's Anonymous follows the mantra, "One day at a time." It is a good one. Kris Kristofferson sang, "One day at a time, sweet Jesus, that's all I'm asking of you." The play, *Godspell*, offered us the song, *Day by Day*.

Babies learn how to walk, step by step. Can you remember watching a baby learning to walk? I do. The baby crawls. The baby is comfortable crawling. She can get wherever she wants crawling. Then, she stands. She is not sturdy. She is wobbly. She holds on.

One day she takes a step, maybe two. She falls. She thinks, 'Why do I need to walk anyway. Crawling is all I need.' But, she stands again. Teetering on the brink of a new way of life, she cautiously takes another step. She makes a few. She holds on to things to help ease her on. She falls again. She cries. She tries to take off her big ole shoes.

But, then she tries it one more time. She walks. She looks so cute. Her steps are bowed, halting, itsy bitsy, but she makes progress.

And now look at us. We all went through the same process as the baby. Yet we walk today without even giving it a second thought. It began with step by step.

My sister-in-law cared for her husband for many, many years. He faced a horrific battle with Parkinson's disease for over 30 years. He was in his late twenties when he was diagnosed.

Along the way, I remember someone saying to her, "I don't know how you get through it." And her powerful, oh-so-true response, "I'll tell you how you get through it. You go to sleep exhausted. You wake up the next day. And you get up and do it again."

Here's to all of you who are facing some tough times in life. Perhaps there is no making it better. Perhaps there is no going back. Perhaps there is. Every situation is unique.

One thing that we do know is that day by day, step by step, one day at a time are all concepts to help us ease along our journey. Maybe today you can look out and see some daffodils perkily smiling at you. Maybe they will encourage you in whatever else you have to face. Spring is so good for the soul.

Some Days A Diamond, Some Days A Stone

I loved that song John Denver sang about, "Some days a diamond. Some days a stone." I have been having some stone days lately. There are lots of other folks who have probably been having stone days lately too.

Mine are caused by immobility and leg problems. I am working on finding the cause, relieving the pain and getting on with life. Not such an easy task.

What it all reminds me of, though, is the first paper I wrote for English 101 in College. I wrote about how health was the most important thing in life. You can't always buy it. You can't always control it. Health is a great big ole gift, one we often take for granted. I remember I got a D- on that paper. It has taken me many years to get over that grade. Oh, wait, I guess I'm not over it.

When people get the flu or a bad cold and it knocks them down, it is amazing how life goes on even while they are out of the loop. So it is with what I am going through. I definitely am out of the loop and I don't like it.

There must be some humor here. Let's see. A couple people have mentioned I should check Lyme's disease. I know you get that from mosquitoes but I saw a cute line about flies so I will use that instead. "Flies spread disease, so keep yours zipped."

I also love the one by Ronnie Shakes. "After twelve years of therapy my psychiatrist said something that brought tears to my eyes. He said, 'No hablo Ingles." That one made me laugh out loud. Laughter is healing, don't you know?

Fitness magazine listed the top three things you should do for your health. Not ones I expected, for sure.

Number 1: An attitude of gratitude. Each day we should consciously think of things we are grateful for in our lives. It is even better to make a little list of them. I have a little book I like to do this in. If you do it, write down whatever comes into your mind. Don't judge it.

Number 2: Laugh. Ray Acuff said, "My health is good. My age is bad." I can relate to that.

It is a wonderful thing for us to be around folks that make us laugh. It is so good for our soul, spirit and health. And it makes us smile too. Talk about a bonus.

When you think about your life, past and present, and the people you love spending time with, I bet those people have a sense of humor.

If you go to lunch or break and you laugh, when you return to work you will be 20% more productive. Four out of five business executives prefer to hire someone with a good sense of humor. When two people do the same exact job, the person with the sense of humor will always excel. Pretty powerful stuff.

Number 3: Get outside. Didn't this one surprise you? It did me. A bit of fresh air - no matter if it is snowing, raining or sunning can lift our spirit and energize us.

So, my friends be grateful, laugh and get your bod outside. Life is all about savoring the moments, whether we are having a diamond day or a stone day. Life and health are precious, indeed.

The Pleasant Present

While in a store the other day, my daughter showed me a small T-shirt which had three pictures on it – a little duck, another little duck, and a moose. The wit of that touched us as *Duck, Duck, Goose* was always one of our favorite games. And, as we were in Maine, where moose pretty much run the joint, it seemed right, fitting and quite delightful.

That morning we had passed a road sign with a flashing light on it. "High rate of moose crashes next seven miles." Not five, not six, but seven miles. I have never seen a moose running around on the road. I have really not seen many live moose anyplace. Usually I see them stuffed on some hunter's wall. The thought of being hit while driving, by a running moose, sounds especially nasty. It makes our prevalent Michigan deer crashes seem rather minor, though I know that's not always so. Some things give us pause.

Some things make us laugh, especially when they get messed up. Returning home, our pontoon lost one of its letters. It had always worn a label, "Bass Buggy". However, somehow, somewhere, it lost the B on Bass. So now you look at it and have to chuckle. In reality, we never did catch bass in it, so it is much more accurate now.

There are many things that make us laugh and pause as we rush through our days. It is good to give them a minute or two, consider them and enjoy them.

The other day my littlest grandson wanted to say the dinner prayer. He said, "Cheers everybody. Here's to God and all the things he did to us." Not exactly as we might have put it, but delightfully fresh and to the point.

I just finished three days of "Nina Camp", my version of grandparent camp. I decided this year to be a bit more on top of things, so I asked the boys right off, what rules they thought we should follow. The one who led the prayer above offered with gusto, "No punching and no farting". Yup, two rules I hadn't thought of, for sure. Some more things to make us laugh and pause.

My friend and former pastor, Phil Salmonowicz, sent me some fun things to share. Here goes.

Half the people you know are below average.

Hard work pays off in the future. Laziness pays off now.

A clear conscience is usually the sign of a bad memory.

And lastly, when everything is coming your way, you're in the wrong lane.

Summer is rushing by. Fruit and veggies are coming on strong. School days are looming. Paul Goodman said, "Enjoyment is not a goal; it is a feeling that accompanies important ongoing activity." And Oliver Herford sums it up, "There is no time like the pleasant."

Enjoy. Laugh. Pause. Refresh. Have some blueberries and ice cream. Listen to an outdoor concert. Lie in the sun and read a book. Linger and laugh with someone you enjoy. Walk a lovely trail. By all means, have a pleasant present.

Young Fun

School Bells Are Ringing

If you are reading this column, chances are you have been to school. We all have memories of school and we all made it through school. We survived. Life goes on in the adult world. But, sometimes, we need a reminder of what it is like for those little ones going to school for the first time.

My grandson, Louie, went to kindergarten. On the first day, he leapt off the school bus, raced to his folks. "Mama, it was the best day ever. I love did it!" Lou is at that cute stage where he adds a "d" to the end of his verbs. You don't want to correct him because once it is gone, it is gone and he will talk boring like the rest of us. My daughter, Cara, would always say, "Can my go?" When we remember that it still holds a tender spot in our hearts.

Danny Burns & friends

"Love-ding" things does not always last, though. Sometimes the glow fades fast. On the second day, Louie got off the bus a lot slower. He slumped over to his parents and said, "MAMA! School is so long. It's like prison!" We're not sure how he knows what prison is like and we really don't want to know.

Stephanie tried to excite her little guy. "Sterling, guess what. Preschool is tomorrow." He said, "Again!" She lovingly explained, "Sterling, you will be going to school for probably the next 23 years." Big silence and then, softly, morosely, "Oh."

That is like little Hunter who said after his first day, "You mean I have to go every day?"

Little kids aren't always enamored with school. When Maddie was 15 months old she began a long battle with Leukemia. She won, but during the struggle she spent most of her time at Devos Children's Hospital with nurses and doctors. She grew accustomed to adults and became grown up very quickly. When she went to preschool she was very disappointed and told her mom she wasn't going back. When she was asked why, she replied, "It's just a bunch of little kids."

A teacher I know in Texas tells her little classes that if someone misbehaves, they will have to disappear. That means, in her class, that they put their head on their desk, cover it with their arms and stay like that until she tells them they can reappear. Little David went home and said, "That is so stupid. Anybody knows you can't disappear by putting your head on your desk!"

At Forest Hills this year, the bus drivers were talking to the kids giving them a bus safety lesson. The bus driver did a great job explaining all the rules and procedures and then asked, "Does anyone have a question?" Cute little Sadie raised her hand very politely and asked, "Did you ever balance a mouse on your head?" Say what?

That reminds me of a senior citizen that spoke in a classroom to little ones. He talked about retirement. When asked if they had any questions, a little one said, "Do you miss your hair much?"

My grandson, Danny, came home from his first day in second grade and said, "This was the best first day I ever had!" "How was your teacher," his mom asked? "She was so nice. She didn't yell at me. She just said, 'You are interrupting the class.'"

"How many times did she say that?"

"Oh, not many. Maybe 5 or 6 times." Okay then.

A friend sent me a Pickles cartoon which showed a grandpa and a little one sitting, talking after school.

"How's school going?"

"Good, but my friend, Paul, has to be neutered."

"Neutered?"

"Yeah, and he doesn't like it at all."

"Are you sure the word wasn't tutored?"

"Yeah, maybe." That's like the Far Side cartoon of the dog in the car, hanging out the window. He yells to another dog chained in the yard. "Ha Ha, Biff, I'm going to the vet to get tutored." Surprise, surprise.

And to end the first week, a Grand Rapids school secretary emailed this to the staff. "We made week one . . . milestones: 6 lost teeth, 6 batches of ice, more than 40 band aids, one student who took the wrong bus home."

There is nothing like children to make us smile. They tug at our heart. We have all been there. I will close with this cute story.

A three year old boy was telling his grandma that he had learned the whole alphabet. "What is the first letter," she asked? "A." The proud grandma said, "That's right. What comes next?" "All the rest of them," he replied.

The Heart Of A Child

Recently on the national news they told what the best selling new car was for the past year. Can you guess? It was the red and yellow plastic Little Tyke and it sold more than any car in America. Never underestimate the power of kids, right?

Of course, if we listen, there are words of wit and wisdom that kids keep giving us.

A teacher I know had a second grader say to her recently, "I'm going to go to a baby wash this weekend." The teacher was obviously puzzled. Then she realized what the girl had meant. She was going to a baby shower. Is that sweet or what?

Danny & Louie Burns

One day last fall my daughter-in-law was trying to explain to the 5 year old about poverty. She told him that some people don't have houses to live in. He said with a big quizzical look on his face, "What do they do? Just stand around in their drive ways?"

It is a new world for kids. They are way ahead of us. Who hasn't had a child, some even preschoolers, help you with your remote or computer? My little friend, Emma, came home from pre-school and said, "Mom, you know Peter doesn't even know what Facebook is?"

We are always working on teaching kids about manners and politeness. My three year old grandson was at a restaurant staring at some people. His aunt tried to bring him out of his trance by saying to him, "Manners." He never blinked, kept staring and said, "I stare please?"

When my husband retired, the college gave us an old huge framed photo of him that was taken many years ago. This same little guy looked at it, scrunched up his face and said, "Why you wearin' all that hair on your head?

I have a friend who recently turned forty. She has three children, ages 8 to 13. She was working at the school recently and a child said to her, "Your daughter looks just like you . . . without the wrinkles." Ouch.

When I was a new mom my Grandma sent me this poem. It is handwritten, worn and faded. I cannot make out the author with her handwriting.

The Heart of a Child

The heart of a child
Is a tremulous thing
Lovely and frail
As a butterfly's wing.

Kissed by the beams
Of a summer sun
Or crushed by the word
Of a careless one.

A look or a smile
Will cause it to sing
For the heart of a child
Is a tremulous thing.

Children are precious and with them we laugh, we learn and we love. We worry about the world they will inherit. We try to give them our best selves, our wisdom, our time. And as we go along, we realize that what Dr. Seuss said was probably very true, "Adults are obsolete children."

The Making Of A Champion

It began like this. "Mom, I want a cow. I want to be in 4-H." His mom sensibly replied, "Jake, you can't have a cow. We live in a cul-de-sac."

That is one of my favorite verbal exchanges ever. I love the cul-de-sac part. The mom and son above are my friends, Jacob and his wonderful mom, Amy.

The journey from that conversation to today has been filled with every emotion and tons of work. Today Jake and his Black Angus steer were named Grand Champions at the county 4-H Fair. This was Jake's first time out and what an experience it has been – for all of us.

Jake Homich

167

The 4-H kids don't find out the time they show their steer until the morning of the show. We waited by the phone like a baby was about to be born. When the call came with Jake's time, my husband and I rushed to the fairgrounds to watch him.

We sat with lots of friends and families of other 4-Hers. It was over 90 degrees in the shade. There was a lot of love and dedication sitting in those bleachers and standing around those fences. Kids were riding horses and being judged in the next ring. A lot was going on in every direction. Many, many kids participated. I am writing about Jake because he is the only one I knew. I am sure each 4-Her has an equally wonderful story.

Jake and the others were judged on their showmanship. Their steers had to be well groomed. The kids were brushing them as they went. They were also scratching their bellies with long show sticks. The steers have to stand a certain way and the judge sizes them up from the back. I had to think how glad I was that I don't have to have someone size me up from the back. Gosh, just the thought.

The steers also had to hold their heads up in the right way. The show men are supposed to be smiling and relaxed as they lead their animals around the ring. I didn't see many smiles. The kids all seemed to be anxious and worried that they would do something wrong. Someone might have been smiling, but I have to confess, I only had eyes on Jake. I felt like a proud mama, even though he is just my friend.

The judge had them move this way and that way and then asked them each a question about their cow.

She then put them in order and announced them. No one mentioned or acknowledged that one big ole cow took a big ole dump right in the walkway of the ring. I, of course, was quite anxious about it and worried that someone would step in it. No one cleaned it up. No one grabbed a wet one to clean up the cow. Such is life down on the farm.

Later, Jake's sister, Maddie got to show the cow with her big brother by her side for guidance. When Maddie was questioned by the judge, she smiled like a ray of sunshine and put on her Maddie charm. She's got lots.

Amy told us, "This is the most wholesome thing ever. Everyone cares about the kids and making it a great experience for them. So many people helped Jake along the way."

As we sat on the bleachers, I thought about 4-H. Though my mate and I were both brought up on dairy farms, neither of us were ever a part of 4-H. Our loss, I think.

The 4-Hs stand for: head, heart, hands, and health. Who could find fault with those? 4-H began at the beginning of the 20th century with a focus of "hands on learning and personal growth of the members".

The 4-H educational philosophy is "Learning by Doing". Their mission is "to empower youth to reach their full potential, working and learning in partnership with caring adults". Their motto is "To Make the Best Better".

There are 6 million 4-H members in America. It is in every county in every state and in 80 countries around the world. There are 60 million alumni of 4-H and currently there are 518,000 4-H volunteers.

I love the 4-H pledge. It is one we could all work on daily in our own lives. "I pledge my Head to clearer thinking, my Heart to greater loyalty, my Hands to larger service, and my Health to better living, for my club, my community, my country, and my world."

When the morning competition ended, I talked to Jake. He was beyond thrilled at his Grand Champion Award. He asked, "Can you come to the livestock sale tomorrow?"

That got me thinking . . . about burgers. And that reminded me of a great burger recipe my daughter, Donna, made on the 4th of July, "Herb and Cheese Double Burgers". Donnie also recently raved to me about a blue cheese burger she made. Both recipes are in the back of the book. Just fire up the grill.

Calvin Trillin said, "Anybody who doesn't think that the best hamburger place in the world is in his home town is a sissy." I don't know about that, but try one of the burgers I mentioned and think gratefully about all the dedication and love put into beef by 4-H kids.

Glorious Food

Chocolate Lessons

Phyllis Diller was a hysterical comedian. One of the funniest things she said was, "I like to serve chocolate cake because it doesn't show the dirt." Hah!

Do you remember the day someone came out and said to the world, "Chocolate is good for you!"? Did you throw yourself on your knees, look up to the sky and say, "Thank you, Jesus!"? Neither did I . . . but I wanted to . . . I think I did in my mind.

Valentine's Day is upon us. Lent is still at bay. This is our window. We can eat chocolate guilt-free. Unless, of course, you're one of those really weird folks who don't like chocolate. I met one once. I couldn't relate. I mean, really. That's like not liking dogs. It might be a sin. I don't know.

For years, I ate chocolate. I just opened mouth, inserted, chewed and swallowed. It was good. I liked it, but I was missing out. I did not realize there are levels of chocolate and that some is better than others. Fine chocolate is just that – fine, mighty fine, even!

In the last few years, I have gotten some education. I now know the difference in fine and not so fine chocolate. I also have learned how to savor it. May I share that with you? Here goes.

First, put it in your mouth. Okay, you knew that. Let it melt against the roof of your mouth to feel the texture. If it is fine, it will be velvety smooth. Roll the chocolate over your tongue, allowing the flavors to permeate your mouth. You should first notice a nutty, roasted chocolate flavor, followed by sweetness and other flavors. Lastly, enjoy the aftertaste that lingers on your palate. Ahhh . . . enjoy this slow pleasant process.

Note that at no point does it say to chew. Of course, with nuts you may want to chomp a bit.

I want to share with you three of my favorite chocolate companies. First, Vosges offers unique divine chocolates. They add a variety of spices, including bacon and chili peppers. Nay, nay, I stay away from those. However, most of theirs are at the top of my list. You will definitely want to savor them as you eat them. You can find them on the web or in gourmet shops in Grand Rapids. They have a couple stores in Chicago, and if you love chocolate, they may be worth the drive. They even make candy bars.

Second, is See's Chocolates which began in 1921 in Los Angeles and remain a west coast standard. Detroit Metro airport has a kiosk. You can also find them on the web.

They aren't as unique as Vosges. Their selection is more standard, but they are still fine.

Third, is close by and fabulous - Koeze's Nut House in Grand Rapids. Grandpa Koeze came from the Netherlands. His son began to make peanut butter, which is now sold all over the world. They sell a variety of fine chocolates, but my favorite is called Cream-Nut. This was featured in Oprah's Favorite Things and several fancy magazines. I gave many at Christmas and I think people are still licking their lips and going, "Ahhh". The Cream-Nut comes in milk or dark chocolate, with peanut butter or without. The peanut butter is the kicker. Go for it. Your taste buds may send you a thank you note.

Now for the health matters. There is a growing body of credible scientific evidence that chocolate contains a host of heart-healthy and mood-enhancing phytochemicals, which benefit both mind and body. Yahoo, you say?

Chocolate is a plentiful source of antioxidants which reduce the ongoing cellular and arterial damage caused by oxidative reactions. Chocolate inhibits the oxidation of LDL cholesterol. If you eat a small bar of dark chocolate daily, it can reduce blood pressure in people with mild hypertension. This just keeps getting better.

The University of California has found that chocolate thins the blood and performs the same anti-clotting activity as aspirin. So instead of having a baby aspirin a day, you could try a taste of heaven. Dark chocolate is best because it has less sugar.

Chocolate also has remarkable effects on the human mood. It boosts brain levels of serotonin. People who are depressed have lower serotonin levels. Women typically have lower serotonin levels during PMS and menstruation, which may be one reason we have strong cravings for chocolate during these times.

So, with all this tasty information, I hope you will savor some fine chocolate soon. I have a favorite fabulous recipe for Chocolate Banana Bread. It was a cover picture on Chocolatier Magazine. I don't like banana bread or cooked bananas, but this is much higher level than that. It is made with several fine chocolates and it's easy. The recipe is in the back of the book. Enjoy!

Kookie, Kookie

Just when you think you've seen it all. I'm talking cookies, of course. At my age, I really did think I had met all the cookies there were to meet. But then yesterday, my friend, Donnie, told me about ones she had just made. She gave me four to take home. Lucky for me, my husband was gone overnight so I got to chow down all four of them. I know it would have been nice to save one, or even two, for him, but I couldn't. I just couldn't. Something came over me and I forgot all about sharing.

This reminds me of a fun sharing memory. We were living on Alexander Street. One Christmas, friends from Nebraska were visiting. Our daughter, Cara, was about three, and did not want to share her toys with their children. Our friend said, "But, Cara, sharing is good . . . they even share on *Sesame Street*." Cara looked at her, little hands on her hips, and said, "Well, they don't share on Alexander Street." Apparently, that attitude is genetic because I got into those four cookies and it turned out they didn't share on our new street either.

Cookies really are one of the most wonderful things in life. They are medicinal. They make you feel better. They can be like a counselor and make you forget about your problems. They are social. Every visit is better over a plate of cookies. They are warm like a hug. I could go on and on.

I have loved *Sesame Street* since it began. I actually could still watch it every day and be delighted with it, but my kids are grown and I rarely do. Okay, sometimes. I admit if I happen to pass it as I change channels, it is very hard to turn away from. But, my very favorite character on it is, of course, Cookie Monster. I love how he says, "Kookie. Kookie," and acts all crazy when he eats cookies. I can relate. Can't you?

Sometimes cookies do that to us. They make us act all crazy. My husband is very sane and disciplined, unlike me, but every once in awhile he will let out a big groan. When I ask him what is wrong, he will explain how he started out to have just a couple of cookies but something came over him and he got all carried away and ate the whole bunch. Kookie. Kookie.

An exciting time of year is always when the Girl Scouts come around selling their delicioso cookies. Who could name one favorite – there are so many. We don't care that the price has risen and the box is smaller. We happily sign up. We like to think it is because we care so much about supporting the Girl Scouts, but we know that is not really true. Girl Scouts. Swirl Scouts. It is really all about the cookie. Kookie. Kookie.

Having battled weight my whole adult life, I also see the dark side of Mr. Cookie. Or perhaps it is Ms. Cookie. Perhaps both. Whatever gender, they appear to be my BFFs but then they turn on me. They are kind of two-faced. They act like our friends but then they can get ugly. I notice it especially when I get on my scale and it yells at me, "One person at a time."

But during the holiday season, we don't care about weight and health issues. We are all about the celebration, the festivities, and the cookies.

There are simple cookies, rolled cookies, drop cookies, bar cookies, complicated cookies, ethnic cookies, family recipe cookies. In fact, the cookie Donnie gave me was one her sister always made. Neither Donnie nor I have ever seen it anyplace else. A new cookie - how great is that? The recipe for Donnie's bittersweet cookies is in the back of this book.

Donnie's sister died of cancer and now Donnie always makes her unique cookie in her memory. Recently, our friend's mom died. At her funeral, her prayer card had her photo and a lovely prayer on one side. On the other side was her favorite cookie recipe. How dear! They told me it is common in the Chesaning area to do that.

So, this Christmas season be sure to have a few – cookies, that is. Enjoy the yumminess of the moment because sure as shootin' January is coming around the corner and you know what that means. All that exercise and health stuff is waiting to snap us back to reality. But for now. . . Kookie, Kookie.

Food, Glorious Food

When we are born, people describe us like food. Some are referred to as having skin like peaches and cream. Some feel downy like peach fuzz. Some have wrinkles and look like prunes. Some have almond eyes, hair the color of carrots or ginger, hair chestnut brown, hair like corn silk.

We play in the cold and people say we have cheeks red like apples, lips red like cherries. Some are lucky to get olive complexions.

People are skinny as corn stalks. Others can be described as beefy, porkers, doughy, all larded up, like stuffed sausage. Women get pregnant and become ripe like watermelons. Risque is nice melons.

Demeanors are the same. He's an ole prune face. She's sour. He's bitter. He's rather salty. She's a hot tamale. He's so bland. She's nutty. He's sweet as pie. Some get all cheesy when they take pictures. Then there are those who are sour as grapes.

Miss Polly is a true southern belle. She always refers to me like food. "Hi, Sugar. How are you sweetie? How's my honey?" She sure can be syrupy, that Miss Polly. I love her!

We are told our shapes are like pears, apples, flat as a pancake, skinny as a string bean. I wish I was like a string bean!

Our lack of courage is called chicken. Sometimes we're called turkeys. Remember the slogan, "No Turkeys Allowed"? I loved that one. I know a lot of turkeys.

People define themselves as, "I'm a steak and potatoes kinda guy." We define others as hot dogs, boring as warm milk. Some are just plain wieners.

Emotions are no exception. Don't get all mushy on me now. The tension was so thick you could cut it with a knife. We get our just desserts. Some things just seem fishy. We don't trust them.

People are named after food. There's the singer Meat Loaf. Was it the TV show *77 Sunset Strip* that had Kookie as a hunky character. "Kookie, Kookie, lend me your comb." Oh, and we can't forget O.J., or can we?

We soup up our cars. We fudge our numbers. When life gives us lemons, we make lemonade. Life's a bowl of cherries, but sometimes it feels like the pits. We get in a pickle and then stew about it. Sometimes we just go out and get pickled.

Today on our altar at church sat a big cornucopia full of gourds. Sadly, as I sat and contemplated in this holy place, I realized I have become a gourd. Gourds are goofy shapes and sizes. They have curves where they shouldn't. They are lumpy. Worst of all, they have things on them, things that stick out, ripples, wart like protrusions. I have those too. And I'm lumpy.

I go to the dermatologist and show him my gourdy things. He just says, "Age, age, age. That will be seventy-five dollars." I hate that. Can't he zap me and make me peachy again? I don't want to be a gourd. I don't want to be a prune.

My son just stopped in. I shared these thoughts with him and he comforted me. "But, Mom, remember, when everything else quits growing, along come the gourds. They bloom late and help to make fall beautiful."

Okay, I think. I feel better now, even though I'm still gourd-like. He has sweetened my pot. It's not so bitter after all. I feel warm and mellow now . . . like a nice cup of steaming hot cocoa. Ah, food, glorious food.

A Helping Of Bad, Badder And Baddest

Food, glorious food was an anthem they sang in the play, Oliver. I love to eat. I love to cook. I love food. However, lately, I have seen a few things that give me pause. I won't give the correct names of the restaurants I write about here - I'll protect the guilty.

This week we were at a place called, Bill Evans. Someone with us ordered the Chicken Noodle Deep Dish Dinner. That sounds safe enough. Isn't chicken noodle soup a kind of medicine?

So her meal comes. There are chicken and homemade noodles in a gravy. Erma Bombeck said, "I came from a family where gravy was considered a beverage." She'd feel at home in this restaurant.

The chicken and noodles are ladled with gravy over a heaping pile of mashed potatoes which lies on top of a large hearty biscuit. Can anyone say, "Carb"?

I also noticed on their menu that you could treat yourself to deep fried apple pie fries for a light dessert. It has fruit in it. It must be healthy.

Recently, while at Shorthorns, a restaurant in Grand Rapids, I got the idea for this column. One of their deserts was deep fried cheesecake. I looked at the waitress and said, "Say what?" She said, "I knowwww. We can hardly keep it in stock."

A restaurant in Brooklyn, New York, serves all their desserts deep-fried. They make deep-fried Twinkies, Oreos, Mars Bars and even Reese's Peanut-Butter cups. Just the thought of it makes me remember I'm out of Imodium AD.

My friend goes to a restaurant which is a chain called Arm Heaven. Remember the names have been changed here, folks. They serve deep fried mac and cheese and deep fried cream corn. Their main beverage is Kool-Aid in a variety of flavors. When I asked my source what she had, let's call her wide throat, she said, "the deep-fried mac and cheese – and I'm not kidding, it was really good." Yikes.

We just returned from 4 days of driving through the southeast where one sees a lot of Cracker Pail and Waffle Home restaurants. One special was fried chicken and waffles. Folks cover the whole thing with syrup. But, of course.

Someplace I saw a pancake stuffed with bacon and cheese. A restaurant in New Jersey has waffles stuffed with Genoa salami and Swiss cheese. Get out!

Ziggy, the cartoon character, found wisdom in a Fortune cookie, "You'll be hungry again in an hour." Oh, no.

Burger Queen boasts double whoppers and triple whoppers. The original whopper just wasn't enough.

KFD now offers a Double Down sandwich which consists of bacon, two kinds of cheese and sauce between two pieces of fried chicken. That's right, folks, the fried chicken is the bun. Whew. Stephen Colbert said, "It is served with a dollop of heart attack. This is deep-fried madness, breaded insanity, a sandwich that lacks all sandwichness."

Our own Fifth Third Ballpark has come up with the baddest food yet, at least according to my serious source, "Wide Throat". This little burger has been featured on NBC's *The Today Show*, ESPN's *Sports Center*, and *Man v. Food*, among other places. Let's see, how do I explain this? Here goes.

First, you take one pound of dough to make a sesame seed hamburger bun. You next put on about a cup of chili. You use five 1/3rd pound burgers. Get it? Fifth Third. You use five slices of American cheese. Periodically you stick in some salsa, some nacho cheese, Fritos, lettuce, tomato (for health purposes), and sour cream. You can add jalapenos as an option. When you are done, you should have a burger that weighs in at about 4 pounds and is about 4800 calories. Who needs the fat count, at this point you might as well wing it. One reporter quipped, "The smell alone is 250 calories". The cost for this treat is about twenty buckaroos and it could feed four. However, if you eat it all by yourself, they will give you a free T-shirt. Well, heck, that would be worth it then.

This bitty burger can also be followed by deep fried Pepsi. What, you say, is that? It is a batter made with Pepsi instead of water or other liquid. And guess what? Then they fry it and roll it in sugar.

All these unhealthy food options remind me of an Orson Welles quote. "My doctor told me to stop having intimate dinners for four; unless there were three other people."

The Way We Were . . . And Are

Making Our Own Magic

Bev Geyer & Jose Olivieri

I have a very dear friend, Beverly, that I consider my mentor. She gives me clear advice when I ask. She loves and supports me unconditionally. She is a terrific role model. This year my friend turns 75. Recently I asked her if that was bothering her. "No," she said, "I have an exciting plan. Each month I am doing something very special in honor of my birthday year." What a great idea, I thought. Why don't more of us do that?

This month I had a birthday. Not a big one. Next year will be a big one as it will end in a five. We all know that big ones end in five and really big ones end in zero.

When I woke up the morning of my birthday, I had an attitude of gratitude. I counted all the blessings in my life. This colored my entire birthday and I never felt bad about getting another year older.

I made a decision to work hard this year to get stuff done that I have wanted to do for ages, stuff that never seems to get done. I thought how great it will feel to turn that big number 5 next year if I have accomplished these things. Since then I have felt filled with renewed enthusiasm and purpose.

Bev has taken her birthday focus to a higher level. She proves to one and all that we are never too old to twirl.

In January she got a tattoo on her shoulder. A solid feminist, her tattoo is of a women's equality symbol.

In February, she and her daughter went to Oprah's favorite, The Miraval Spa in Arizona. They attended programs based on Dr. Andrew Weil's mind, body, spirit concepts.

Bev and her husband just returned from her March experience. They hiked down into and up out of the Grand Canyon. She prepared for months to accomplish this feat.

In April they are going to Paris for ten days. She has always wanted to go there. "April in Paris."

Future birthday months will include learning to kayak, walking the Mackinac Bridge on Labor Day, and going on a balloon ride at the Albuquerque Balloon Fest in October.

One month she plans to have a complete physical. She will also review and update her will, make her funeral arrangements and write her obituary. She wants to do this so her kids won't have to scramble trying to do it later.

Another month she will go on a silent spiritual retreat to focus on what she wants in the rest of her life.

One month she will reaffirm her marriage vows and thank her wonderful husband for the years they have shared and for those they will share in the future.

Bev intends to take one month and go on a girlfriend tour where she will visit all the women who have contributed so much to her life. She wants to tell them what they have meant to her and why and thank them.

To finish her birthday year celebration, she plans to self-publish a book, with photos, of her 75th year, how she spent it and why. She is also in the process of writing the story of her life for her only granddaughter, which she will also self-publish.

Her whole year of celebratory experiences is based on what she calls "a mission of gratefulness for the life I've lived and hope for the life I have left to live."

It is easy to see why I am drawn to this woman. She is so full of life and such a great example for the rest of us.

Letty Cottin Pogrebin said, "The fastest way to age is to disengage, to settle into well worn grooves in life. We can't be young again but we can be new. We can't do anything about the length of our life, but we can do something about its width and its depth."

As she was dying, my dear friend, Nelda Cushman, summed up her life in this way. "Life is sometimes tragic, mostly magic, but all in all it's been a great ride."

Whether we are 25, 35, 49, 55, 64 or more, we can all take Bev's example to heart and make it work in our own lives. It is up to each of us to find our own magic and make our life wide, deep, and a great ride.

The Pain And Joy Of Class Reunions

Just met with a group of my high school classmates to plan our blank-blank reunion. If I told you how many it was, I would have to kill or at least hurt you. There was only one person I have seen through the years. The rest I didn't recognize and they probably didn't recognize me either.

We have all reached the age where going out is good but coming home is better. We can sing along with most elevator or grocery store music. Some are retired. I was tired yesterday and will likely be tired again tomorrow. Does that mean I'm retired?

Gerry once told me that he was okay with consonants but had trouble with his bowels. I am sure he was joking, but that could sum up the high school reunion crowd.

I thought it might be fun to ask people if they had any stories from their high school reunions. One told me, "I hate to go to those. It's just a bunch of old people!" I gotta agree. When I saw my classmates get out of their cars at our meeting place, we might as well have had "old" stamped on our foreheads.

I had a bad experience with my 15th high school reunion. I had just had my third baby and lost a bunch of weight at Weight Watchers. I was feeling like I looked pretty good. When I walked in, the classmate who was registering us said, "Gosh, Maureen, I never thought you'd get fat." This was after my great weight loss success. I talk a good self-esteem spiel, but I gotta tell ya, I never got over that one. As other reunions came up, I could just never face going - no matter what motivating talks I had with myself. I know I am a decent motivational speaker, but I wasn't good enough to undo that damage - until now, that is.

I have another humiliating memory from that reunion. When everyone stood up to introduce themselves and their spouses, I said, "I am Maureen and this is my first husband, Don. The minute it came outta my mouth, I knew it shouldn't have. I knew it wasn't right or funny, even though everyone laughed. Today my friend, Carol, said, "The most shocking part of my tenth reunion was that a couple had already been married three times. I had foot in mouth disease. Turns out it has been a chronic illness.

When we went to one of my husband's high school reunions, he was off visiting and I was wandering around alone and bored. To ease my boredom I went up to a woman and said very excitedly, "Remember me?" Of course, she couldn't because I had never seen her before. She covered though. She said, "Well, not by your face, but I remember your voice." At the end of the night I did go and confess to her and we ended up having a good laugh together. Maybe it wasn't right to do that but believe me, I was really, really bored.

Jackie told me today that at her 55th high school reunion they all got together to have a group photo taken. The young perky photographer said, "I can't see you very well. Could the back row stand on the folding chairs?" We had a great laugh over that. Jackie said she could barely get up out of the chair, let alone stand on it.

My cousin told me she didn't want to go to her high school reunions anymore because her breasts had gone south and the real problem was that one went towards Detroit and the other towards Grand Rapids. What can you say? She's family.

That reminds me of a cartoon I just saw. The woman in it said, 'My body ain't what it used to be - even when I'm naked, I still wanna slip into something comfortable." Sadly, I can relate.

Some people go to every high school reunion. Some go to none. I guess if you go to one, remember this quote by Michael Pritchard. "You don't stop laughing because you grow old; you grow old because you stop laughing." Be sure to take your sense of humor when you attend class reunions. Laughing with others and at ourselves is the only way to go.

Ricky And Wrinkles

I love to get a personal note in the mail - handwritten address, no computer label. You know it's going to be special and it makes you feel really good. Ummm.

I got one the other day. Of course, my heart went pitter-pat. 'How nice is this,' I thought. The positive thoughts kept up until I opened it.

Oh, Man! It was a glossy sheet of an ad for wrinkle cream. At the top, handwritten to make it special, it said, "Maureen, this really works." Of course, no one signed it.

I immediately thought of all the people I see who must be looking at my face thinking, "OMG – does she need wrinkle cream or what?"

What woman hasn't at my point in life, taken the skin on the edge of her face and pulled it back and admired how great she would look if it would stay that way. Unfortunately, we always have to let go and so does the skin.

This reminds me of having someone look at photos of you when you got married or were younger. They always say in a shocked disbelieving tone, "Is THAT you?" Inferring that there is no way on this earth that they could recognize you in your old photo, not even a glimpse of you. They are such jerks.

So I take my handwritten mail insult and go on with my day which ended with my cousin, Sandy, and I going to a "Ricky Nelson Tribute Concert". Sandy and I went to Coopersville High School together. We are five years apart but shared some of the same music era. The concert was Ricky's music sung by his twin boys, who are now in their forties. Sigh.

The first thing that hit me was – what are all these old people doing here? I'm telling you, it was like going to a class reunion! Sandy and I immediately agreed that we didn't look like we belonged there.

People hobbled in and the auditorium filled. The twins came out and the audience never moved. No movement at all, not one bit, just still silence as they watched and listened. I thought to myself, "I don't feel like I've gone to a garden party and am reminiscing with my old friends."

Many of you readers have likely quit reading this by now. You don't know who Ricky Nelson is or was and you can't relate to wrinkles. Many of you have kept on. You remember. Some of you are even wondering where you can buy some of that wrinkle cream. Email me and I'll give you the phone number, suckers.

When I was in the fifth grade, the first record (a flat round thing you could play music on – really!) I ever bought was by Ricky Nelson. It was a flip side hit – *My Bucket's Got a Hole In It / Believe What You Say*. Ricky was considered a Teenage Idol and was a teen star on the T.V. hit, *The Ozzie* and *Harriet Show*. Elvis was new and big then, but parents were afraid of Elvis and his wild wiggles. Ricky didn't wiggle. American parents could trust him. He was like the boy next door, though not my door. The boy next door to me didn't look that good at all.

Ricky Nelson is the only person ever to have had a number one hit on the charts, *Poor Little Fool*, a number one T.V. show, and be in the number one movie, *Rio Bravo*, all in the same week.

As the years went by and Ricky was no longer at the top of the music charts, he went to Madison Square Garden to perform in an oldies show. When he came out on stage, he didn't look like the boy next door anymore. He had long hair and played new tunes. He was booed off stage by 20,000 people. From that experience, he wrote his biggest hit, "Garden Party".

My dear friend, Marcy, went with me to see Ricky perform in Grand Rapids shortly before he was killed in a plane crash. It was in a dive bowling alley on Division Street. As much as we loved seeing him (he was still cute - believe what I say) and he could still sing the old songs, but how sad to see him in such a dismal venue. He seemed like a *Poor Little Fool* who likely lived in *Lonesome Town*.

So back to last week during the show. There was an intermission during which all the people stood up, slowly, very, very slowly. Then they just stood there and waited out the time until the second set. It obviously took way too much energy and effort to walk out into the lobby. What made me laugh was that as they stood, they were all rubbing themselves – hips, backs, knees, all the sore spots. I said to Sandy, "Well, maybe these are our peeps after all. "They were boomers who were obviously all boomed out.

As we sat waiting to leave in the slow moving parking lot, we talked about the old tunes, the old people and the wrinkles. We both agreed. "You can't please everyone, so you've got to please yourself."

Getting Older

I have never considered doing away with myself . . . until today. It went like this. Well, actually, it began a couple of days ago.

I went to a doctor who happens to be a friend. It also happens that I have known him since before he was born. His parents are very dear friends. I love this guy like family.

You need a bit more background here. I am also in a women's group - twelve women. Our ages span quite a bit but probably they range 10 years on each side of me. Age is no matter here. We gather, laugh, share and bond. Oh, one more tidbit. One of the members is younger. I don't know how much. I truly don't. I don't care. No one does. We all love her and I think it is vice versa. I have always believed that once people graduate from high school, you can be good friends with anyone, no matter the age difference. Sometimes age difference even adds to a good relationship.

So last Tuesday I am being treated by this doc, who is great at what he does. We are chatting and begin to talk about this friend of mine. He tells me how much he likes her and that he had asked her recently why she is part of this group. As he put it, "those older women".

I am a bit hit by this remark of his. I have never thought of that perspective. The idea that someone wouldn't want to hang out with us because of our age - Good Lord. I still think of us as young (at least not old) and vital and wild and crazy and wonderful. I could go on and on.

So that settles like a dim bulb in the back of my brain. I don't forget about it but it isn't all that penetrating. Then today the big one.

A wonderful man comes to do some work for me. I really like him and he is also excellent at what he does. We have known each other about six years. I have no idea how old he is. I feel like we are adult peers, if you know what I mean. I know he has a 19 year old. I also know he is younger than me, but no matter, right? I don't even think about age with him.

He is chatting with us. He is in one room. My spouse and I are in the next, sitting at the table. He is telling us about his parents. They are in Florida, and he makes it sound like that is what old folks do. As Jerry Seinfeld once said, "My parents didn't want to move to Florida but they turned sixty and it's the law." He tells us his mom fell. Then his dad fell. He says another remark about their elderly status and jokes about whether or not they can still live alone.

At this point, I do a foolish thing. I should have known better but I did not see it coming. Honest. I asked him how old his folks were. When he told me, it turns out they are a couple years younger than my mate, which is a couple years older than me. In other words - about our age.

And that is when ending it came to mind. I quietly said to my husband, "You know that big butcher knife out in the kitchen? Go get it for me, please. I want to slit my throat."

I will now fess up a bit more. No, I won't. I just wrote out how old I am but then decided to delete it. I don't know you that well. You might turn against me. I don't feel old. Well, once in awhile I notice things like I hurt more, but it goes away. It is sort of a daily thing like sunshine. Oh, wait, that isn't so daily, is it? I also don't have the energy I used to, but I still have lots and am always being told I need to slow down.

What else do I notice about my age and my peers? I notice when we get together we often talk about doctors, ailments and meds. The thing I really notice is how much we all enjoy discussing this with folks who can relate. That would be each other.

I notice another thing and I don't like this one as much. People often talk about the way things used to be. I am leery of that one. I think it can be a trap and one needs to be careful to not fall into this habit too often.

Someone said, "It takes about ten years to get used to how old you are." Perhaps that is the problem. Perhaps I am old and am just not used to it yet. I like living in my personal la-la land. Until every once in awhile when someone hits me with a comment of reality. And who needs that?

Memory Keepers

Am I the only one that gets hit by emotion? It comes out of nowhere. You are totally feeling and acting normal and doing normal things. Along comes some memory. It could be on T.V. or a song you hear. It could be when you see someone in a crowd that reminds you of somebody you loved. In reality, it could be anything.

Once I saw a woman in the crowd at a parade. She looked like my Nana who had been dead a few years. Instantly I was all choked up and my eyes began to tear. Everyone knows there's no crying in parades.

Perhaps you are minding your own business, working on a project, not paying one bit of attention to the T.V., when Sarah Mclachlan begins to sing on that dog commercial. You know the one. OMG! Instantly I am all emotional as every dog I ever loved before is going through my pathetic mind. Couldn't they have put some other singer in that ad? Rod Stewart, Bob Seeger or some other rough voice would have worked fine. Why did they have to torture us with the voice of an angel? I'm telling you. The master mind that put her voice on that ad should be running a political campaign. Minds like that are extremely aware of what makes people tick and feel.

You might have seen the *Modern Family* episode on T.V. The mom and two daughters are all on the same emotional hormonal cycle. To prove this and make it realistic, the three of them are shown sitting on the sofa and sobbing as they watch that dog commercial. You don't see the commercial. You don't hear the words. You just hear that lilting angelic voice singing that song in the background. Immediately you are on the emotional roller coaster with the T.V. characters. As we watched it, I said to my husband, "Those writers really know people and are tuned in to what can make America cry at the drop of a hat."

So, I got thinking about this on Easter Sunday. I was at my daughter's house. She was preparing dinner. I was looking at a magazine she had just told me to read. Colleen had a CD playing of some old country tunes.

George Strait began to sing, *Amarillo by morning*, up from San Antone, everything that I got, is just what I've got on . . . ". I was immediately drawn in to it, singing along. It is one of my old favorites and every time I hear it, I love it. I said to my daughter, "I love this song."

She exuberantly replied. "I know. I remember the night you brought the CD home and Dad was gone and we played it and sang it over and over all night long."

In a second, I am right back there. I see us. I hear us. I remember dancing around the kitchen, singing our hearts out. And then it came, out of nowhere, the emotion. Soon tears were running down my face which I really didn't want anyone to see. I was having a very happy day, after all. I was not sad in any way. But that emotion, it gets ya every time.

And that was when I thought about the fact that our memories are most alive when they are shared by others. We remember. They remember. It is good. One of the best times we have is when we share old memories with people. We laugh. We even add to the memories. Sometimes we distort them a bit, but that is usually okay. No harm done. They still make us feel good.

Yes, we are memory keepers for each other. When we share them it can be a beautiful thing. They can bring emotion, sometimes tears, often laughter, but almost always – good feelings. They are a testament that our life is and has been good.

In our church there is a hymn I love. It goes, "We remember how you loved us . . . " And that is what makes sharing memories emotional and precious. It's all about the love.

"Amarillo by mornin', Amarillo's where I'll be…"

The Hills Are Still Alive

Every once in awhile I ask people for thoughts for my column. I usually get good response, but never have I gotten the response that I did with this request. People of all ages and from all over responded. What was I asking? I asked if they had any special memories about *The Sound of Music*. Do you?

In 1965, *The Sound of Music*, won 5 Academy Awards. Many believe it to be the best movie they have ever seen. It is filled with great morals and became life altering to millions, myself included. Faith, believing in who you are, destiny, trusting your instincts, not compromising for what you believe in, love and joy are all part of the message so beautifully crafted.

Seven unknown children, 34 year old Canadian Christopher Plummer and a newcomer, British Julie Andrews (28 and a brand new mother) were the stars. Who can forget them? Maria, the Captain, Lisle, Friedrich, Marta, Louisa, Kurt, Brigitta and Gretl.

I met my husband while *The Sound of Music* was showing at the Midtown in Grand Rapids. I think I saw it there 18 times. I wore the soundtrack out. I believe I remember every word to the dialogue and the soundtrack, but I wasn't the only one affected by this magnificent movie.

Carol and Pete also saw it at the Midtown. While driving home, they decided to name their baby, if it was a girl, Lisle - they did.

Fr. Fred feels *Climb Every Mountain* helped him decide to become a priest.

Kathy will never forget watching Julie Andrews singing and running through the hills. It was the first time she really thought about the importance of children and family.

Gayle reminisced about the characters and how deeply we felt about them. The snobby Baroness, the handsome Captain Von Trapp. The painful rejection between Lisle and her soldier. The love and chemistry between Maria and the Captain. Gayle was not alone in wanting a flowing dress like Lisle wore as she danced in the gazebo.

Mary remembers taking her babysitting money and sending her parents off to see the film. They hadn't gone out to see a film in over 20 years and she treasures being able to do this for them.

Gisela and Ron spent many weekends in Salzburg, Austria, and visited all the places the movie was filmed. In 1969, Ron was in Viet Nam and saw the movie. He wrote Gisela a long emotional letter afterwards. Soon he found out their son had been born. The movie remains very special to them.

The Sound of Music film lives on through community theatre. Hollie played a nun in it twice, once she was pregnant. What??? What??? Her mom, Char, was in over 50 performances. She also said it is the only play that has never lost money. There is always an eager audience for *The Sound of Music*.

Jody was a nun in the 1977 Central Montcalm production and recently her daughter, Taylor, was a nun in the Greenville High School production. Lizzy played Lisle in that production and actually turned 16 on opening night. How cool is that? She is 16, going on 17, innocent as a rose …

Pat still finds herself singing the farewell to friends – *So long, farewell, auf weidersehen, goodbye.*

My niece, Charity, in New York City, said she watched it over and over and wanted to be Lisle. One of her favorite memories is coming and finding her older, macho teenage brother, standing on the sofa, singing *The Sound of Music* at the top of his lungs along with Julie Andrews on T.V.

Sadly, in 1997, Julie Andrews had a botched throat surgery and lost her voice. She has since written 24 children's books. She said, "It is true, when God closes a door, He always opens a window." That line has gotten me through many things in my life and still does.

A beautiful deaf woman got hearing through a cochlear implant. The first song she ever heard in her life was Julie Andrews singing The Sound of Music. She said, "Can you imagine? The hills are alive . . ."

A man remembers being in Viet Nam for a year during the war. He watched the movie 127 times because it gave him peace.

Some challenges faced while filming the movie - the two little girls each lost front teeth during it and Fredrich grew 6" in 6 months.

The Sound of Music will always remain one of our very favorite things. When we got married, we used the film's wedding march. When I was at a huge crossroads with my faith and knowing what to do in my life, *Climb Every Mountain* inspired and guided me.

For many of us, we not only know the movie and songs by heart, they are in our heart. We want to share them with our children and grandchildren. *Edelweiss* can still choke us with emotion. *Do-Re-Mi* can still lift our spirits. And when the dog bites, when the bee stings, when we're feeling sad, we simply remember our favorite things . . . and then we don't feel so bad.

The Way We Were

So imagine graduating from high school, moving away almost immediately, and never returning . . . until today . . . sort of. I never lived in Coopersville. I only went to high school there.

I have just returned from a picnic of about twenty gals from my high school class. I could only remember half of them. The rest I didn't have a clue. The names meant nothing. The faces were strangers. In my defense, it was a big class.

Perhaps the hardest part wasn't the part where there was no recognition. The hardest part may have been that even after they told me their names, a minute later . . . I couldn't remember what they'd said.

Those that I remembered, I was delighted to see. It had been many, many moons, after all. My children are almost twice as old as I was when I last saw these people.

The funny part was the ones I did remember, and remembered me, came up with all kinds of memories they had of things we did in high school. I did not share most of those memories. I had memories I shared with them. They did not remember mine.

Our past is like a puzzle. A bunch of pieces connect to make a picture. Other people hold some of the pieces, though, and together they can help us make a picture of our whole life.

Barbra Streisand sings in my head. "Memories like the corners of my mind, misty watercolor memories of the way we were. Scattered pictures of the smiles we left behind, smiles we gave to one another for the way we were. Can it be that it was all so simple then or has time rewritten every line? If we had the chance to do it all again, tell me, would we? Could we?"

We have a layered life, don't we? We have our babyhood, our pre-school years, our elementary, middle and high school years, college years, single years, married years, parenting years, later years. We have our family, our friends, our community, our church folks, our work cohorts. We live in different places, different cities, different states, different countries. Our lives change as we get in and out of interests, habits, experiences, neighborhoods, jobs. Our lives end up being a whole bunch of memory pieces.

I am always struck with the way that members of a family, brothers and sisters, have such very different histories and memories and yet they lived in the same home with the same parents. The shaft of life hits all of us in different ways. We look back and can't believe we experienced the same things and yet so differently.

As we visited today, we did the usual thing in these kinds of situations. We asked about this one and that one. Some had died. Some had disappeared. We shared thoughts about teachers we liked and those we didn't. We laughed. We smiled. It was nice, after all. We agreed to meet again in a year and get more of our class to come. They even decided to invite the guys.

So in the end . . . "it's the laughter we will remember, whenever we remember the way we were".

In The Spirit

Learning To Fly . . . Again And Again

A couple years ago we had a special treat. Right outside our bathroom window a robin made a nest and had two babies. We named them Pat and Mike, though we couldn't tell them apart. We watched them grow and enjoyed every minute of this visual adventure.

The very best part was when I happened to see the last baby and his Mom standing on the edge of the nest. The mother flew away. The baby teetered and flapped and off he went, flying in a faltering huff and puff kind of way. I was in awe. To get to see a bird fly for the first time, that's quite a rare and wonderful thing to see.

Right now we are having a similar adventure. A very large robin has had four babies in that nest. One tried to fly today but landed thud on the cement and just sat. My husband picked him up to put him back in the nest. When he did, two robins attacked him in a very upset tweeting way.

The nest is teeny and barely holds the four babies, especially the one that we call Chubbo. He's way bigger than the rest. At night, though, the mama flies in and sits on top of all four of them as they all sleep.

I was thinking today of how those babies have to learn to fly on their own and we all do, don't we? Sometimes we learn to fly off like many high school seniors are doing now - flying out of the nest, off to schools, off to jobs, off to independent lives.

There are other times we have to learn to fly on our own too - when we move far away and don't know anyone; when we become parents; when we suffer loss in our lives. There are many times we need to learn to fly solo or at least in new ways and in new directions. These can be very scary times. The unknown can make us hesitant and afraid.

I think of my life as a pie with several wedges. Each wedge represents different parts of my life – family, work, health, home, etc. Recently a wedge was pulled out. This left an empty spot. What to do with it? How to fill it?

I decided to buy something to have in my home or yard that would remind me of this new time in my life, but had no idea what that would be. I thought I would know it when I saw it.

Not long after this, I went to see my friend, Marty, who was recovering from knee surgery. You might say she was learning how to fly again.

I stopped to get her a gift. As I was browsing, I saw a sign and began to cry. I knew I had found what I needed. It was a quote on a sign, one that I have read and heard many, many times. It is a good quote but it had never really touched me in a deep, personal way before. Of course, I bought it and it sits right in front of me as I write this. It gives me strength and a big hug as I glance at it. It reminds me of that baby bird learning to fly solo.

Learning new ways to be, to feel, to live, aren't just for the very young. Life is a journey and we are called upon in many ways to learn, grow and change. Sometimes these are easy things to adjust to and sometimes they take a lot of effort, time, prayer and support. The best we can do is to keep on keeping on and keep on doing the right thing. I know some of you are also in situations right now in your lives where you need to learn to fly in a new way. Perhaps this quote I bought will help you as you, like me, learn to fly again in new directions and in haltingly, teetering, flapping, huff and puff kinds of ways. Here it is.

FAITH

When you come to the edge of all the light you
have known and are about to step out into the darkness,
faith is knowing one of two things will happen . . .
there will be something to stand on or you will be
taught to fly.

I expect by the time this is printed the baby birds will have flown off to live their new lives. May God bless the rest of us as we also fly off to live new paths put in our lives. God speed.

Lord, I Hope This Day Is Good

There is a hymn I love called, *Lord, I Hope This Day Is Good*. It continues . . . "I feel empty like you knew I would. I should be thankful, Lord, I know I should, but Lord I hope this day is good."

We want good days, of course. What part of that is God's? What part of that is ours?

People sometimes use God like a spare tire. They kind of keep him in the trunk and only use him when they are flat. It is better for us and those around us if we embrace him often – daily and throughout our days.

My daughter, Colleen, gave me roses recently for my birthday. They were in a vase for days and looked lovely. But when I removed them, the water was yucky, stinky and stagnant. I think that is how our life can get at times. We can be like a vase, holding stuff within.

I have a funnel I use in my kitchen. It has a big hole on the top and a small hole on the bottom. It is a good example of how we should live if we want good days. When we live like the funnel and open ourselves up to our God and let him in, we are at our best.

Recently a friend's kids had seriously misbehaved. Before dealing with them, she went outside to clear her head and ask for God's guidance. Then she went back in and felt she handled it better than she would have without doing that. Her God worked through her to parent them.

Taking the funnel thought further, the other part of what we need to do to have a good day, is to let God flow through us to others. We do this in many ways.

With our eyes – we look at people and really see them.

With our mouths – we smile at people. We speak to people and our words have the power to heal, comfort and encourage.

We pray. My friend called last week to ask me to pray for her son who is seriously ill. As she said, "We are prayer warriors for each other." It is a wonderful thing in life that when times are really tough, we can call upon others to pray for us. I have seen many miraculous things happen when folks pray.

Our words also have the power to hurt and discourage. In a song Cher sang, "Words are like weapons. They wound sometimes." I think words are like toothpaste. Once it comes out of the tube, you really can't get it back in. We may wish we could take words back. We may say we are truly sorry for words we have said. However, the reality is that once said, they have a life of their own and they can continue to hurt someone for years.

With our ears – we listen, really listen, and hear people. Sometimes the best gift I can give is to listen. It can be a gift of healing.

With our hands we act. We write notes and cards. We touch, hug, and hold. We do for others and when we do for others, we do for God.

With our time – we give our very life. Nothing is more precious to give.

Anne LaMott says her most used prayers are, "Thank you. Thank you. Thank you." And "Help me. Help me. Help me."

When we feel empty, it is good to take stock of our blessings. Last year someone I thought was a friend hurt me deeply with words. As I tried to work through that, one thing I did was to make a long list of my blessings. "Thank you. Thank you. Thank you." It certainly helped ease my pain.

Barbara Bush spoke at my daughter's graduation from college. She ended her talk with, "Why don't we all try to do a little good every day?"

Michael J. Fox ended a T.V. interview with, "If everybody would just do the next right thing . . . " These are both wonderful thoughts to try to live up to.

We are the hands, eyes, mouths and ears of God. If we are like a funnel and open up ourselves to his grace and guidance and then let him flow through us to others, we will likely be on the road to a good day, no matter what life brings.

Oh, Lord, I hope this day is good.

The Generous Gift Of Time

Generosity, what does it mean to you? What does it mean to me? We often relate it to money, but when I asked myself what it meant to me, I got a completely different kind of answer. That answer surprised me.

Rather than asking myself how I am generous to others, I thought of how others have been generous to me. Immediately, these two instances came to mind.

It was nearly twenty-five years ago. I was in Louisville, Kentucky, with my husband and his board. They were there for a convention and I was there to tag along and relax. The first night I got a phone call telling me that my younger brother had committed suicide. This was, as calls like this always are, devastating and shocking. I doubt anyone is ever prepared for calls like this.

The next morning, when our group heard the news, one lady said she was not going to attend the meetings, but would instead spend the day with me. When I think of generosity, this act is the first thing that comes to my mind and what a strong comforting memory it is.

We spent the day walking and talking. Mostly she listened. Sometimes we cried. Her generosity was the compassionate giving of her time.

Before this, I would have considered her a friend. After this, we had a much deeper bond. Time is an invaluable gift. It is priceless. I have never forgotten her gift and what it meant to me then and still means to me now.

Fast forward to the present. My second thought of when someone was generous to me was also about the giving of their time.

After years of emotional struggle with a parent, I needed to go talk with them. One of my daughters took off work and went with me for a four day trip to do this. We spent the four days doing what needed to be done. It was, for me, a very painful time.

What my daughter gave to me in a most loving way was her compassionate ear. She listened. She encouraged. She helped me think straight. She loved. She gave me more than that, though. She gave me four entire days and nights. She gave me her very precious time. This is truly generosity in action.

Most of us have some sort of cable television these days. We turn on the T.V. and can watch hundreds of things. Sometimes, however, a storm will knock out the cable. Sometimes there is technical trouble and our cable doesn't work. I am sure if we didn't pay our bill (which, I might add, costs way too much) that our cable would be shut off. If our T.V. set breaks down, we lose our access. If our power goes out, we lose our access. So although all of this is available to us 24/7, there are times when our access is shut off and we can't get anything but silence and a blank screen.

As I think of generosity and the gifts of time that have been so lovingly given to me, I think of God and his generous gift of time.

Since I was little, I have prayed to God. I am sure you are the same way. Never, not even once, has God shut off my access or power to reach Him. I pray and he listens. I ask and he listens. I beg and he listens. I rant and he listens. I cry and he listens. No storm affects this open communication. Never does he put up a barrier of technical difficulties. He never makes me pay a bill for the privilege. His power never shuts down, even if I do. There has never been a time when he is not available to me. I am never left with blankness.

God always has time for me - 24/7, day after day, month after month, year after year. From the get go He generously and constantly offers me his gift of time and compassion.

Everyone you talk to these days is busy, busy, busy. People are all rushing. To give someone time is harder than ever. It seems to be so hard to come by. Our time is truly one of our most generous gifts.

Kahil Gibran said, "It is when you give of yourself that you truly give." To give our time is to give ourselves.

I am so grateful to God for always being generous to me with his time and always giving me access to his power and love. I am also grateful to the people that have so generously given me their precious gifts of compassionate time. I need to be sure I follow their examples and generously give my time when I see it is needed.

As Mother Teresa reminds us, "If we worry too much about ourselves, we won't have time for others."

Choosing To Believe

We often say, "I have faith in you. I have faith in them. I have faith that it will happen." We encourage people with, "Keep the faith. Have faith." When someone is faltering we even say, "Have a little faith, good buddy." Okay, maybe we don't say the good buddy part.

We have faith in family members. We have faith in spouses. We have faith in our children. We have faith in friends. We even have faith in many strangers.

When I was a child I believed in Santa Claus. I had faith in him. One Christmas eve, in the middle of the night, I saw him. He crawled in my bedroom window and I lay in bed with my eyes wide with excitement. The vision was full color and extremely real. You may think I am a bit goofy here, but I am speaking the truth.

Some would say I was dreaming. Some would say I was imagining. But, for me, all these many, many, many years later, I can still see him coming in that window. I was full of faith in his reality.

The faith of a child is a beautiful thing. So is the faith of an adult. When we have faith, we kind of go out on a limb. Though faith can be strong, it is also nebulous.

I have a strong faith in God. Most people I know also have a strong faith in God. We may be on different paths on how we believe, but the fact that we do believe is the same.

I also have friends who do not believe. A very few are down and out atheists. Many of them, however, are agnostics. They don't really believe or not believe. Mainly they aren't sure. They don't really know. They question. They wonder.

Mother Teresa said, "Prayer begets faith." In my life I have had struggles. I am sure you have had struggles too. I have prayed from the get go and God has always answered me.

I pray for little things – really little. You know the kind – lost keys or shoes, to help me find where I am going (I would use my GPS but she doesn't like me and I don't care much for her either.) I pray for medium things – help my child, help my friend, help me, help, help, help.

And then, of course, I pray for big things, huge things. Usually those are very personal, too personal to write here.

I pray with expectations. I expect God to answer me. And I am never disappointed. Oh, sometimes I am disappointed that the answers aren't quicker or what I want, but I have faith that God knows best. I trust His decisions and his timing, even though I may not be all that happy about them.

Many times when I pray for something and it doesn't come through as I wanted, I later see that God had better things in store for me. The future held something greater than I had ever thought of or prayed for. My vision was very small compared to God's.

The other day my friend shared a neat thing with me. She said, "The day before my son was born, if God had told me that he would be giving me the gift of a child tomorrow and that I could pick it all out in detail. I would have picked this and that and none of it would have been as great as the gift my son turned out to be. I could never have imagined what great things God had in store for me."

Isn't that a great example? We need to get out of the way and let God do his miracles in our lives. We need to have faith that God has great things in store for us. We also need to have faith that God knows more than we do.

St. Augustine said, "Faith is to believe what we do not see, and the reward of this faith is to see what we believe." I cannot tell you God is real. I cannot confirm that there is a heaven. I cannot tell you anything for sure, except for this. I choose to believe. I know that throughout my life, I have prayed and I have gotten answers. I feel God guiding me. I hear God speaking to me when I am quiet and listen to the voice in my spirit. Sometimes I believe God speaks to me through other people. I am never sure where or how he will speak to me, but I know he will and does. I just have to be open and listen. I have to put my faith into action.

When Oprah interviews people, she often asks them what they know for sure. What I know for sure is that I have a strong faith in God. God is active in my life. I feel God's presence and guidance all the time, in little things and in giant things.

The other thing I know for sure is I am not sure. I don't have tangible proof. What I do have is perhaps stronger than that. I have faith.

Hear, Oh Lord

Near where I live is a glorious wooded trail. There are huge trees and the sun filters down through all the leaves as you walk. I think of it as a spiritual place. God, for me, is definitely present in that setting.

When I am alone there, I like to pray and listen to God. When I do this, a hymn always plays in my head, the same hymn, over and over.

"Hear, oh Lord, the sound of my call. Hear, oh Lord, and have mercy. My soul is longing for the glory of you. Hear, oh Lord, and answer me." This song helps me open up to God. It helps me to center myself in prayer. It calms my spirit.

Mercy – it seems we all want it. Yet, what is it, really? Mercy is pretty complicated. Mercy is a sister to forgiveness and justice. It is also loving kindness and compassion. Some forms of mercy are easier to do than others. The most difficult is showing compassion to one who has harmed you.

Abraham Lincoln once said about someone, "He reminds me of the man who murdered both his parents, and then, when sentence was about to be pronounced, pleaded for mercy on the grounds that he was an orphan."

I often remember Pope John Paul II showing mercy to the man who tried to assassinate him. Remember how he visited him in his prison cell and forgave him? That was mercy in action, for sure.

In 2004, a former student of my daughter's was killed in a car crash. Joey Teater, 12 years old, was hit by a twenty year old nanny driving a Hummer and talking on her cell phone. When the driver was in court, Joey's mother showed mercy by not wanting the girl to go to prison. I remember thinking what a beautiful example of mercy that she showed the world and how very hard that must have been.

Spiritual acts of mercy are directed toward the soul. Corporal acts of mercy are directed toward the body. We are called to minister both.

When it comes to giving mercy, both corporal and spiritual, we can think of St. Francis. "Make me a channel of your peace..."

Recently I have been aware that one form of spiritual mercy is listening to one who has lost someone they love. They tell you the story of how it happened, going over the details again and again. As I have learned more about loss, I have become aware that this is a necessary part of healthy grieving. We can listen, again and again and it is a merciful gift of comforting the sorrowful.

Mercy is visiting the sick or shut-in. It is being there for others who are suffering. It is being there when we don't have a thing we can do to make it better and when we don't have any words of comfort to offer. Just being there is often a tremendous act of mercy. We don't always have to know what to do or say. Mercy rises above that. Sometimes showing up is enough.

Mercy can be words of encouragement and praise to one who needs both. With honest, verbal mercy, we can sometimes be the wind beneath their wings. I am always struck by how words we utter can really make a long lasting difference to someone. And that works both ways. I know the words of others have really, really given me long lasting help and that they likely never knew that their words were so taken to heart.

A hug can be mercy. Sometimes all I have to offer is a hug, but that, also, can be enough. We have all gotten a big hug from someone and felt, 'oh, I needed that.' It is a wonderful thing.

Mercy is stepping in when we see someone is being bullied or sticking up for others when they need it.

Sitting and praying with someone who is dying is a beautiful act of mercy. Even when the person seems to be totally unaware of what is going on, I think they know.

I believe these acts of mercy help lead them out of this life into the next. We can ease their journey.

In this day of hard, financial times, people need assistance in so many ways. When we help by sharing our time, treasure or talent, we are often showing mercy. We can help serve soup. We can help nail a roof on a Habitat house. We can babysit or elder sit. We can. We can. We can. There are endless ways to show mercy where it is needed.

If you aren't sure where to begin, perhaps singing or saying the song can help you hear God's nudges. "Hear, oh Lord, the sound of my call. Hear, oh Lord, and have mercy. My soul is longing for the glory of you. Oh, hear, oh Lord, and answer me."

The Grand Miracle Of Forgiveness

It is said that we teach most what we need to learn. I needed to learn to forgive.

I went to a class and the instructor asked who had a resentment they would share. My hand was up quickly and I was chosen. I told about someone who had hurt one of my children seven years before. The class loved it. They identified.

I was quite proud of myself until the instructor asked, "Why haven't you forgiven her?" I was speechless. What a dumb question. When I finally thought of an answer, I said, "Because if I forgive her, she'll get away with it." I could see everyone agreed.

The instructor just got worse and said, "She got away with it seven years ago. You've been keeping that alive all by yourself." She told me how my resentments affected everything I did, said and thought. I immediately decided to resent the instructor too.

Her words gnawed at me. I knew she was right. I should let the resentment go, but I had no idea how to do it.

I am Catholic. I am educated. I have gone to counseling. One would think I would have learned to forgive somewhere along this road. But no one ever told me how. They just said, "Do it."

I went back to the instructor and said, "I have decided I want to forgive her, but I don't know how. What do I do with all these feelings?"

What a wise woman she was. She prayed with me and then taught me three steps to forgiveness. I have used them many times. I found I had a long list of resentments I needed to let go of, some since childhood, some more recent.

The three steps the instructor taught me have changed my life.

Step One: The Act / Decision

We decide intellectually that we want to forgive them. It is a decision we make to ourselves and our God. It doesn't feel good yet. We are still in pain. Lao Tzu said, "The journey of 1000 miles begins with a single step."

Mother Theresa said, "A true test of faith is whether or not we can forgive." It has also been said that asking God to help us forgive is the highest form of prayer.

When I was a young mother, my grandma sent me a poem by an unknown author.

Let Go and Let God

As children bring their broken toys with tears for us to mend,
I brought my broken dreams to God, because he was my friend.
But then, instead of leaving Him in peace to work alone, I hung
around and tried to help with ways that were my own.
At last I snatched them back and cried, "How can you be so slow?"
"My child," He said, "What could I do? You never did let go."

Letting it go is difficult. When we make that decision, we don't have to like it but we do have to be sincere.

Step Two: The Process

We need to feel/process all our feelings in this situation. We have to feel the hurt, anger, grief, betrayal, resentment, hate, or whatever emotions we have. We may need to write about them, to talk about them, to do whatever we can to work through them in positive ways. Once a counselor told me to walk and consciously think of my anger. It was a much more aggressive walk and a positive release.

When you see a man on the top of a mountain, you can bet he didn't fall there. Feeling our feelings takes time and can be very painful. In the film, The Prince of Tides, Barbara Streisand says, "Tears won't bring him back, but they might bring you back."

Sidney Simon says in his book, Forgiveness, "When we shove our feelings under the carpet, they just make ripples that we will trip on." Feeling our feelings is tough work but it liberates us. Hopefully, our pain will ebb.

I have a physical scar where I was cut. In the beginning, it hurt and was tender. Now it has healed over. I still see it. I know it's there and where it came from, but the sting is gone. So it is with our emotional scars. They heal over. They no longer give us pain when we touch them. They just become part of who we are and our life journey.

A counselor once told me, "Everyone has a cross to carry in life. These are just part of your cross." Put in that perspective, the carrying of them doesn't seem so heavy.

Step Three: The State of Forgiveness

I believe that forgiveness is a God thing. I believe that if we do the first two steps, God will do his magic and bless us with the state of forgiveness. Often when we least expect it. Sometimes when we think it is impossible.

Inner peace is created by changing ourselves, not the person who hurt us. When we forgive we look at them through new eyes. We see them, we remember, but it doesn't hurt us anymore. We may even wish them well and go on our way.

We are imperfect people and we live in an imperfect world. Pain is inevitable. Suffering is optional. Forgiveness is one of the hardest things we will ever be asked to do. Is it worth it? You bet. Because we are worth it.

Marie Balter was locked in an insane asylum for years. She wasn't insane. Marlo Thomas portrayed her in a TV movie. When she was released she said, "I would not have grown one bit, if I had not learned to forgive."

Though forgiveness is a personal journey and a gift we give ourselves, the benefits radiate to our families, our friends and our world. I love the short prayer, "Lord, give me the guidance to know when to hold on, when to let go and the grace to make the right decision with dignity." When we are able to do this, a grand miracle is performed.

****

Forgiveness is a choice. We can choose to harbor hurt and resentment or we can choose to heal and give ourselves the peace we deserve. Don Juan, in Journey to *Xtlan*, said, "We either make ourselves miserable or we make ourselves strong. The amount of work is the same."

Hurts come in all shapes and sizes. They come in different ways. Sometimes folks mean to hurt us. Sometimes they don't even know they have.

What do we need to forgive? Not irritations. What we need to forgive are deep personal hurts. We need to forgive actions, what people have done, not who they are and what they are like.

When I began my journey of forgiveness, I really didn't want to forgive. I just wanted the pain to end. I wanted to feel healed. But to do so, I had to let it go and quit licking my wounds. Sometimes, I think it is harder to give it up than to go through what happened in the first place.

One woman shared that her counselor asked her, "How long do you want to bleed over this?" Is holding on worth the price we are paying? Would we rather be right than happy?

There are some people who are very difficult to forgive. Perhaps they're still mean and nasty. They're never sorry. We want them to beg for forgiveness. They don't. We want them to pay, to hurt as we have. They don't. Some of them even die and leave us with the whole burden.

A wonderful thing to learn is that we don't need their repentance to forgive. It is really not about them. It's about us, our healing, and our future.

Often we want two things. We want to keep our anger and we want to have peace. We can't have it both ways. The word forgive means to give up.

There are some important things that forgiveness is and is not. Forgiveness is not forgetting. We don't get amnesia when we forgive. Often we need to remember so we can protect ourselves.

Forgiveness is not trusting. We don't have to become a fool to forgive. Some people should never be trusted. Others we may be able to trust again. Each situation is unique.

Forgiveness is not understanding it all. I want to understand everything, to talk it through. That is usually a fantasy. We need to accept confusion as we forgive.
Forgiveness is not tolerating, excusing, or condoning. When we forgive we are not saying it was OK, nor are we saying we will allow it to happen again. Our forgiveness does not let them off the hook. It is not absolution. They remain responsible for what they did.

Forgiveness can't be forced or phony. We can't forgive because it's our duty or someone told us to do it.

Getting even doesn't work. It's a game no one wins. When we forgive, we quit playing the game. We walk away. We leave the score unbalanced. We surrender . . . our resentment. We win . . . peace, joy and healing.

Forgiveness can't wait for the circumstances to be right. They may never be.

We need to limit our expectations of forgiveness. We must accept imperfect forgiving. Perfection locks us up. We may not get a rosy ending. We may never be best friends again. We may not kiss and make up. We may not like them again. We may have to let them go out of our life. We can still get peace.

There is no one way to forgive. We can forgive in many ways: face to face, by letter; by actions, silently within ourselves. Every situation calls for a different approach.

Forgiveness occurs one step at a time and sometimes they are just baby steps. Be patient. Forgiveness can't be rushed. The deeper the wound, the longer it takes. Forgiveness is not an event, it's a process. Even when you feel it's not coming, don't give up. There is only one thing that can prevent you from forgiving and that is your will, simply refusing to do it. It is not "you would if you could". You can. It is in your hands.

Pray for the person you need to forgive, perhaps even out loud. You can do it through clenched teeth. You don't have to like doing it. You just have to mean it. It's like priming a pump. It opens you to God's power and allows Him to perform His miracle and free you of the hate, resentment, anger and pain.

Portia Nelson wrote an autobiography in five very short chapters.

"**Chapter 1:** I walk down the street. There is a deep hole in the sidewalk. I fall in. I am lost. I am helpless. It isn't my fault. It takes forever to find a way out.

Chapter 2: I walk down the same street. There is a deep hole in the sidewalk. I pretend I don't see it. I fall in again. I can't believe I am in the same place again, but it isn't my fault. It still takes a long time to get out.

Chapter 3: I walk down the same street. There is a deep hole in the sidewalk. I see it there. I still fall in. It's a habit. My eyes are open. I know where I am. It is my fault. I get out immediately.

Chapter 4:   I walk down the same street. There is a deep hold in the sidewalk. I walk around it.

Chapter 5:   I walk down another street."

Do you need to walk down another street? Most of us have hurts and resentments we need to heal. We have the power to choose healing or harboring. Lao Tse said, "If you do not change directions, you may end up where you are heading." Is that where you want to be?

(This column won first place with the Catholic Associated Press.)

Real Role Models

If Life Were Fair Awards

Recently I received an Associated Press award for my column. I was thrilled but had to identify with Jack Benny who said, "I don't deserve this award, but then I don't deserve arthritis either." It got me to thinking. What should we get awards for? I put the question out to some folks and got some brilliant and fun responses.

I think we should get awards for going places when you don't really want to but know you should, also for saying no when you want to say yes and saying yes when you want to say no.

I would like an award for continuing to exercise through all these seasons and years. There should be an award for living in a state without enough sunshine and remaining perky about life. Of course, all the anti depressants everyone takes do help with Michigan's perkiness level.

I would like, but do not really deserve, an award for folding and putting away laundry in a timely basis. However, the timely basis might keep me from getting this award.

Here are other's ideas:

"Eating the leftover dessert so that others in the house don't cheat on their diet. Smiling and saying thank you when your mate tells you how to do something you've been doing quite well for many years". Bev

"There should be an award for parenting and one for raising teenagers! I also want an award for mastering technology. I have conquered a computer, cell phone, smart phone, digital camera and a GPS, but I still can't figure out how to cancel the timer on our microwave or set the radio station buttons in my car. And the microwave has a help button that I can't figure out. The best help button I have found is a teenager." Kim

"I think we should get a time spent award for the amount of time we spend looking for glasses, cell phones, car keys, etc. We should give an award to the person that has to answer our questions of 'does this make my butt look big'? 'Is my hair all right'? Oh, and an award for answering all the questions our kids ask us: 'when will we get there; how many bites do I have to eat; how many days till my birthday; how many days till Christmas; can so and so spend the night; what do I get if I clean my room?' I also think we should get awards for interesting words. You know, when you open your mouth and interesting words come out that had nothing to do with what you meant to say." Laura

"I'd like an award for when someone steps on your foot or bumps into you. They say, 'sorry', and you reply, 'oh, that's ok', but it is not okay and you spend the evening with an ice pack all night." Carol

"There should be an award for most holes in the tongue – for being the best at biting your tongue and not saying what you are really thinking. Or the most mold growing in the fridge award. Or the longest overdue book award. Or how about an award for getting the farthest into a store with your dress tucked into your underwear before you notice it. Oh, wait, that's too personal. I'd win." Gayle

"I have always thought the MVP award at high school football banquets should go to the mother who picked up, dropped off, cheered on, bandaged up, and sat through all kinds of weather just to watch a football game with her kid in it." Kean

"I want an award for not being politically correct all the time. We could call it the Maxine award." Rae

"What about awards for the natural aging process . . . greatest sag or best receding hairline?" Darci

"Some days I deserve an award for getting up and getting dressed. My husband wants an award for the occasional staying put and shutting up." Hollie

"I think I should win an award for still thinking I'm young enough to keep up with my kids when my body proves otherwise." Candy

So, there we are, lots of creative ideas on what we should get awards for if life were really fair, but then again, it isn't.

Lessons From A Real Giant

Maureen & Fred Meijer

When I was a kid, I loved to read fairy tales. In some there would be giants and in my mind I saw them as huge, tall, great big creatures – inhuman. Now I am grown up and I know what giants are really like.

They can be short, slender, normal looking and maybe even walking with a walker. In my adult eyes, Fred Meijer was a giant in every good sense of the word.

So much has been said and written about Fred already, but I want to write about the lessons we can learn from this giant. If followed, his lessons can make all of us better people. How did he teach them? By living his life, of course. We all lead in three ways: by example, by example, by example. Fred did a great job of that.

Lesson 1: <u>Laugh easily and with gusto</u>. Fred punctuated every conversation with lots of laughter. He joked easily, often about himself. He laughed with people, never at people. Are we laughing enough?

Lesson 2: <u>Set the tone</u>. A few years ago, Fred told me how he still went to the office every work day. He said his job was to set the tone. And, boy, did he! There was nobody more excited about Meijers than Fred Meijer. His tone was enthusiasm and it was contagious. How is the tone we set in our lives? Are we enthusiastic, pessimistic, optimistic, grouchy or joyful? Whatever we are, we are also contagious.

Lesson 3: <u>Brighten the world with a smile</u>. Oh, you may not think that is much of a lesson, but let me tell you, try going without one and see how life feels. It is hard to imagine Fred without a smile, because he was usually wearing one.

Lesson 4: <u>Give back</u>. Fred lived by John Kennedy's words. "Ask not what your country can do for you. Ask what you can do for your country." Yes, Fred was one of the richest Americans, but his things didn't make him happy, his ability to give did. Fred gave and gave and gave. He gave encouragement, kind words, opportunity, and, oh yes, lots of money. We could sum it up by saying, Fred Meijer gave generously always.

Lesson 5: <u>Never forget where you came from</u>. We all know that home is where we start from. Fred started from Greenville and he never forgot it. Fred was a regular at events in Greenville. He lived in Grand Rapids and loved it, but he loved where he came from too. He was proud of his heritage and his history.

Lesson 6: <u>Work hard</u>. I love the fact that Fred worked right up until he died. What a blessing for him and what a blessing for the world. Many times, especially in the beginning of his career and life, he gave up experiences and events because he felt he had to work instead. His work ethic was strong. The world could really be a better place if we all worked that hard.

Lesson 7: <u>Praise others</u>. Fred handed out praise as happily and as often as he handed out Purple Cow ice cream cards. One Friday night I was home alone. It was about 8:30 at night. The phone rang and it was Fred. You can imagine my surprise! He said he had especially liked one of my columns and had copied it to give to people. He then went on to chat about other things I had written, encouraging me all the time. When I hung up, I was stunned and honored. I could not believe that on a Friday night, when there is so much to do, that he would take the time and effort to call me with praise. I know I am just one of the many thousands of people that he praised. I am also quite sure that we each remember his praise and encouragement with fondness. We can pass this lesson on if we remember to praise others often.

Lesson 8: <u>Be open minded and forward thinking</u>. Fred hired minorities when it was a novel idea. He didn't seem to see color or sex as barriers. He saw people as people. He saw the world as what it could be, not necessarily as what it was. How do we see it?

Lesson 9: <u>Be a dreamer and run with those dreams</u>. Fred collected sculptures long before the gardens and sculpture park were even discussed. Fred dreamed the concept of one stop shopping before it was a concept. Yes, he dreamed big and then he added the magic to his dreams – work. And a wonderful thing happened – reality.

Lesson 10: <u>Love big</u>. Fred loved his dear wife, Lena. He loved his children and grandchildren. He loved people. He loved life. He loved the road he had traveled and was traveling.

Harry Emerson Fosdick sums up Fred nicely. "To laugh often and much; to win the respect of intelligent people and the affection of children; to earn the appreciation of honest critics and endure the betrayal of false friends; to appreciate beauty; to find the best in others; to leave the world a bit better, whether by a healthy child, a garden patch or a redeemed social condition; to know even one life has breathed easier because you have lived. This is to have succeeded."

If we follow the above lessons that Fred showed us, we can succeed too. It may be that the way Fred lived his life is his greatest gift of all. He was a true giant in the real world.

We Have Been Changed For Good

Twenty-five years ago there was a new girl in town. I was in my thirties. My little one had just made her First Communion. The rest of the kids were busy with band, sports and babysitting. My husband was in the beginning of his presidency. The new girl in town was Oprah Winfrey. She appeared on T.V. weekday afternoons and became part of our family. Now she has left us and what a hole she leaves. Oh, I know, she will still be around and she has her OWN channel and all that jazz, but she has left us as we have known her and many of us are left wondering what we'll do without her.

I am one of the many, many women who LOVE Oprah. I have gotten and read every issue of her magazine. Twice, I have been in the audience on her show. I have shaken her hand as we left. We will never forget how warm and real she was and how she told my daughter how much she loved her outfit.

What is it about Oprah that makes her such a big deal? Barb calls her "an angel among us". Carol says, "She is like one of my best friends, although I have never met her." Oprah has that effect on us. Annette put it so nicely. "She taught me a lot about compassion and love for everyone. I didn't agree with Oprah on everything, but that's how it is with friends, isn't it?"

Carolina, from Spain, said, "Oprah has been a member of my house for 25 years. She's a role model to me." Char adds, "She relates to regular women. She walks our walk and talks our talk. I respect her."

"When I watched Oprah, I never saw color," says Claudette. "I just saw a pretty woman who genuinely seemed to care about everyone. "

Cousin, Maureen, sums it up. "Oprah is my HERO . . . the essence of inspiration and survival. One of the greatest humanitarians of our time, she lifts us all. She took all of the skeletons out of the closet, dared to share them, and opened the floodgates of pain, shame and despair for millions of people. She gave them hope and healing. She taught us to find our inner strength, to believe in ourselves and each other. She was our special friend who knocked on our door just when we most needed to know that we still counted and that someone still cared."

I loved that Oprah was honest about her struggles with weight. As Bunny said, "If someone as brilliant as Oprah can struggle with weight and hold her head up high, so can I. Many of Oprah's issues are the same as mine. She has found strength from her tribulations and because of her, so have I. She has developed character rather than be crippled by her past, and because of her, so have I. Oprah is an over-comer." She has shown us that we can overcome too.

Gayle feels, "With all Oprah's wealth and wisdom, she is still human, full of heart and humble. She touches humanity."

Hollie had an especially personal encounter. In 2000 her son was very ill. Hollie went on the Oprah Show with her personal story of gratitude. A limo took them from Greenville to Harpo Studios. They stayed at the Omni Suites Hotel. "Oprah and her people understood that this was a once in a lifetime experience for us and they made sure we felt like royalty. I cannot say enough about Oprah. She is the real deal and I will miss seeing her every day at four."

My daughter, Colleen, said, "I think Oprah makes us want to be better people because she's always striving to be a better person. That might be with health, career, relationships . . . but the aim is always towards our best self." Tyler Perry said of Oprah, "She pushes her destiny to its boundaries with the wind of God at her back." She taught us how to do the same.

And then there is the "reading, reading, reading", as Connie puts it. Oprah has had 70 book club choices. I read most of them. She made reading and discussing books cool again.

When Oprah received the Kennedy Center Honors Award in Washington, D.C., Chris Rock quipped. "I look out and see the most powerful person in the world. And sitting next to her is Barack O'Bama."

Personally, what I love about Oprah is her openness, honesty, quick wit, spirituality, intelligence, and caring example. I have laughed out loud with her. I have cried with her. I have grown with her. I am now in my sixties. My children are well into adulthood. My husband is retired. Oprah has been part of our journey.

What do I know for sure? I know I am going to really, really miss Oprah. I also know that she has taught each of us that we are strong. We are enough just as we are. We can go forward with grace and make a difference in the world. We've had the power all along. We just needed some "Aha" moments to realize it.

In the play, *Wicked*, they sing, "People come into our lives for a reason, bringing something we must learn, and we are led to those who help us most to grow, if we let them . . . because we knew you, we have been changed for good . . . you'll be with us like a handprint on our hearts." Thank you, Oprah. You are at the top of our gratitude journals.

Learnings From A Local Legend

"What we need in life is a roof over our heads, some good love and peanut butter in the pantry." This is wisdom from Ty Hallock, given to him by his Grandpa Tucker. Ty followed this with, "I grew up rich, not in material things but in the important things."

Ty Hallock

Ty Hallock is a Greenville High School graduate who played football for Michigan State University, the Detroit Lions, the Chicago Bears (Da Bears), and the Jacksonville Jaguars. He is now retired as a pro athlete and works in commercial real estate. Ty spoke the other night and I thought I would share some of his wisdom with you.

Ty got bags and bags of mail from teams all over the country that were interested in him playing football for them. He ended up choosing Michigan State. He said, "I thought it was so cool during the recruiting process. Then it wasn't so cool. You gotta show up and work, work, work. You're pushed to your limits."

"You have to have some God given ability, but potential doesn't win the race. Potential does not keep you around. Being smart and adaptive does keep you in the game. You have to see what's happening and adjust. And then you have to keep getting up. Everyone loves someone who gets knocked down and gets up and gets back in the game."

He advised, "If you don't know, ask someone, ask the best, ask the ones who are successful at what you want. There are tons of things to be learned from other people."

He quit football and returned a couple of times. He said, "Quitting is a temporary place."

Ty said the influences we have along the way are really the keys to our successes.

"I learned a great lesson from my Dad, when I took his car after I had been forbidden to do so. I totaled it. All he asked was if we were all okay. When he found out we were, he said, 'I can replace a car but I can't replace you.' He never yelled at me. Lesson learned – my parents loved me unconditionally, no matter what I did on and off the field!"

"Relationships matter," he stressed. "Family is the true treasure." He talked about how his entire family all get together once a year and have "Pass the Salt Shaker" time. "When you get the shaker, you have to share what's going on in your life and how you are doing. And everyone listens and values where you are in your journey in life." This sounds like a great idea for all of us.

He made a serious point about saying, "It never ever came to my mind to use performance enhancing drugs to help me succeed in football. There are lots of roads to go down, but there is no substitute for hard work." He said he is honest with young people when they ask him questions and he is proud to say he never used drugs.

Ty believes that "high school football should be an educational experience". He feels that "sports do not need to be practiced all year long in a mandatory way". He thinks, "Kids need some breaks". He feels, "High school athletics should be in the business of building kids up regardless of talent level". He says, "I'm a builder, not one who beats the kids down. I don't believe in being wrecking balls to kids in athletics, especially in high school and younger ages."

"Football was great fun but it's not everything. Football doesn't define me." He believes in perspective. "I often look around and think, is this really important? Is it the end of the world if one rival wins over another?" Good sportsmanship is more important along with several other lessons that sports ultimately teach us. "It's not okay to lose and be a jerk."

Ty is warm, bright and real. He gave an emotional from the heart talk. As I listened, I thought of watching him grow from a kid who hung out with my kids to this fine man. He, like all the other people in his family, is a super person. He had experiences most people don't get to have. He grabbed the ball of athletic success and kept his touch with reality. I left his talk thinking how he has been a Yellow Jacket, a Spartan, a Lion, a Bear and a Jaguar. More important than all of them, though, I would sum him up as one cool cat. And we can all learn a lot from cats.

The Blessings Of Courage

Courage – I ask myself when I have had it. I am still saddened by a time I didn't have it. It was a grey Friday, November 22, 1963. I was sitting in business math class at Coopersville High School. Over the intercom came the news that President Kennedy had been assassinated. The teacher went on with our class without acknowledging what had happened. I sat there and felt strongly that we should pray. I felt compelled that I should lead them in prayer. I wanted to. I knew I should. I just did not have the courage to do it. I was sixteen. I hadn't developed enough courage yet.

I have some courage now. If I hear someone tell a racist joke, I will tell them it isn't funny and they should never repeat it. That takes courage, I think.

I recently had the courage to walk the Mackinac Bridge even though I am very afraid of heights. I am not sure I was really courageous, though. I had an army of friends and family praying for me. My dear Aunt Mary prayed to different saints to be on each side of me and to take all my fear away. And, they did. I had no fear as I walked. I am smart enough to know that all my courage as I walked was the answer to the many prayers offered for me. It was a gift.

I watched my mother be courageous when she got Guillain Barre Syndrome and had to very painfully learn to walk all over again.

My friend, Cheryl, says, "I believe our faith foundation holds us up when we need it. We may look for other things to help, but we find they don't last. God puts people in our path to lead us. We need to be open and willing to listen." Cheryl knows of what she speaks.

In 1993, Cheryl woke up to pounding on the door and screaming. "Kelly has set herself on fire." Kelly was her 29 year old daughter who had been suffering from mental illness. Kelly had gone to a park with a can of gasoline, doused herself and tried to burn out the demons inside her. Kelly was a very devout Catholic. Cheryl does not believe she was trying to commit suicide, but that the voices inside her told her to do it.

Years later, Fr. Phil Salmonowicz told Cheryl, "Christ fought demons. The mentally ill also fight demons." These words gave her great comfort and the courage to go on.

Life is not always fair. Cheryl now has another daughter that is mentally ill and Cheryl is raising her son.

Cheryl said, "You ask why. Why? Why? You want God to come down and say, 'This is why'. But he doesn't. I don't understand God. There are no answers on this earth. I don't know why. But this is earth, this is not heaven. God doesn't tell me why, but he does give me the courage to go on. I go on for the rest of my family."

Cheryl continued, "I take great comfort in Psalm 139, 'You made all the delicate, inner parts of my body, and knit them together in my mother's womb.' I am so grateful I got to have Kelly for 29 years. What a blessing! My other children give me peace. I begin each day with a prayer and turn my will and life over to the care of God and know I can never be lost from his spirit."

Maya Angelou says, "Courage is the most important of all virtues, because without it we can't practice any other virtue with consistency." When I look around me, I see lots of courage and these courageous people are great examples for us. As God has blessed them with courage, they bless us with examples. I know from them, that as I need more courage in my life, I can rest assured that God will not let me down.

Thank you, Lord, for being the fountain of courage when we need it. I am also reminded of something Mother Teresa said, "I know God will not give me anything I can't handle. I just wish He didn't trust me so much." Amen to that!

I Need A Hero

Remember the movie, *Footloose*? Remember the song in it that said, "I need a hero"? I am thinking we may need a hero now.

It is a sad time in hero world. It is an even sadder time for fans of heroes. Who wasn't shocked at the Tiger Woods fall from grace? Heck, I'm still shocked at the David Lettermen mess.

The nasty war featuring Jay Leno was just as shocking. I am not a Leno lover nor am I a Conan fan. But, hey, remember when Jerry Seinfeld said he was quitting because it was best to quit when you are on top? I think Leno must not have heard that remark. He left NBC on top. I watched his farewell show. I even got teary with the emotion of it all.

Today it seems farewells are not really that. They are more like pauses in reality, pretend farewells - all hype but no reality. I can think of several singers and sports stars that retired with big fanfare and then later returned to their respective careers. Some, like Brett Farr, took pretty big hits in the mocking departments when they returned.

But lately it seems like there have been lots of folks falling from their lofty perches. The most recent is John Edwards. I saw Edwards speak in Grand Rapids. He was oozing charm and likeability. He made sense. He seemed honest and trustworthy. I really liked him. The night I saw him, he was ending his campaign and giving his support to Barack O'Bama. He was rousing. And then the fall from grace. And what a fall it has been.

Watching the 20/20 show with all the details of the Edwards scandal made me sick. I actually found it hard to sleep afterwards.

There was a book after John F. Kennedy died, Johnny, *We Hardly Knew Ye*. It referred to JFK dying so young before he got to live his life out. But as I think about John Edwards, it could have been written about him. John, we hardly knew ye, for sure.

I look at the little children I know and I wonder what they will think about heroes. Who will their heroes be? Who will we look to for heroes in the future? Do we need heroes?

Perhaps heroes are not people we don't know. Perhaps they are people we do know but don't realize that they are the true heroes in life.

Perhaps heroes aren't just media made but life experience made. John McCain is a hero for surviving years as a POW and there are lots of unsung heroes defending our country in foreign lands right now.

Lettermen, Leno and Conan are certainly not heroes, but they are stars. Sometimes it is hard for us to realize the difference. The media likes to put up stars as heroes.

We like to glorify. It is a perfect match. The media puts them in front of us. We hold them up. Tiger Woods and Muhammad Ali have certainly been sports heroes and their athletic greatness put them there. What makes a hero? Is it something that they do that others have not? Or something that we can't imagine ourselves doing?

I don't know what this all means. I just feel a bit disillusioned in the hero department of life. I don't know who will be knocked off their hero throne next. There always seems to be a new shocking news story that takes the focus off the last one. Lettermen gave up the spotlight to Tiger. Tiger gave up the spotlight to Leno. Leno gave up the spotlight to Edwards. And so it goes. There's always a new one around the corner.

I watched Conan's last show on NBC. I don't really care for his humor style but I really liked how he ended his show. He said, and he directed this especially to young people, "All I ask is one thing . . . please do not be cynical . . . it doesn't lead anywhere." A great message for all of us, especially in these times of heroes falling like rain.

At the Grammys, Michael Jackson was quoted. "In a world filled with hate, we must still dare to hope. In a world filled with despair we must still dare to believe."

So, let's not get cynical. Let's dare to hope and believe in the goodness of people. The world is full of real heroes. Some of them we know, some of them we don't. Some of them are in the media. Some are not. Perhaps the best place to find heroes is in our own little corner of the world.

The Grand Temple

What is it that makes people stand in line for three hours in the freezing cold? To hear an autistic professor from Colorado State University speak? Really? Really!

That is if the professor is Temple Grandin. Who? Temple Grandin is a woman, a professor, a Ph.D., one of 25 heroes in the 2010 *Time* Magazine list of 100 Most Influential People in the world and a renowned scientist who "lives on the autism spectrum". I recently heard her speak.

Temple Grandin

I am a movie lover. HBO did a movie called *Temple Grandin*. I had absolutely no idea what it was about, but I have faith in HBO, so I taped it. I never watched it. It sat in my DVR. My girls watched it, loved it and encouraged us to see it. Finally, we did and we were blown away. We began campaigning. "See the movie, *Temple Grandin.*" We didn't really tell people what it was about. You couldn't explain it and make it sound nearly as good as it was.

Unsurprisingly, *Temple Grandin* won 7 Emmys including Best T.V. Movie, Best Actress, Best Director and Best Supporting Actor. Claire Danes, who played Temple, just won a Golden Globe for Best Actress. At both award shows, the real Temple Grandin sat in the audience. "The movie was very authentic. I helped create it. Claire Danes portrayed how I think and feel very accurately."

Temple cannot be described by regular Hollywood labels. She is not socially cool. She didn't speak for her first years. "I would have ended up in an institution if mother hadn't helped me. Mentors are essential. I needed hands on learning."

"I had to sell my work, not myself. I had to learn social skills." Once she watched an engineer show his detailed drawing to a group. She told him it was "pigeon do-do". Her superior made her go and apologize for her rude behavior.

"I told him I was sorry I was rude. I did not tell him his idea was good."

Temple describes how she thinks. "My brain works like Google. Each concept is in a file folder in my mind. I had a file for cats. I had a file for dogs. Then my neighbor got a dachshund. It looked like a dog but it was small like a cat. I was all goofed up. I figured out it had a nose like a dog. Then I realized so do bears."

"If you tell an autistic child not to run across the street, you need to tell them that means in different places or the child will think, 'Don't run across the street at home'. The child will think it is okay to run across the street at school or at the neighbors."

"I can't do well in a restaurant with ten T.V.s going on. I can't do well in a church with lots of loud music. Autistic people are sensitive to fluorescent lights."

I did not expect Temple to be humorous, but she was. She used a power point and showed slides of her brain compared to a normal brain. They were clearly different. "I think in photo realistic pictures. I am a total visual thinker."

In the movie it shows that if someone mentioned shoe, her mind would rapidly go through pictures of all the shoes she had ever seen in her life. I know this is hard to imagine. You've got to see the movie.

She explained, "If you said map, I would first think of the roll down map from my elementary classroom, the puzzle of the world I once had, then I would see England and my visit there . . . "

"A normal person thinks in vague pictures. Their mind drops out the details. Autistic people focus on the details. How do you think?"

Jake went with me to hear Temple. Jake is 13 and has a special interest in her famous ideas on working with cattle. After her talk, we sat and discussed it. We looked at the big clock which was near where we sat. We looked at it and saw the basic clock. We didn't notice details – like the advertisements all over it, the decorative iron and design. We tried to see it like Temple. What a unique thought process to try.

She said, "It is impossible for me to multi-task. If the phone rings it takes me longer to shift my attention between one thing and another "

She showed print jiggling on a page and said, "That is how autistic people see words on a page".

"There were always autistic people. The fifties had more social rules. People said please and thank you. They did things a certain way. Today society has less rules. That is hard for autistic people. Kids are addicted to video games and computers and they don't do anything else. They need to get outside, play and be creative. The mouse isn't connected to the brain in the same way that hands are."

"Half of Silicone Valley has Aspergers. You wouldn't even have computers without all the people with Aspergers. Those social talky people would never have invented it."

She advised students, "Go out and show all the good stuff you can do. Find a niche and make yourself really good at it. Ability has to be developed."

Someone asked her. "Is any mind normal?"

"I have thought about that," She paused, "If so, it is very boring."

You may be interested in some of her books, especially "Thinking in Pictures / My Life with Autism".

Jake had won Grand Champion at the county 4-H Fair. It was his first 4-H experience. After Jake saw the movie and was excited about it, I wrote Temple at Colorado State and sent his photo and an article about him from the newspaper. I asked her to send him a note of congratulations and that it would be super if she included a photo of herself. I knew it was a long shot.

A few weeks later I received a letter to Jake with her photo on the front. It said, "Dear Jake, Congratulations on winning the Grand Champion.... Keep working hard and achieve your dreams. Best Wishes, Temple Grandin".

After we heard Temple speak, we got in line to have her autograph books. Jake said, "Thank you for your note." She looked at him and asked, "How's 4-H? How's school?"

I know it may sound crazy to other boring social talky brains like myself, but I swear she knew Jake from the note and photo. She remembers everything visually, everything. Her mind is a grand temple.

Smile Because It Happened

Today I waved good-by to my friend who is moving to the Seattle area. There were about a dozen other friends there, but I was selfish and only thinking about my own sadness. You see, my friend has been around the block a few times, yet she is still full of life, zest and courage. I asked her, "Do you think you will return to visit?"

Dotti Rackliffe

She looked up and laughed, "Good heavens, how do I know? I'm 90 years old!" She will turn 91 in May but nothing really gives that away. Oh, she is battling serious cancer. She chose to give up chemo because it was horrible for her and she decided she didn't want to live like that. At this moment, her cancer has quit growing.

Many of you have guessed by now, I am talking about the wonderful artist, devoted volunteer, and fun lady, Dotti Rackliffe.

Dotti was a modern woman before women were liberated. Her mother was way cool, too. I remember her saying to me, "Don't even begin to think about getting old until your baby turns 50!" I never forgot that and on days when I ache away, I remember her wisdom and feel better.

Dotti has never been shy. She pretty much tells it like it is and you end up happy to hear it. Friends drove her to the airport. One shared, "Dotti never "asks" you to do favors for her. She just "tells" you what she needs done and asks you what time would work for you to do it."

When Dotti was 50 she learned to ski, and when her husband retired, they moved to Austria for ten years. When she returned, she threw herself back into being a vital, active part of this community.

In the early eighties, Dotti was a main player in women's festivals. She was always there to help women become all they could be. And that is at the core of why I am so sad to see this woman leave. She really gave me a leg up when I started out.I had been speaking professionally for several years and audiences were asking for a book to take home. I told Dotti and she immediately said, "Let's do it!"

I wrote the book and Dotti illustrated and published it through her graphic arts company. She also backed it financially until it paid for itself. Luckily, that didn't take long. I remember her sketching and saying, "Look at her? Here she comes. Oh, isn't she cute?", as she was coming up with the main character in the book. Fun to watch creativity at work.

We sat at her kitchen table and bounced titles off one another. We decided on Run with your Dreams and that was that. That little book went on to sell somewhere around 100,000 copies and to also be published in Spanish, French and Braille. It became an Amway Book of the Month and is still sold regularly today. As I think of my friend, Dotti, I know I owe her a lot. I went on to write five more books, but would I have ever done that without the support, enthusiasm, encouragement and belief in me that Dotti gave so lovingly and sincerely? I think not. I wouldn't have known how to get started. I would have left my dream on the shelf. With Dotti, I was able to not only run with it, but make it a reality.

Dotti lost a breast to cancer. She lost a baby. She lost a beloved mate. The thing that knocked her flat, though, was when her 40 year old son, a minister with a young family, died of a heart attack while jogging. She told me she had laid in bed for a long, long time. "One day, I looked up and thought how horrible it all was and how I was justified to be wallowing in my grief. I said to myself, 'Okay, Dotti, you can lay here forever and cry, or you can get up and do something for someone else to make the world a better place.' And I did." I have used that message many times in my talks. We all need to be reminded of her inspiring perspective.

Hollie said, "Dotti inspired me because of all she has been through and yet is still able to find beauty and joy in life. She also taught me that the best view is from the front of church. With her leaving now, I have to remind myself of the saying, 'Don't cry because it's over, smile because it happened.' "

By the time Dotti left, strangers all around the airport were caring about her and wishing her off. The most beautiful thing, though, was watching Tom, a 6th grader, hug her long, tightly and with great love, his eyes welled with tears. Tom has suffered serious health problems and Dotti had formed a very special bond with him.

As Dotti flew off to the next adventure in her great big life, I thought of what a bright spot she is in the world. She left a cadre of people waving and crying, but to also leave children crying because you are going – that is a life well lived, indeed.

Run with your new dreams, dear Dotti. We have been blessed to have you in our lives, for sure.

What A Difference A Person Makes

There is an old song that says, "What a difference a day makes." I was just thinking what a difference a person makes. Oh, we already know that, but it keeps rearing its lovely head wherever I turn.

We drove to church today and passed a fun unique ice sculpture. Each year Dan pours water over some old Christmas trees and voila - a lovely ice sculpture for all to enjoy. Dan is a man that is all about helping others. He is an avid volunteer, especially with Habitat for Humanity, but mainly, he's a great fun-seeker. Wherever he goes, he spreads sunshine, laughter, caring and conversation. What a difference Dan makes.

I just returned from a two mile walk for Africa. For my part, I did nothing but walk, enjoy and write a check. However, a wonderful young teacher, Mary, did all the real work. Mary has recently taken two trips to Africa to work with children in schools and help where she saw need. She organized a nonprofit organization, *To: Africa, From: US*, and is now raising money to build classrooms and a school kitchen for two Ugandan schools. She is raising $10,000 to do this and is over half way to her goal. What a difference she makes.

A couple weeks ago, I attended the ordination of David who became an Episcopal priest. David is active with the library and other causes, but this wasn't enough. David has now followed the nudge to become a full-time pastor. Wherever David goes, he brings a calm joyful spirit. His wife, Merry Kim, brings joy and brilliance, as well. I have always wondered if her parents looked in her eyes when she was born and named her Merry or if it was just divine intervention. However it happened, Merry Kim is definitely the epitome of merry. What a difference David and Merry Kim make.

As you look around in your own lives, who are the people that first come to mind that make a positive difference in your world? Some get awards, but many do not. Many just quietly make a difference and that makes all the difference in the world. Perhaps we can radiate some of their sunshine right back at them with our words of appreciation.

At David's ordination, another pastor said, "God is within every human being we encounter. There is such joy in a community of good people. There will be moments when we sing, and moments when we weep, and they all come together in a unity of love. And that love is so needed to build up our broken world. This is a great day. May God grant us all the willingness to love with good cheer and rejoice in peace and justice."

What a difference one person can make. As Gandhi challenges us, "Be the change you want to see in the world."

Near And Far

Foreign Language Blunders

Oh, boy, it is hard enough to understand each other when we speak the same language. Add in a different language and most Americans get confused.

While in Spain I bought an apron which reads in Spanish, "Nina - Queen of the Kitchen". My grandboys call me Nina. When I told my friend who speaks fluent Spanish, she corrected me. I had said, "Nina - Queen of the Pigs". In Spanish, cocina is kitchen and cochina is pig. So close but yet so far apart.

I asked others to share some of their fun language blunders or ones they had seen. Many of them were hilarious but inappropriate for me to put in this column. One I loved was from Dan in Muskegon. "I don't try speaking in any other language. If I was hitchhiking in Mexico and somebody stopped, I would say, 'Amigo, I need a ride-o into town-o'. I have tried that technique of speaking Spanish myself. Sometimes it works. Sometimes it doesn't.

Gail moved to Florida and kept asking how to adjust the pool controls. She was saying, "Donde esta las controles para la pescadore, por favor?" She learned later she was asking how she could turn on the fisherman.

Susan lives in Madrid but is from Connecticut. She has seen many fun ones. Translated to English on a Spanish menu was "frightened eggs" for fried eggs, hanging on a hotel room door "Do not molest", and instructions at a seminar "When you finish completing your documents, stuff them in the holes of your pigeons." What???

A military friend was with a bunch of soldiers in Germany at a McDonalds restaurant. One soldier was trying to order McNuggets which were sold in quantities of 6, 9 or 12. He asked for nine. The clerk kept asking what he wanted. He kept repeating, "nine Mcnuggets". They went back and forth for a long time and someone finally told him that in German nein means no. He was asking for no Mcnuggets. Ahhhh.

It is common in Spanish for people to mix up "tengo hambre" with "tengo hombre". The first means I am hungry. The second means I have a man.

Gary visited a Paris restaurant. He asked a lot of questions to which the waiter kept saying, "Oui" which means yes. Gary felt he had done well with his order until he received two complete meals.

In Spain, my husband thought that the common public sign of a man running was the sign for restroom. He realized, much to his distress, that it was the sign for exit. Dixie wrote me that in German the word for exit is ausfahrt.

Lance said the Chevy Nova didn't sell in Mexico. When they checked into why, they realized that in Spanish nova means "no go". He also had a friend who worked as a guide at the Henry Ford Village. He was nervous and his first tour was a bus of Spanish folks. As they passed the Thomas Edison lab, he got the translation wrong and told them, "This is the very building where Edison invented the electric vagina." After the bus roared with laughter, some kind person corrected him.

Gary was lost in a Moscow subway. Each stop had the same name and he was so confused. And then someone told him that sign said, "Watch your step".

Steve often travels to China and Taiwan with work. In these countries, they teach English as a second language. Early on the student chooses an English name that they use for the rest of their lives. He says they are often amusing. Some he has enjoyed – Rainbow Chen, Magic Hwa, and the quality engineer named Cheerful Wang. Steve says sometimes it is very hard to maintain your professional manners and etiquette, also not to laugh.

Elaine had a Russian exchange student who asked what she wanted to do that day. Elaine said she would play it by ear. A few days later the student said, "Today we will play it by eye".

A friend visited Spain and went shopping for very large sofa pillows. She walked in and asked for "cojones mas grandes que tengan". This translates to the biggest ones you have. The word for pillow is cojines. You will need to look up cojones for yourself.

Ah, yes, it is a wonder that we get along at all with people who speak other languages. A young student at the Spanish immersion school in Grand Rapids heard his teacher talking in English on the playground. "Oh," he asked her very surprised, "you speak person too?" If we can remember that our languages sound very different, yet we all do speak person too, the world just might make it.

How'd You Get So Funky?

Okay, I am taking a big risk here. I'm setting myself up. I'm not sure I should go on, but maybe, just maybe, some of you can relate. The rest of you who will read this and think you are all that and a bag of chips, the ones who will feel all full of yourselves, we will just refer to you as smartypants from here on out.

"What in the world is she talking about?" you ask. Just that– the world.

In particular, Egypt. My question to you, and let's be really honest here, is this. When you first heard of the revolt in Egypt, how many of you knew exactly where Egypt was? I have asked this to many folks in the past 24 hours. Some knew. Some did not. No one wanted to admit it.

A doctor looked at me rather amazed and said, "Of course." Tom said he knew, but then fessed up that he did look it up in Wikipedia to be sure of all the details.

Linda and Gisela each said, "Yes, I knew because I have been there." Okay, that obviously gave them a leg up.

Cindy said, "I know it is by Israel because that is where the Holy Family fled." "Oh, yeah", I said, "I remember that story. I just never thought about it much." It is hard to relate that story to the 6 o'clock news reports of revolt.

Frankly, I have never thought about where Egypt is. When I do think about Egypt, I first think about Steve Martin and his irreverent Egyptian song, *King Tut*. "How'd you get so funky? Did you do the monkey?" And later in the song, "Born in Arizona, Moved to Babylonia, King Tut."

I also think about the Nile River and the pyramids – at least I know they are in Egypt, except for the pyramid Steelcase built in Grand Rapids. I have worked in that one several times.

I, of course, think about Cleopatra. Elizabeth Taylor was so beautiful. Wasn't she? I know the budget for the movie, *Cleopatra*, was 2 million. They spent over – 44 million. That was mucho dinero in 1963 dollars. I also know Marc Anthony was played by Richard Burton. Something you may not know, all you smartypants who knew where Egypt was, there is a remake of *Cleopatra* in the works and it may star Angelina Jolie.

Oh, and I know other things about Egypt, too. I have seen *Joseph and the Amazing Technicolor Dreamcoat* many, many times. I own the CD and the DVD. Actually, I think my grandsons and I know the words to every single song. If not all the words, we could come pretty darn close. Is there a contest for that?

I know Pharaoh was a bad boy and he looked like Elvis. Or was that just in the play?

I know other things about Egypt. When you look it up on Google, the second thing that comes up is Egypt Valley Country Club and I've been there many times. I've also been to the Egyptian hotel in Vegas, the Luxor. Does that count? Okay, I just walked through the lobby twice. Whatever.

I don't know anything about Egyptian food. I haven't seen any Egyptian food cookbooks. I do know that Roz Lawrence said, "The best way to lose weight is to get the flu and take a trip to Egypt." I don't know who Roz Lawrence is, though.

I know the book, *Cleopatra: A Life*, was one of the 10 best non-fiction books of 2010. I also now know that Cleo, as I like to call her for short, was not a beauty. She spoke 9 languages and murdered one of her siblings. Cleo! Cleo!

I know that when we were in Spain last year, many of the T.V. ads were about traveling to Egypt for a trip. I know the Brits we met there travel to Egypt regularly for vacation. Hmmm, never thought about doing that.

So, am I ignorant because I asked my husband where Egypt was when the revolt began? I don't think so. I am like a whole bunch of Americans. It isn't so much that we don't know. It is more that we have never thought about it.

I know where odd countries like Muldova and Andorra are because I have had a personal reason to know. I guess I have never had a personal reason to know where Egypt is before.

Remember the 9-11 song by Alan Jackson, *Where Were You When the World Stopped Turning*? In it he sings, "I'm not sure I can tell you the difference in Iraq and Iran." For many of us, until we have a reason, our personal maps just say, "You are here." How'd we get so funky?

Looking At The World Through Different Eyes

Danny Burns   Louie Burns

Some of you know that we lived in Spain before we moved here. We recently returned for a month. We didn't tour or sightsee but got an apartment on the southern coast and absorbed ourselves into their culture and life again. It was interesting to note some differences in our American and Spanish cultures.

They were in the midst of enjoying the most rain they had had in fifty years. So the rain in Spain fell mainly on the plain, and the mountains, and the sea, and us. However the sun did come out nearly every day and there was no snow or ice.

One thing that tickled me was posters advertising a benefit, "Flamenco for Haiti", definitely something we don't see in the U.S.

Apparently Spain, and many other foreign countries, did not get the memo on the bad effects of smoking, which was rampant. It seems everyone smokes everywhere. Pregnant women were smoking. A guy next to me in the store paying for groceries was smoking. Restaurants were full of smoke. And the amazing thing is they smoke much harsher cigarettes. It felt like entering the world of *Mad Men* on T.V.

We were there during the Olympics. The T.V. had Spanish, Swedish and British channels. How funny to watch the Olympics through their eyes. America is mentioned about as often as U.S. coverage mentions France.

Commercials on T.V were often about visiting Egypt or Morocco, unusual for us.

The Academy Awards were not on regular T.V., but they did show reporters interviewing the actors as they left. No one wanted to talk to the international press and none of the major winners did. When they did get an actor to stop and chat, the actor kept looking around for someone else to talk with. Their announcers were at the very end of the line and the authorities kept yelling at them that if they crossed the line one more time, they were going to be kicked out. This all came through on their news broadcast.

Many restaurants don't open until 8 p.m. and don't get busy until 9 p.m. Those late meals may be why the siesta is still thriving. Nearly everything closes for a few hours in the afternoon. Even school kids go home for the break.

Things we did not see: Starbucks, baked potatoes or ranch dressing. They don't use butter or oil on their bread, but eat it dry. Desserts are not big, nor are their people.

Most people live in apartments. Cars and dogs are small. Walking is a national pastime.

Some things are universal, though. Cell phones were everywhere and people in restaurants were talking on them loudly. Teens were texting.

The thing that gave me the most pause was the grocery stores. They had grocery carts like we do, but they were chained. You had to pay to use them. You got a little basket for free. I couldn't help wonder about that - certainly different than our American big box mentality.

One night we saw a bullfight on T.V., live with instant replays. See him stab the bull. See him stab the bull again. Yup, he really did stab him! One more time.

Animal rights activists are up in arms over the bullfights. But like our politics, there are two views. Some see it as Art. Recently on 60 Minutes, two Spanish bullfighters were interviewed and one of them had been fighting on the show we watched. He did so well that they cut off the bull's tail and both ears as trophies. He carried them around the ring waving them as the crowd waved hankies and cheered.

Just because they stab the bull over and over until he falls dead, drag him out of the ring bloody, then cut off his ears and tail and wave them around as trophies – why do they think that's barbaric? It certainly is different than watching golf on T.V.

You know the song, *We are the World*. Well, it turns out that is not true. We are just a corner of the world. Spain is more like the United States than it is different. However, we each have our own uniqueness and flavor. Ole.

Lost

We lost our son twice. Once was at a campground in France next to a raging river. All of a sudden the nearly 2-year-old boy was gone. We called and searched to no avail. We knew if he had gone in the river there wasn't a prayer of survival.

After an interminable time, we heard someone yell, "And don't come back in here!" as they kicked him out of their tent. Ahhh. Thank you, God.

The second time we lost our son was at Festival of the Arts in Grand Rapids, Michigan, and he was about 7.

As we arrived, I mentioned if anyone got lost there was a booth for lost children. Of course, I never expected anyone to need it. We were attentive parents, after all.

But, later, we looked around and saw no son. We, again, called and searched to no avail. Finally we went to the lost children's booth and there he sat coloring. Luckily he had remembered my mentioning that booth. I remember he sat there looking so brave but when he saw us he burst into tears. Being lost is a horrible thing. Fear is a giant.

My husband got lost on his very first day of school. He was just 5 and so excited about school that he jumped off the bus at the wrong school and then got to the door and panicked as he realized he didn't know where he was. He was alone. He was lost. Fortunately an older cousin saw him and helped him get where he needed to be.

Being lost is a horrible thing. Fear is a giant. It must be an especially huge giant for a lost child.

I got to spend a few days with two lost boys. Their story is different. Their families didn't save them. Their families had been killed.

These boys were left abandoned, alone. They were the age of my grandson, who just started kindergarten. They didn't have backpacks or snacks to ease their journey. They didn't have nice tennis shoes to walk in. They walked without help from anyone. They walked and they walked and they walked. They walked for years.

They walked with hope in their heart. Hope for survival. It turns out that staying alive is a great motivating force even when one's life is grim and horrific.

For a moment, think about telling a kindergartner you know that he should go off for, let's say, 10 years and be on his own. He should scrounge the earth for his food and water. He should sleep on the ground. He should not worry about the lions and other wild animals that might attack him at any moment. He should just keep a positive attitude and a faith in God that all will be O.K. Someday. Some year. Maybe. If he's lucky. Or blessed. Or both.

You might also remind him that if, and when, he meets adult strangers that they can't necessarily be trusted. They may offer something nice but then turn him into a slave.

They might also kill him. Yes, the adult stranger might be just as dangerous as the hungry lion.

But don't be dismayed, you might add. You may end up in a good place. You could even end up in America. You might even write a book on your time being lost. Who knows, maybe someone will begin to call you "the lost boys". If you really dream big, you could end up in Greenville, Michigan, telling your unbelievable story to a whole bunch of people.

These people won't really be able to fathom what you will tell them. Their lives will have been quite cushy. They will eat lots every day. They will sleep in beds. Those beds will be in houses with roofs and those houses won't fall down when it rains. They won't have to walk anyplace because they will all have cars, even the students will have cars.

And, you will find this hard to believe, but all the children get to go to school. They will even feed them at school. They will even have books and paper to write on at school. And pens and pencils to write with.

I know this is all very hard for you to imagine, but it is true. So, keep the faith, my sons. Keep walking and walking and walking. And then, walk some more. And if you survive and you get to this place they call Greenville, if you truly do all these things, be careful as you tell your story. Because as T.S. Eliot said, "Humankind cannot bear very much reality." But then again, you must go ahead and bravely tell your story because these people need to hear it. They need to know what the world is like for others and that they have been lucky or blessed or both.

****

The Lost Boys above wrote a book called, *They poured fire on us from the sky.* More than 900 people heard them speak about their experiences. There were some unbelievable things they didn't share in their talks, but shared easily as we chattedover the three days we spent with them. Here are some of those things.

Alephonsion said, "One day I really thought I would die from the lion. Because there were so many dead children lying around the land, the lions got the taste for human flesh. This day the lions chased me and I raced up a tree for safety. The lions wouldn't leave. They waited. After a long time I threw a piece of tree down and hit one lion in the head. They then slunk off and I was able to come down." He, of course, was just a boy.

He woke up in bed one night and between him and his brother was a snake. He also got up one night in his hut and heard an odd sound. He stepped on something strange. His brother got up and, as they had no electricity, lit a torch so they could see what it was. It was a big boa constrictor. "I think it came into our hut to eat rats."

They described their huts proudly and said some were as big as Applebee's Restaurant.
Benjamin said they would often see deadly poisonous spiders and one had to be careful not to step on them as they would also be in their huts.

One day Aleph saw a boa eat a goat. It swallowed almost the entire goat when his mother came out and banged something on the snake. It coughed out the goat which lay stunned and nearly breathless. After days, the goat recovered.

Benson, who wasn't with them in Greensville (which is how they pronounced it), but is Alephonsion's brother, lives with them in San Diego and co-wrote the book. He remembered something their mother always said to them. Each day as the planes bombed their village, she would say, "They pour fire upon us from the sky." Thus, the book title.

Benjamin flew into New York City from the refugee camp on September 11. He looked out and saw the towers on fire. Then they were diverted to Canada. He thought that was what America must be like. He was used to war.

They said seeing other children with legs all swollen was a normal sight and meant they had been bitten by snakes. Once bitten, they would die. It would take about three days and then they would begin to foam white at the mouth. Then death. My daughter, Donna, asked him, "What would you do then?"

"We didn't do anything. We had nothing to do. We just knew they would die soon."

Once they referred to being caught by the bad army and being forced to be their soldiers. They did not go into further detail on this.
There were so many horrible things they experienced. Even though the audience wanted to hear about those things, I don't think they can spend their days reliving that. They have to move on. The horror would be too much to keep retelling it.

As I took them to Saginaw for their next talk, someone asked them, "Do you ever have bad dreams of it all?" Benjamin said, "Yes, of course."

Alephonsion said, "Do you mean nightmares? Oh, YES, I have them all the time. They never stop."

Many people asked me, "What happened to the girls?" The girls were raped and murdered or taken as slaves.

Our friend in Lansing works with the United Nations and was in the refugee camp they were in. He was there for months interviewing 500 boys. Each wrote or told their story of survival for him. He then was part of the group that chose who got to leave. He has copies of all those stories, which are called "applications for resettlement". One, Paul, said, "We lost most of our friends on our exodus, leaving them behind with vultures feasting on them merrily."

He goes on, "One wonders how men as young as I could manage such a dangerous journey. It was God's Power that really directed and gave strength." He says that he used to hope for peace in his country but then came to lose hope in that dream and "Now I want to apply for new and permanent citizenship. Thank you for your consideration." He signs it with his name and ration card number. They all had a ration card number and that is how they were known in the camps. Alephonsion and Benjamin were in the camp for 9 years.

How would I describe these boys? Positive, faith-filled, great senses of humor, easy to talk to and relate with, handsome, caring, gentle, very bright and well educated, wanting to learn all the time. Yesterday they asked Donna, "What is a DVR? How does that work?" And they intently listened to her explanation.

Alephonsion mentioned books he had just read: *Eat, Pray, Love, The Secret Life of Bees, The Audacity of Hope*, Bill and Hillary Clinton's auto-biographies, and on and on. He said he likes to read the lives of people so he can learn about life. My friends in Lansing who have had ten lost boys live with them said, "You begin thinking you are helping them but it turns out they help you. You become a much better person and you realize you have been greatly honored to have had this opportunity."

My daughter, my husband and I feel we have been greatly honored to have been able to spend time with these two young men who are in their twenties now. And as we hugged good-by I told them, "I hope our paths will cross again." And with a tear in my eye and a lump in my throat, I thought, and if we do, I will be the lucky one.

Alephonsion Deng, Mureen, Benjamin Ajak

New York State Of Mind

This past weekend, my niece got married In New York City – on a rooftop in Soho. It was a way cool experience for us and one with glaring differences from our normal life.

We overheard someone say, "Yeah, the bride is from a small town in Michigan." Of course, that small town is Grand Rapids, which we think of as a big town. It is the second largest city in our state, after all.

I can see where they're coming from, though. To New Yorkers our area must seem small. New York City has over 8 million people. The entire state of Michigan has about 9 million. Grand Rapids has about 188 thousand. Translate that to a different view – New York City has about 67,000 people per square mile, Grand Rapids has about 5,000 per square mile, and to get an even clearer perspective, Montcalm County has 82 people per square mile. So, I guess, coming from their point of view, we are small.

Some other interesting differences: you can't talk on a hand held phone while driving; you can't smoke while driving; and you can't put on make-up while driving. That did not seem to distract the driver next to us who was filming a video while he drove.

My husband and I have thought we would love to live in New York City if we could afford it. Of course, that is never going to happen – the affording part. Everything in New York City is more expensive. A movie is 13 buckos. Can you imagine what popcorn and a drink costs? A cocktail can run $15.

New York City is a young people's city. The average New Yorker walks 3-4 miles a day just to do what they have to do. I didn't see many overweight people living there. Also, although I am sure all codes are met, nothing that we did or saw seemed very handicap accessible. I was mighty glad I had both of my knees replaced.

I have a fear of flying. Oh, I fly when I need to, but I don't enjoy the thought of what I'm doing and turbulence can instantly bring on a rosary, terror or even spontaneous tears. After being in New York taxis for a couple of days, I told my husband that I needn't have worried about dying in a plane. Clearly my life was much more in danger in a cab. And in the midst of all the taxis driving like maniacs, there were lots of bicyclists pedaling along just inches away from the reckless drivers . . . and they weren't even wearing helmets. I could hardly watch.

I read that there are 170 languages spoken in New York City. We went to Mass in Spanish. The mass after ours was in Chinese, and it was full. While on Canal Street, people kept accosting us, yelling at us in Chinese, wanting us to buy things. My daughter and I both found ourselves answering in Spanish, then laughing at how crazy that was. People do weird things in uncomfortable situations.

My niece who lives there said, "There are no Meijers, only small corner shops for groceries and pharmacies. There is no one stop shopping. You have to go to several stores to get what you need and then lug it all for blocks." Did I say it is a young peoples' city?

There seems to be some creative job opportunities, though. In the midst of the constant crowd on the streets of Times Square was a woman, a very old, wrinkled, and extremely worn out woman making money in the most resourceful way. She billed herself as the Naked Cowgirl. There is a naked cowboy down there, but we didn't get to see him. She was more than enough to take in. She wore a skimpy pair of bikini underpants made out of American flag looking fabric and a map of the city stuck in her crack, I mean back. She wore a cowgirl hat and boots and nothing else, except a couple of pasties on her breasts. Oh, I forgot. She also wore a guitar. In the American way, tourists would give her a buck to take a photo. I didn't pay her but I did take some shots. I knew it wasn't right. The devil made me do it.

In spite of the things I have mentioned, it's a fabulous city with everything - everything to do, everything to see, and everything to experience. We loved it. But I gotta say, it did feel wonderful to return to small town Michigan.

Martin Mull said, "The town where I grew up has a zip code of E-I-E-I-O." At least we are bigger than that. And we have a Meijers too!

Viva Las Vegas

Many businesses hold conferences at The Shack located in Jugsville, near White Cloud. This weekend I was in Las Vegas with my three daughters celebrating one of their birthdays. I have been to Vegas three times and I really think it should switch names with Jugsville.

No matter where in the whole world you are from, Las Vegas is the opposite. Rita Rudner says, "Everything is legal in Vegas. The only people in jail are those who litter."

You don't see clocks in Vegas. Many times you have no idea what time it is because casinos and hotels are so mammoth. You could walk for days and never see the sun. People get disoriented. You can hear folks say, "I think it's 4 a.m., guess I'll go have lunch."

There is an anthem that seems to permeate the Vegas atmosphere. Whatever you do here stays here – anything goes.

You look at people dressed in crazy get-ups. You wonder, 'did the airlines lose everyone's luggage?' It is clear that what you can wear in Vegas, would probably not work in your home life.

Everyone says this is a really bad financial time in America. People all across the country are without jobs. You wouldn't know it in Vegas. The planes are full. The taxis are full and can't keep up. One taxi driver told me, "I think we are as busy as we have ever been."

Restaurants are full. Shows are full. Streets are full. And, of course, casinos are full. Wherever the hard times are in the good ole U.S.A., Vegas didn't get the memo.

Las Vegas is the wedding capital. Over 100,000 people get married there each year. Unfortunately, the divorce rate is said to be way higher than normal. I heard that it is at 75%, but who knows if you can believe what you hear on the streets in Vegas. You might not want to bet on it.

Casinos are not my thing. Well, I like the hotels. I just don't like the casinos. I don't like to gamble. I never want to throw my money away. It seems so crazy. I know you can win. One of my daughters won 80 bucks quite quickly. But I am afraid to take the chance. When it comes to money, I am quite sure I don't have the luck of the Irish.

It always makes me feel sad to see the casinos full and people feeding the machines and tables with their hard earned cash. Most folks don't look like they have money to burn, yet burn it they do - burn, baby, burn.

Kent Andersson said, "I felt sorry for myself because I had no hands until I met a man who had no chips."

People sit gambling for hours. They toss money away for entertainment. There seems to be a kind of "betters rule". Play till you win and when you win, play till you lose it. I know what it is like to have eyes bigger than my stomach. Eyes in the casinos are like that. They seem to always see themselves winning more than they ever win.

I gambled once on this trip. I ordered liver at a nice seafood restaurant. What was I thinking? Who knows! I guess I was in a gamblin' mood. I lost. I should have had the fish or a V8 or anything else. I would have been better to not even have ordered. At least then I would have saved my money. That was the extent of my Vegas gambling. Losing is losing, no matter how you look at it.

I do love the shows in Vegas. I had to laugh that Cher, Garth and The Judds were all having their "last" shows. We had seen Cher, Garth and The Judds each do their last shows years ago. In fact, we saw Cher do her last show two years in a row. Last doesn't mean what it used to mean. I think it now means - times are rough, we gotta get back to work.

The only show we saw this time was comedienne, Rita Rudner. She had some wonderful lines. She said when she works she hires an impersonator of herself to babysit so her daughter never knows she's gone. She said, "Vegas is the only place in the world where you can go to the top of the Eiffel Tower and look down on Rome. It is also the only place in the world where you can take a gondola to The Gap."

Yes, Las Vegas is definitely a world like no other. It is a crazy, wild, beyond glitzy, unnormal kinda place.

Each of us has different likes and dislikes. You may be like me and not like to gamble, but rest assured, there will be other things you will enjoy in Vegas. And remember Jimmy Jones' advice. "Make a bet every day, otherwise you might walk around lucky and never know it."

Times Like These

It is always good to pause for a moment and reflect on how good our life is in Michigan. Oh, I am very aware of the negative. But, hey, look around your sweet self. You are likely reading this in one of the most wonderful and beautiful states in the union. Michigan deserves a moment of pause and praise.

Kid Rock performed his song, "Times Like These", at the American Music Awards. He knocked my socks off, got a standing ovation from the sold-out crowd, and more than did Michigan proud.

In a show full of flash and pop, Kid rock stole the show with just a stool and a microphone. He not only proved less is more, he proved nothing can be as moving as true passion and caring. Videos ran behind him with scenes of Michigan. Though much of the focus was on recent economic problems in Detroit, much of it was on the beauty of our fine state.

"I heard them say they're shutting Detroit down. But I won't leave because this is my hometown. It's times like these we can't replace and it's times like these we must embrace. Even though it's bittersweet and it brings us to our knees. It makes us who we are in times like these."

I thought about what he was singing and I thought about how much I love Michigan. Do you? Have you thought about it lately?

I grew up in the country in Ottawa County. We had to go 7 miles to get milk. Oh,

I guess we had the option of going out to the barn to milk the cow, but you couldn't get cookies with her.

I lived for a few years in Grand Rapids, a shining star in our state, for sure. Actually, as I travel the country, I think Grand Rapids is a shining star in the whole country.

I lived in East Lansing and enjoyed one of the two greatest universities around. How cool is Michigan that we sport both MSU and U of M. As much fun as we have with rivalry, I am so proud to have both be a part of our state. All you have to do is visit other states to see how blessed we are with these and the many, many beautiful colleges and universities we take for granted. Not every state has these options.

I have lived in small town U.S.A. for most of my married life, a.k.a. Greenville. People who live in bigger cities have no idea how cool this kind of life is. Almost everyone I talk with agrees. We love the values, advantages and lifestyle of our small town.

Growing up on the west side of Michigan, I took for granted that all you had to do to get an apple was walk out the door and pick one off a tree. All I had to do to get berries was cross the street, bend over and pick them. Veggies were abundant in the garden. Talk about the greening of America, wherever I turned there were fruits and vegetables. I never really appreciated this until my friend, Alison, in California, went on and on about how she couldn't believe we grew up with cherries and apples. For her, they were an expensive luxury that had to be sent in from places like Michigan.

We take for granted the sportsman's paradise that surrounds us. Wanna ski? You got it. Wanna golf? We have over 800 pristine courses. Wanna fish? Are you kidding me? Turn right, turn left, go in any direction and don't forget your bait.

Want to go boating? Want to go to balloon fests? Want to swim or walk the beach? There are something like 200 lakes in our county alone. Michigan has the world's longest fresh water coastline. We sport some of the highest freshwater sand dunes in the world. We are blessed with shimmering beaches that you can walk and walk and walk.

Like light houses? Michigan has more than 100. Want to camp or picnic? Michigan has more than 99 state parks and tons more city and county parks.

We have islands. They range from rustic, like Beaver Island, to Victorian fancy. Mackinac Island boasts the Grand Hotel which is America's largest summer resort hotel and more than a century old. It is written up as one of the best in the country and remains *Somewhere in Time*. But don't bring your car, the horse will take you wherever you need to go if your legs or bike can't.

While driving recently, I actually saw buffalo roaming. We also have moose, bear and deer. In fact, if you want to see a deer, just go park your car on a road and one will come out and smash into you, pronto. I promise.

Michigan is clean, green and beautiful. If you don't believe it, visit another state and you will immediately be stunned by their litter. Michigan just says no to litter.

Michigan is so cool we even have our own stones. Right, Petoskey?

When I had a major birthday a couple years ago, my family took me on a mystery trip . . . to Detroit. It may not sound glamorous, but we saw fabulous plays, ate fine meals in wonderful restaurants, visited Greek Town, and stayed in the Renaissance Center. We took the People Mover. We felt safe.

So, thanks to Kid Rock who makes us pause and be thankful for our Michigan. 'This is our home and it's times like these we can't replace. It's times like these we must embrace. Even though the hard times are bittersweet and bring us to our knees, it makes us who we are in times like these.' Ah, yes, I'm very thankful for Michigan.

A Toothpick, A Beer Cap, A Nail And Some Ice

Give me a couple toothpicks and I will likely stick them in a cake to see if it's done or I may pick sweet corn out of my teeth. That's about the extent of my toothpick use.

Give me a beer cap and I'll toss it.

Give me a nail and I might pound it into a wall to hang something.

Give me some ice and I'll put it in my glass or on my sore body.

What I won't do with toothpicks, beer caps, nails and ice is think of making art. That brainstorm will never hit me. It will not even be a glimmer in my radar of thought.

Greg Lewis, from North Carolina, is not like me. He saw a toothpick and thought, 'if only I could get 86,999 more of these, I could sculpt a mermaid.' Who thinks like that? People who enter ArtPrize think like that – and lots of them.

ArtPrize in Grand Rapids is an annual fall event. Nearly 1,800 artists from around the globe have artwork displayed – free for the world to come see. And lucky for us, we are the world.

Where else can an artist from Gowen display their artwork with artists from Poland, Israel and Russia?

Greg Lewis took 18 months to craft his toothpick mermaid. She is beautiful, breathtaking, really. She began with one toothpick that became her lips. Hundreds then formed her face. It took months to sculpt her trunk. She has long golden fingernails, all toothpicks. Her curly hair enthralled me. How in the world did he do it? Her scales used 32,250 toothpicks.

Another gifted artist took 1,000 pounds of nails to form a life size lion and other animals. They stand in their beautiful glory.

It took Derek Maxfield and Randy Finch nine months to make colored sculptures out of 3,500 pounds of ice. They could have made a baby in that time.

ArtPrize is interactive in many ways. Besides all the oohing and ahhing, people can sit in laid back seats and listen to things. People go into some of the artwork to participate with it. "Accord" is a metal sculpture that plays tones as you move in front of it. Twenty pianos are placed around the city inviting you to "Play me. I'm yours." I watched Eva, Avery and Gracie, ages one to three, as they sat together playing a tune to their own drummer.

One man is a sculpture in bronze. You think he is not real and then he moves. Even his eyeballs look bronze. He comes to life and gets the audience to move with him as he talks to them. Then all of a sudden, he freezes again. Awesome to watch.

A Grand Valley State University student from Lowell took 43,000 beer caps to make a six foot tall cactus in gold and silver. The caps were donated from local breweries. Thank God. That's too many beers for even a college student to drink.

Lori Hough from Freemont used papier-mache to make a lifelike mama and baby giraffe. I wish I could have brought them home. They warmed my heart like a big hug.

Most of the artwork is so unusual that I can't find words to describe it to you. Janice Arnold from Olympia, Washington, made an enormous ceiling hanging out of felt. It had to be experienced as you walked through the art museum hallway and it hung above and over you. She was there, as many artists were, and I did that dumb thing people do. I asked Janice if she knew my friend from Olympia. How fun that she did know him well. It is a small world after all.

Lorna Poulos sculpted an ornate 6 by 8 foot gold gilded picture frame and also painted the lifelike scene on the canvas, "The Last Dance".

Maybe one cannot see all the art exhibited. But one can have an absolutely wonderful time seeing all you can. I would encourage you to try hard to get to ArtPrize. Go downtown Grand Rapids and park in a lot. It will be worth it, trust me. Get out and start walking. Art is everywhere, inside and outside. Signs easily show you where to go.

I love fruit, but how hard would it be to decide if I like a banana more than a juicy orange or a crisp fall apple - really impossible. Add to that kiwi, raspberries, blueberries, mango, pineapple. My list goes on. I have a lot of favorites.

Thus, with ArtPrize, how can we choose which one is best? We can't. They are all winners. Some we like more than others, but we appreciate all of them. And we appreciate the time, talent and creativity so gloriously displayed.

One piece really did knock my socks off, though. I love black and white photography. Ryan Spencer Reed from Ludington has done 21 framed photos of battered Detroit. They will stay in my memory for a very long time and it was a privilege to see the young man from another small town that did such creative work.

So I suggest you run, don't walk, to ArtPrize. On a scale of one to ten, it is a 99. Bravo to everyone involved. It is one more blessing for living where we do. Don't miss it. Your day and life will be richer for the experience.

Holidaze Throughout The Year

A Slow Start

It always takes me a couple weeks to go from an old year into a new year. I like to think it will only take me a day or two for this transition but reality bites. Each year I kinda lose half of January in anticipation of January.

Am I alone on this crazy journey? I still have to end all the Christmas card stuff. There are some decorations still up. I have a couple gifts left to exchange. The new calendar is not up to snuff yet. Why do we say up to snuff? Yuck. And, I am really exhausted from the whole holiday ordeal, as nice as it was. Perhaps I should have asked for a box of energy for Christmas.

So anyway, along with this whining over my sluggish start to the New Year comes this mental hanging on to last year. In that process I am still thinking of all the folks who died last year and how they touched us. Those T.V. and magazine lists always get me. Farewell lists of who died last year.

Walter Cronkite - Mr. Trust. Who will ever get over the shock of him saying, "President Kennedy died at 1 p.m. central standard time." His sincere demeanor. The tear and the lump in his throat were something that touched us forever. He was the gold standard for newsmen.

Paul Harvey. Years ago I was fortunate to go with some local folks to hear him speak. There were several motivational speakers and he came on late in the day. I tell ya - when he walked out on stage and bellowed, "Hellow, America" - wow. All I can remember is he had me at hello, for sure. The thrill of those words from his booming unique voice was really something you never forget.

Farrah Fawcett. She was an angel. Now she is another angel. I liked her. She may have been the first female sex symbol to wear tennis shoes, jog and carry a gun. What I really remember the most about her was that poster. You know the one. Was it plastered on your teenage son's wall too? And then who expected her to turn into a great actress, but she did. In the movie, The Burning Bed, she put a face on domestic violence for all to see.

Paul Newman. Be still my heart. He had it all. And I love his salad dressings too. Patrick Swayze, Andrew Wyeth, Karl Malden, Ted Kennedy, American soldiers in Iraq and Afghanistan and Millard Fuller, the founder of Habitat for Humanity. All gone.

Eunice Kennedy Shriver, the founder of Special Olympics. I took my girls to volunteer for the International Special Olympics. It was an event that changes you.

Mary from Peter, Paul and Mary. "Where have all the flowers gone." "If I had a hammer." "Puff, the magic dragon." I am seeing my life flash before my eyes. What a loss. Peter and Paul alone just won't cut it.

A few years ago she was on my plane going to Philadelphia. I saw her and wondered if it was Mary. One tip off was she was tall, built like Mary, had long blond straight hair. The real kicker was she was in first class and I, of course, wasn't. I saw Paul meet her. It could have been Peter. It was the short one. We ended up, just the 3 of us, in the elevator together. I tried to hold myself back but I couldn'tl, so I asked them, "Are you Peter, Paul and Mary?" They gave me a look like, "DUH." They could have said, "The answer my friend . . . "

We took some of our kids to see them perform once. I remember my kids knew the words to every song and I felt so proud. When they sang, "Blowin' in the Wind" to the packed house with lighters lit all over in the dark, it was one of the most moving memories. They were part of the history of our lives.

So, the year is over. Farewell to it and them. We look ahead. We wonder what this new year will bring. We know life will change. We wrap up all this end-of-year, beginning-of-year stuff and we jump back into the ring. But as I end this bit of melancholic remembering of people, I am also remembering a quote by H.G. Wells. They were his last words, actually. "Go away. I'm all right."

Looking Back

Ah, another year gone, another year beginning. How sweet it is!

At this time of year I always love all the end of year lists – the top ten movies, the top ten books, the top ten news stories . . .
What about our personal lists? What were our top ten "things"? As we got Christmas letters, folks often covered their year high points. This is a week to contemplate our own past year.

I spent half the year worrying about my husband's upcoming retirement. Someone today asked me what I had been worrying about. I think it was about two things. The big ending of a life we had known and the big beginning of a life we had never experienced.

Now, after being six months into our new life, I find it to be quite wonderful. Change is good and this has been a year full of lots of new growth for both of us.

Growth is one of life's most special gifts. There is no standing still in life. One is either going forwards or backwards. Bob Dylan said, "He who is not busy growing is busy dying". The gift that change gives us is growth. Sometimes we don't ask for the gift. Sometimes we don't want it. Sometimes life just pushes us into it. Ready or not, here it comes.

At the end of each year I like to make a list of the ways I have grown in the previous year. It is rewarding to see the new things tried and accomplished, even the small steps taken toward new growth.

I love the thought that we are surrounded by our comfort zone, what we know and do comfortably. Then we try new things, meet new people, go new places, and our comfort zone expands. We become more and we never go back to the way we were. We have grown and it is permanent. It is good.

When we look back at our year, it had new music, new T.V. shows, new books, new movies, new plays. We met new people. We learned new games. We went new places. We tried new things, some good, some bad, some mediocre.

Some of us had health issues. Some we care about survived huge health scares. People we care about passed. All of this makes us realize that our health is a gigantic blessing and one we must tend to in the New Year. Exercise will be a must for many of us and it should be for the entire year, not just for the January after holiday fitness craze.

The past year full of friends and family, and the love and support they gave us, makes us realize that people are life's very best thing. Oh, and dogs. Let's not forget about the dogs. And for all my cat lovin' friends, the cats too. And for all my horse lovin' friends, the horses too. So let's not forget about tending to the people and animals in our lives. We need them. They fill our cups. And our water bowls.

A special blessing many of us had this year was meeting the two lost boys from Sudan. Yesterday, Alephonsion, called from California to wish us a happy holiday. He said that he really doesn't know much about this holiday stuff as they didn't have holidays before. He said he wanted to call us because we had touched his life this year. All I could think was that it was the other way around. They touched our lives in precious ways. But he made me realize that we also touch others and many times we have no idea when we have done so.

So in looking back, who touched us this year and whom did we touch? What were our high points? What ways did we grow? What are we especially grateful for? Who came into our lives and who left our lives and how did that change us? What are our best memories from the year?

As we begin a new year, what should we change, what should we stop, what should we begin? Looking at our physical, emotional, intellectual, and spiritual sides, how should we move forward in each of these areas.

A Prayer for the New Year

Please bless me in this New Year. Help me to be a good person. Please enter my heart and remove all anger, fear and pain. Help me to forgive and begin anew. Refresh my spirit. Please bless every person and situation I will encounter. Thank you for the past year and this upcoming year. Help me to live this new year with grace, dignity, purpose and goodness. Help me to make a positive difference and to be a good example. Thank you for this opportunity of life and this new year to grow in. Amen

Just One Big Change

I am making some major changes. I should have done it years ago. Basically, it is just one change, but it's a big one.

I am changing January 1 to February 1. January 1 is just too much pressure for me. I mean, we just got through major holiday stress. I'm not really what you could call through it, either. There are still things to return, some things to arrive – yes, gifts are still "in the mail" and we are patiently waiting. Okay, impatiently, but definitely, waiting.

For instance, the book my daughter ordered for me on how to change my life is back ordered. Not a good omen. But then again, I feel rather back ordered myself.

So much holiday residue to finish off. There are holiday decorations sitting like remnants around the house. And dealing with the guilt about that big metal Santa I kept forgetting to set out – and, in fact, never did. He's still in the basement in a corner. How long do I need to feel guilty about that?

There is a big pile of gift bags and wrapping stuff that I notice every time I glance under my office table. It just lays there and silently says, "Put me away, would ya?" I try to ignore it. I'm waiting for the energy to come so I can deal with it. The energy seems to be having its own vacation someplace else, certainly not in my body.

Discussing this concept with my friends today, they agreed. January 1 is too soon to begin anew. As a friend put it, "For one thing, we still have all those goodies to finish up." Amen to that.

I wonder what folks who begin diets on January 1 do with all the left-over goodies. Do they toss them? That might be a sin. Do they give them away? I don't know anyone who really wants them. Everyone I know has their own left-over goodies. Yes, we need to eat those left-over goodies. That is the only right thing to do. We are no quitters!

There are holiday thank you notes to write. That is for those who still practice the ancient art of putting pen to paper, instead of putting finger to computer key. How long can we wait before it is too late to send them? Time is always on our backs.

There is the organizing of our holiday notes. You know - the lists of people you sent cards to, the lists you bought gifts for, the food you made. I always do lists. I have only once, though, in 43 years of wedded bliss, remembered where I put those very helpful lists when I needed them the following holiday. There is a trick there, I'm sure. It just keeps eluding me.

There are all those things you got half price at the after holiday sales. You need to decide why you really bought them and where you should put them. The why is sometimes the hardest part. Oh, yeah, I remember. They were half off.

Then there are all those people you put off seeing. You know, the ones to whom you said, "Let's get together after the holidays." And you meant it. Doing it, however, is much harder to accomplish. The intent is sincere. The reality of getting it done is not as easy as it sounds.

There is that big ole pile of holiday music you have to put away. And as you do, one needs to decide which ones to keep and which ones to give. This is a hard chore because after the holidays, you really don't want to listen to any of it one more time.

I guess what I want January to be about is regrouping my life. Oh, I want all the New Year goal stuff to become a reality. I just need some time to ease in to it. I think I need a few naps. I need to chill – and I don't mean outdoors. I need to be done with all the holiday after glow. Perhaps it is more dim than glowing, but you know what I mean. I also need time to really think about all the ways I want and need to change my life, all the goals I need to set and reset.

Changing your life takes energy, focus, clarity of purpose. Basically, it takes everything we've got. We need time to ease on into this.

I am not sure who ever decided January 1 would be the beginning of our new better life and higher self. Is it the same person who said we would just get all excited over New Years Eve and want to stay up late, kiss everyone around and drink champagne with gusto? Is that person retiring soon? I think they should. In my life, this philosophy is not quite as relevant as it once was. In fact, it hasn't been relevant to my life for many, many years. I think it could even be another one of those myths played on us by the media.

I am guessing that more people would stick to their New Year goals if they began them in February. This is such a wise concept; I am shocked it hasn't been suggested sooner.

So, for all of you who agree with me, let's just all agree to begin the New Year on February 1. Let's unleash our old January 1 bondages. Let's write our own life journey in our time frame. I feel free-er already. I feel energized, well, a tiny bit.

Should old acquaintance be forgot? Nah, but perhaps January 1 and all the hype of what it means should be. Happy New Year – just a couple more weeks before we begin it on February 1. Prepare ye, prepare.

Top Of The Mornin' To Ya

Being St. Patrick's Day is upon us, I thought I would toast the Irish a wee bit.

So, this Irishman walks out of a bar . . . no, really, it can happen.

Why are the jokes about the Irish always about drinking? My husband's family is 100% Irish and they don't drink . . . that much!

For the Irish, a seven course meal is a six pack and a potato. That's not true for everyone – I don't even like beer.

Mickey worked at the brewery in Milwaukee. One day he fell into a vat of beer and drowned. His co-workers went to tell his wife. "Bridget, we hate to tell you this, but Mickey fell into a vat of beer today and drowned."

"Oh, me God," she said, "Did he suffer much?"

"I don't think so. He got out three times to go to the bathroom." Okay, so that isn't true, but it is funny.

A guy came home late and drunk. He fell and landed on his bottom, breaking the whiskey bottles in his back pockets. He was cut and bleeding on his backside, so he put on some Band-Aids and went to bed. The next morning, his wife said, "You were drunk last night, weren't you?"

"Why would you say such a mean thing?"

"Well," she replied, "it could be the open front door, or the broken glass on the floor, or the blood trailing through the house, or your bloodshot eyes, but mostly . . . it's all those Band-Aids stuck on the hall mirror."

Now the Irish are known for more than their drinking. Yessiree, Paddy.

Paddy was in a hurry and looking for a parking spot. Being religious, he prayed. "Lord, take pity on me. If you find me a parking spot, I will go to Mass every day for the rest of me life and give up me Irish whiskey."

Miraculously, a parking spot appeared. Paddy looked up to heaven and said, "Never mind, I found one."

An Irish couple drove for miles, not saying a word. An earlier discussion had led to an argument and neither wanted to concede their position. (When I read that part, I said to my husband, "Been there." He also knew it well.)

As the couple passed a barnyard of goats, mules and pigs, the husband asked sarcastically, "Relatives of yours?" "Yep," the wife answered, "in-laws."

The Irish are also known for fighting. "Is this a private fight or can anybody join in?"

I sent out a request for Irish jokes and got lots. Most I couldn't print, but I gotta say, I did enjoy them.

Lloyd wrote about his Dutch, Catholic, Scotch-Irish, and Protestant ancestry – a mixed marriage, as he called it. He said his father had great Irish wit and always said that the bag pipe was invented by the Irish and given to the Scots as a joke . . . and the Scots haven't caught on yet.

The Irish are known for their limericks. This is a favorite of ours. It's best when read aloud.

> "There once was a man from Hyde
>
> Who fell through an outhouse and died.
>
> His unfortunate brother fell through another
>
> And now they're interred side by side."

This isn't really Irish, but it is true. When I heard Temple Grandin speak, a man got up and talked about how he wanted to be a scientist and never work with people, because he didn't like people and didn't want to have to see people or talk to people. She interrupted him and said, "What work do you do?" "Oh, I'm a Catholic priest," he said. That brought the house down. And to top it off, I knew that priest and he probably should have become a scientist. I'm pretty sure he wasn't Irish.

My son said he frequently thinks of Irish luck. He believes there really is an unbeatable optimism in Irish people and he is often reminded of his Grandpa Burns upbeat perspective. "It's like stepping in dog poop in your bare feet and thinking how lucky you are not to have your good shoes on."

The joke I received that made me think of doing this column was this.

A hooded robber robs a bank. As he carries the bag of money out, an Irish customer grabs off his hood and looks at his face. The robber shoots and kills him. He then looks around and says, "Did anybody else see my face?"

After a few seconds, another Irishman tentatively says, "I think me wife might have caught a glimpse."

Enjoy St. Patrick's Day folks, whether you are Irish or not. Have a few good laughs and maybe some green beer or a Shamrock Shake. I will close with this.

When creating men, God promised women that good and ideal men would be found in all corners of the world . . . and then he made the earth round.

That God, he's such a joker.

Perhaps he's Irish.

Hope, A Purposeful Life And A Satisfied Soul

I heard a study recently that 23% of Americans go shopping on Sunday, 85% watch at least 4 hours of T.V., 42% socialize and 23% go to church. Tomorrow is Easter Sunday. What does that mean? It means churches will be full, very full. Why? Because there will be that influx of folks who come twice a year – Easter and Christmas.

Easter also means chocolate bunnies, Peeps, decorated egg hunts, wonderful dinners and bonnets. Well, it doesn't mean bonnets that much anymore, but some of us remember when it did.

This all leads me to thoughts that are ping-ponging around in my brain. This morning I gave a talk at a Lenten breakfast. First I sang a song and then talked about the words in it. Believe me when I say - I don't consider myself a singer. I did it because I think it is important to push myself to do things out of my comfort zone. That was way, way out.

So, yesterday I asked a friend, Hilda to pray for my upcoming song/talk. I said, "Will you pray that I don't make an ass out of myself?" She said, "You mean, again?" We had a good laugh, but we knew it was true.

That reminded me of a prayer I once saw, "Lord, please save me one more time." I need that one on a pretty regular basis.

I saw a sign, "Why pray when you can worry?" That's another perspective. I've also read that if there were no God, there would be no atheists.

For years I have wanted to use this quote by Kurt Vonnegut, but have hesitated as I was not sure how it would be taken. Today I am going to go for it. It is "I tell you, we are here on this earth to fart around, and don't let anybody tell you different." I think that's funny, but, also, not true. I think we are here with more purpose than that.

Rabbi Harold Kushner has a *Prayer for the World.*

"Let the rain come and wash away the ancient grudges, the bitter hatreds held and nurtured over generations.

"Let the rain wash away the memory of hurt and neglect. Let the warmth of the sun heal us wherever we are broken. Let it burn away the fog so that we can see each other clearly, so that we can see beyond labels, beyond accents, gender or skin color.

"Let the warmth and brightness of the sun melt our selfishness so that we can share the joys and feel the sorrows of our neighbors. Bring forth flowers to surround us with beauty. And let the mountains teach our hearts to reach upward to heaven. Amen." Now that's purpose.

A billboard I saw said, "You know that love your neighbor thing. I meant it. God"

Maya Angelou says when she wonders what she should do, she thinks of what her grandma would do or say to her. "She'd say, 'Just do what's right. You don't really have to ask anyone.' Right may not be expedient. It may not be profitable, but it will satisfy your soul." Ah, what a wonderful thought . . . satisfy my soul.

Maya goes on, "Try to be the best human being you can be. Try to be that in your church, in your work, in your family, in your community. Do it because it is the right thing to do. People will know you and they will add their prayers to your life. They will wish you well." I love the thought of people adding prayers to my life. And they have.

"Try and live in such a way that you will have no regrets. This is your life. This is your world. You make your own choices. Make it a better world where you are. It can be better. It must be better, but it's up to us."

Compare that to Mark Twain who said, "Always do what's right when people are looking."

So, as Easter rises in the morn, what does it mean to you? Where will you be celebrating or will you?

Do you relate more to Kurt Vonnegut or more to Maya Angelou? If you have faith in God or a special religion or a higher power, does it satisfy your soul? Does your life purpose carry you on?

Perhaps this Easter, as we look at our divided troubled world and country, we will feel better remembering what Steven Spielberg said when asked what his favorite movie ending was. He replied, "Hope."

I close with wishing you hope, a purposeful life and a satisfied soul. May we all do what's right to make our corner of the world a better place.

Unclear Of The Concept

I have a cartoon I love. It shows a guard locking a prisoner into a cell. The prisoner sits down on his cot and says perkily to his cell mate, "Now what?" The caption just reads, "Unclear of the concept."

My friend has a 2nd grader in Grand Rapids. For Lent he decided to give up saying, "Poop and butt." I thought this was so cute. It made me wonder what other funny things people give up for lent. Are any of them unclear of the concept?

Pastor Jones knew a woman who gave up strawberries, which were impossible to find anyway. She also gave up mountain climbing, but she lived in Maumee, Ohio, where there are no mountains. She didn't let her faith inconvenience her in any way.

One lady gave up Bud Lite – but not beer. Josh gave up smoking last year, but he doesn't smoke.

Pastor Mike heard of a guy giving up ice cream, so he just drank malts all lent. Candy once gave up "ice cream with chocolate and peanuts on top. I could eat ice cream and I could eat chocolate and I could eat peanuts, but I couldn't have them together."

A gal in Grand Rapids gave up dairy, but not sour cream, ice cream, cheeses or yogurt – basically, she just gave up milk, which she hates.

Don wrote me that Alec Baldwin said, "I'm going to give up my Catholic guilt because I normally thrive on it."

Jenny said that her 5 year old gave up french fries and she really, really loves french fries. Her parents had told her we need to give up something because Jesus gave up his life for our sins. Since, she has been asking a lot of questions about how this really went down. How'd he die? What does that have to do with my french fries, etc.? She is not sure her sacrifice is worth it and she has assured her parents she will never give up french fries again.

Kelly said she always gives up watermelon because she really loves it. My daughter, Cara, also gave up watermelon. When my other daughter asked her, "Do you really eat it that much?" She replied, "No . . . therein lies the genius."

Pastor Karin gave up food one day a week during lent. She said she wasn't sure that had been a good idea as "when you're hungry, you can't focus on anything but being hungry."

Janet thought of giving up wearing make-up, but decided that would be more painful to others than to herself. She had thought that then, like Jesus, she could come out on Easter with full make-up on and go, "Tah dah!"

A lady told me she gave up chocolate . . . after 8 p.m.

One lady decided to eat only one dessert. A friend asked her, "Per day?" "No, per meal."

An esteemed local gentlemen, who will remain anonymous – but I will hint that he was recently a mayor – decided to give up second desserts. Recently he was at a luncheon and the dessert was cookies. He had only one, but of course, that really wasn't enough. So he had a second. Someone next to him said, "I thought you gave up second desserts." Ever the politician, he retorted, "I made the regulations. I can amend the regulations." If you see him, be sure to tell him you didn't recognize him here.

My grandson, Danny, asked if he could give up going to church. Gayle's children wanted to give up three things – homework, chores and spinach. She gave up Facebook responses, but not, of course, Facebook. Marty wanted to give up snow.

Jody gave up saying a very naughty word. "That lasted only a day . . . well, not even that." She gave up cheese once, but found it "a slippery slope. At first it was all cheese, then, if the cheese was already there, like on a pizza, that was okay. So that didn't work out so well. I gave up beer one year, but then I just drank hard alcohol drinks and got wasted all the time." Life is hard.

Susan has a friend who gave up trying to give up smoking.

I will end with this one I read the other day. A newlywed was feeling amorous. Her mate shook his head and said, "I can't. It's lent." She said, "Well, I don't know who you lent it to, but you better go get it back." Unclear of the concept.

Who's Knockin'?

A doctor held a stethoscope to a small boy's chest. "Can you hear that? What do you think that is?"

The little boy looked at him and said, "I bet it's Jesus knockin'!" Aha! Aren't little ones smart?

Here we are at Lent again. It is time to give God more attention than usual. How's that going for you? Do you hear him knocking?

There have been times in my life when I felt my spiritual side was in high gear. Then there were other times when I felt the world took over and my spiritual growth took a back seat. Lent is a time to stick God back in the front seat with us.

Father Phil Salmonowicz once told me, "Lent is relational. When you fall in love with someone, you spend more time with that person and other things fall aside. Likewise during Lent, we encourage people to spend more time with God and let other things fall aside."

I like to think of Lent as a spiritual refresher time, a spiritual time out. Our churches can be vehicles for this but we each make our own journey. Hopefully, that journey continues when we aren't in church.

My friend, Gary, was a Lutheran Bishop. He told me, "Lent is a chance to step back from our hum-drum thoughts, to go deeper into the spiritual God places in our lives. It is a time to reflect, give up, and give in to God's actions. It is a time to forgive and allow God to renew us and make us whole." I love the thought of "God places" in my life, in my heart and in my soul.

There are so many ways to go about Lent – attending church services, reading spiritual writings, giving up things, doing positive things, letting go of negative things. Lent can ground us and help us remember what is important. It can also be a time to reflect on how we are doing in our spiritual lives and decide what adjustments are in order. We don't have to do our Lent perfectly. God doesn't expect perfection of us.

Personally, I always find it helpful and wonderful when I can go to a play about the passion or some like religious drama. It draws me in. It makes it real. It helps me to center on a personal lent experience.

For many years, we went to St. Alphonsus in Grand Rapids where they would put on an event about the life of Christ. The choir would sing as slides were running behind them. I believe it was called, *His Last Days*. We went with our children several years in a row and each of us was deeply touched and loved it. The one that I never got over was a slide portraying how Mary felt when Christ was crucified. It was going through thoughts she was having as she mentally went over her son's life. The scenes were full of anguish and we could feel and imagine the pain. The one slide that touched me so deeply and I never forgot, was of a young mother with a child in snow suit, hats and mittens. Never mind that there wasn't snow where Christ grew up. Never mind that snowsuits weren't from that time period. What was the exact same was the feelings of motherhood from birth throughout your child's entire life. We can all internalize those feelings and they make Mary's experience come to life within us. It made lent come to life in a new way.

There are many ways to make lent come alive for us. We just need to open up our mind and awareness to find what works best for us. We are all individuals.

When my grandson, Louie, was small, if you held his hand to walk with him, he would move his legs up and down and up and down. There would be lots of motion, but not much of it was moving forward. It was like he hadn't really grasped the concept of "onward, Christian soldier." Sometimes my faith journey has been like Louie's legs - lots of movement but not necessarily any positive growth. Growth is the purpose of Lent. I need to be sure I am not just moving up and down. I need to move forward and grow with God. Do you need this too?

I will close with this. "Knock. Knock. "

"Who's there?"

Lent is our time to look within and see who's knockin'. I bet it's Jesus.

Thanksgiving - Not What It Used To Be

Thanksgiving is not what it used to be. Oh, we still gobble, gobble, gobble, but not like we used to. There are some unwanted guests that come to our table, and frankly, they make it quite a challenge, especially for the cook.

In the good ole days, we cooked, we ate, we were stuffed. It was simple. First you stuffed the turkey, then you stuffed yourselves. A good time was had by all. Easy as pie - oh, yeah, don't forget the pie!

But now the meal planning is full of challenges. Some of us have become lactose intolerant. That means we have a shortage of the enzyme lactase. This is found in basic things like milk, ice cream and whipped cream. I'm sure whipped cream is a basic, right? At least on Thanksgiving it is.

Common symptoms of this problem are fun things like diarrhea, nausea, abdominal cramps, bloating and gas. Happy Thanksgiving. But, all in all, we can take some Lactaid over-the-counter pills and do okay.

That isn't so easy for one of our gang who was diagnosed with Celiac Disease a few years ago. It seems she always had it but no one realized it until a wise doc did a biopsy. Celiac is common with Irish and northern Italians.

A while ago I was in a gluten-free bakery in Grand Rapids and a gal from Italy told me that in Italy, they test newborn babies for Celiac. If they have it, the government pays them a stipend for the rest of their lives because their food budget will be more costly and their national diet is heavy with pasta, bread and other wheat products.

Gluten is a protein found in wheat, barley, rye and sometimes oats. If you eat gluten, it permanently damages the villi in your small intestine which enable you to absorb nutrients into your bloodstream. There are a whole bunch of very serious complications that arise from this and there are no drugs which work for it. A gluten-free diet is the only solution.

Let's see now. How does gluten play into Thanksgiving? Well, there is gluten in rolls, gravy, pies, cakes, cookies, salad dressings, and, of course, that Thanksgiving star – stuffing. And don't forget the green bean casserole that is a staple for Turkey day, full of gluten.

On a normal day, some other foods one cannot eat are pizza, pasta, breads, cereal products, coatings, and beer. I made a soup a while ago which I was sure was gluten-free. My daughter got sick after and asked what was in it. I told her, but was sure I was "clean" with my cooking of it. Not so. Turns out canned chicken and beef broth have gluten in them. Who knew? I tell you, this gluten stuff is insidious.

There has never been a better time to have this disease. The world is now full of information and gluten free products, but they are costly and a challenge to find and use. And then some of them taste like cardboard; however, cardboard is gluten free. Add to the above dilemmas that another family member has recently been diagnosed with sugar diabetes. Ah, another whole ball of wax. Of course, wax has no gluten, sugar or lactose so might be a good deal at this challenging meal.

We all know that sugar is in pies, desserts, wine, alcohol, fruits and on and on. This, too, can be worked around. But it is another challenge. Put these restrictions all together and voilla. It seems like the turkey may be the only thing on the table that everyone can enjoy. And I haven't even mentioned calories and fat contents yet.

It is now time to prepare my menu and my grocery list. I am worn out by the challenge and I haven't even begun yet. I can do this, though. I know I can. I must remember, it is not about the food. Even though the ads tell us it is. It is about the people, the love, the laughs and the time we share together. That's what Thanksgiving is all about.

But as I begin my very careful planning of this holiday, I am reminded that turkey is filled with tryptophan which may make us all sleepy after our feast. As we nap away, we won't care one bit if our dreams are full of sugar plums, dairy or wheat. Until we wake back up to that reality show called life.

The Dirty Christmas Sweater

Okay. It's time to wear the Christmas sweater. There are only 2 and a half weeks to do it. I have already wasted a few days. I'm losing precious Christmas sweater wearing time. I gotta move on this. But, there's a problem.

Last year after Christmas I didn't clean it. Instead I put it on top of my wash machine and thought I could put the task off. After all, it wasn't urgent. I didn't need it for a whole year.

It has some sparkly stuff on it and other cutesy Christmas stuff and I thought it would be a challenge to wash. I also thought it might run all over itself. This project could get ugly. I hate laundry challenges. Who has time for those? Especially if it isn't something you need to wear soon. I've got lots of time, I thought.

Winter went. Spring sallied by. Summer slowly simmered away. Fall fell. Thanksgiving came . . . and went. I think it all went too fast.

My daughter just sent me the most appropo quote by Dr. Seuss. "How did it get so late so soon? It's night before its afternoon. December is here before its June. My goodness how the time has flewn. How did it get so late so soon?"

Embarrassment arrives. Who leaves a sweater on their washer for an entire year? What kind of person does something like that? A lazy person?

I love Mark Twain. He said, "Never put off until tomorrow what you can do the day after tomorrow." Amen to that. He understands me.

If it were only the dirty sweater. But it isn't. If truth be known, and it is by anyone who knows me, I have lots and lots of uncompleted projects. Some of my friends and family say it in a very mocking tone,"Your projects." I sense an Uwwwwwwwww in their snide tone. My children are the worst. Sometimes they rudely refer to them as just "piles of stuff". How nasty and insensitive can they get? I tell ya, I get no respect.

Every once in awhile I get a project completed. I feel like I discovered the Titanic or something. Wheeeeee. Wowwwww. How great am I? No one answers. Their looks say it all.

I like to think, and I think it is true, that I keep making progress on my projects. But then I have to ask myself, is it good enough? Have I gotten enough of these tasks completed or could I, should I, have done more?

I could've done this. I should've done that. I should've done this. I should've done that. I learned early in life not to should on myself. Say that fast about 5 times. The moral: Don't let anyone else should on you either.

I still have piles waiting for me to tackle. I have things that need to be cleaned out, organized, redone. Sigh. They don't look exciting. I don't want to do them. I just want them to be done.

Am I the only one with projects that go on and on and on? Year after year some of them still clutter my life, my mind. They mess up my yearly goal list. I just roll them over from one year to another. Once in a great while I complete a couple and get to cross them off the lingering list. Progress is such a dandy, even when it is slow. The crossing off part is delightful. Yeah! Bingo! I did it!

How are you doing with your projects? What have you set aside because it isn't urgent? What have you put off because it isn't fun to do? What is still waiting to be taken care of because you really don't want to do it when there are so many other things to do?

I'm guessing I am the only one with a dirty Christmas sweater for the past year. You wouldn't be that bad, I'm sure. But, I swear to you, if the cleaning of this didn't baffle me so, I would have done it months ago. Maybe even twelve months ago.

It is probably the fear that holds me back. I fear all the cute décor will fall off. I fear the colors will turn it into a grey drab blob. I fear it will shrink to fit my grandsons. I fear I will lose all the money I invested in this dumb sweater. Can sweaters be dumb or is it the person that buys it that is? The same person that is afraid to clean it.

I need to come to terms with these projects. I need to tackle them. Eliminate them. Not take them into the New Year with me. But first I gotta hurry. There is a dirty Christmas sweater to wash, whether I want to do it or not. And that window of wearing opportunity is clicking away.

The big truth in life: If it weren't for the last minute, nothing would get done.

Say It Forward

We talk about paying the piper. We talk about paying our dues. We talk about paying the bills, but not now. We don't talk about that until January. Now we are busy causing the bills.

We talk about paying others back for something that they did to us. Sometimes it is a good thing. Sometimes it is a bad thing.

A few years ago there was a movie called, *Pay it Forward*. It was about doing good deeds before we need to. The concept was that what goes around comes around. If we pay it forward, the chances are greatly enhanced that what comes back around to us may be a good thing.

Recently my daughter, Donna, who teaches fourth grade, mentioned a concept she was using with her students – Say it Forward. The idea is that rather than doing something forward, we say something.

In the last few days I have visited with several people. Every single one had a story, a dilemma that they were worried about or were stressing or hurting over. Each had something painful that they were carrying around in their hearts.

The problems discussed ran the gamut. Don't they for all of us? Visiting with three friends today, it was amazing how most of us had dealt with issues like divorce, alcoholism, mental illness, blended families, problems with parents, problems with children, fragile self-esteems. We had all experienced mean hurtful things that people had said to us.

In many of these discussions, tears filled their eyes as they shared. People may look good. They may dress well. They may have their hair and make-up done. They may be performing well at work and being nice to others. But what they also have are hurting hearts, painful memories and fragile egos.

The world has more than its share of mean people. Some of them do horrible things. Others don't do horrible things but they do just mean enough things to hurt people deeply. They make others suffer with their words and actions.

As we enter into the Christmas season, we are bombarded with the melee of holiday happiness. Everyone is singing carols, buying gifts, tra-la-la-la-la, la-la-la-la. Snoopy is doing his holiday special. Everyone is wishing everyone a happy holiday.

So, as the holiday season enters full blast, along with the snow, let's do something new along with all the other good things we buy, give, sing, celebrate, eat and drink. Let's try that new concept – Say it Forward.

Here's how. Look around you each day. Who do you see? The people you live with, the people who do things for you, the people you work with, exercise with, live near, worship with – the list goes on and on.

Open your eyes and minds wide. Praise when you can. Thank when you can. Say kind words when it might help. Listen with empathy and encouragement. Offer words of kindness. You might punctuate it all with a hug and a smile. Wowser, this is just getting kinda crazy, isn't it?

Say it forward as fast and as sincerely as you can. Even if it is out of character for you, go ahead. It won't hurt. I promise. And if it does, the pain will begin to ease the minute you see the other person's face as you say it.

Try this for the morning. Try it for the rest of the day. Try it tomorrow. When you go to bed at night, ponder your Say it Forward experiences. Go to sleep. Get up and do it all over again.

Concentrate this whole holiday season on Saying it Forward. You might like it and want to live like that from here on out. Tra-la-la-la, la-la-la-la.

Einstein said, "A human being is a part of the whole called the universe. He experiences himself, his thoughts and feelings, as something separated from the rest. This delusion is a kind of prison for us. Our task must be to free ourselves from this prison by widening our circle of compassion to embrace all living creatures. Nobody is able to achieve this completely, but the striving for such achievement is in itself part of our liberation and a foundation for inner security."

I agree with Albert. He could have also just said, "Say it Forward".

A Cup Of Kindness

We think of Christmas as merry, happy and ho-ho- ho. It is, for most people. But this year, I am very aware of many who are not merry, happy and full of ho-ho-ho.

We took our grandsons to Coopersville to ride the Santa Train. As we left, there was a poster pinned on a door. The poster was for a fund raiser for the family who lost two children last week, when they crashed into the back of a school bus. I didn't realize those were their only children. Their loss is so profound, I don't know how people get through such ordeals.

In the past couple of weeks, and even this week, we have friends burying spouses, sisters. These people leave children and some leave grandchildren. They leave many others who mourn for them.

My friend told me at a Christmas party this week that he is struggling with what to do with his mother who was mentally there one day and the next day she wasn't.

Marriages are ending during this holiday season, while others are in great turmoil, on the edge.

My sibling is one of the many who have been without a job for way too long, yet still have children to make Christmas merry for.

Last week, I went to my doctor. He asked me the dumbest thing. He said, "Do you have any stress going on in your life now?"

I told him he might not want to ask that of any other women right before Christmas. Women are up to their eyeballs with stress, trying to get everything done for everyone they love. I think I even advised him to not ask his wife that right before Christmas. She might just hit him with a Christmas tree stand. The tree wouldn't be hard enough.

Yes, we are stressed, rushing, spending and tired. We definitely need a holiday and a vacation might even be better.

However, we must keep it all in perspective. All the holiday stress and madness is just that. We will likely all look back and think it was a very merry, happy and ho-ho-ho Christmas. But, when we pause and look around us, we see the many who are suffering for many different reasons. This can give us an instant shot of perspective.

As I sat in church yesterday, I thought of the many people I mentioned above. By chance, I opened the songbook to this hymn.

"We are many parts, we are all one body, and the gifts we have we are given to share. May the Spirit of love make us one indeed; one, the love that we share, one, our hope in despair, one, the cross that we bear."

As we begin our personal holiday, let us each remember to do what we can for those we know who may be hurting during this merry time. Whether it be a call, a note, a hug or a prayer – let us each open our hearts. We can't make the problems go away, but we can add a tiny bit of caring.

It is good to remember the words of Stephen Grellet. "I expect to pass through this world but once. Any good therefore that I can do, or any kindness that I can show to any fellow creature, let me do it now. Let me not defer or neglect it, for I shall not pass this way again."

I wish each of you a merry, happy and ho-ho-ho holiday. But, if you are one of those suffering this season, I hope your burden is lightened by the caring of others.

Running On Empty

Years ago I would pull into the gas station. I would say, "Fill-er-up, please. And please check the oil and the tires. Oh, and please clean the windows." Then I would just sit there in my warm car and they would replenish me, or I should say, my vehicle.

It was a grand time and we took it for granted. Who knew that years later we would all be standing in the freezing winds with our chilled bods pumping our own gas? We would be forgetting about our oil and tires and no longer caring if our windows are dirty because, frankly, it is just too darn cold to clean the suckers.

Ah, yes, that kind of service is history. I'm not sure my two younger girls even remember those days. But many of you do.

Today my car tank is full, though it does need oil and for someone to clean those yucky windows. But what needs filling is me, my personal tank. I'm outta gas. I'm running on empty. Can any of you relate?

Last night I realized, 'Oh, no, I have to turn my column in by noon tomorrow and I haven't had a chance to think about it and I don't have a clue what to even write about. Nor do I have any energy, which oddly enough, creativity demands.'

My next thought was, 'I'm out of gas.' That brought to mind the song by Jackson Browne, *Running On Empty*, and it played in my head. It is still playing in my head - probably because I just played it on YouTube.

Part of my empty tank is due to a nagging cold I have had for over a month. Colds do wear us out, even though we keep going. Another cause is having just had a lot of speaking jobs which required a lot of prep time. Add to these all the holiday decorating, cooking, planning, shopping, wrapping, social events – to give just a starter list. I get more tired just thinking about all that is still left to do.

"Running on empty . . . running behind. Gotta do what you can . . . everyone I know . . . everywhere I go . . . I don't know about anyone but me . . . if it takes all night, that'll be all right. . . if I can get you to smile . . . how crazy this life feels . . . I look into friend's eyes, they're running too . . . running on empty . . . I'm running behind." Yes, Jackson speaks to me. And I'm betting he speaks to many of you right now also.

I look ahead and Christmas is a week away - the countdown. I sure do feel down for the count. I know I can get it all done. I'm sure I can. We always do, don't we? We may work "*all night. It'll be all right*".

Speaking with my friend, Julie, today, she says she is also on empty. She says she doesn't feel the holiday spirit yet. She won't see her only child this Christmas. She is wondering how best to fill her tank. If we look around us, we see many "*running on empty*".

I am not complaining. Please don't get me wrong. Life is good - very, very good. I am just tired. The good news is that we can replenish with a bit of R and R. A bit of rest can bring our tank to at least half full and allow us to do what we need to do. It can renew our energy level which will renew our spirit.

Gas and oil are precious commodities. So is our personal energy. We need to use different sources to keep it flowing. Thankfully, they are right around us. The window to look out of to view the beautiful snowscape. The chair to sit in as we prop up our feet for a bit. The cup to fill with a renewing beverage. The holiday music to listen to which helps us get in the mood. The bed to crawl into for a long winter's night. The person to hug which lifts us up. Our higher power to go to for peace in our soul. Yes, R and R is there for the taking. But it has to be taken. We have to go get it. If we don't, we remain on empty.

I'm sure there are many like me who are running on empty right now as we try to accomplish all that December and the holidays mean for us. The good news is that there are stations in our lives where we can go to fill-er-up. And, of course, the fill up is for us, our personal tank – not our car.

When we take the time to refill ourselves, we can change our tune from "*Running On Empty*" to "*all is calm, all is bright. . .*"

Music To Help You Get From Here To There

Louie Burns

Ah, the holiday bustle is upon us. And yet, there are lots of things to enjoy along the way.

Last night I went to hear John Berry's Christmas Concert. His Christmas CD is one of my most favorite and has been for several years. His voice is the nearest to perfect I have heard and Christmas carols spotlight it perfectly. He is a country singer, was most popular years ago. If you are looking for a new CD of standard and beautifuly sung carols, buy his and I doubt you could be disappointed. His Away in the Manger is my favorite.

Each year I try to add a CD or two to our holiday music collection. There are some I love year after year and they are not ones you'd likely expect. Jimmy Buffett's *Christmas Island* brings his typical fun sound and I love the entire CD. It might put you in the mood for a Christmas Margarita. Beware.

Rosie O'Donnell has two different Christmas CDs that highlight other famous singers. Almost every song on both of them is great. Neil Diamond now has two Christmas CDs, but I only have *The Christmas Album*. My favorite on it is *Morning is Broken*, but all the Christmas songs on it are excellent. Of course, with his unique voice what else would we expect?

Sarah McLachlan's *Wintersong* is divine. Another perfect voice and a lovely collection. I also love Jewel's *Joy: A Holiday Collection*. Jewel has a unique special voice making this one of my year after year faves. The Celtic women soar on *A Christmas Celebration*. I also love Vince Gill's *Let there Be Peace on Earth*. It will lift you up. He also has one of the best voices around.

A couple oldies but goodies that our family still enjoys after many, many years are Anne Murray's *What a Wonderful Christmas* and Kenny and Dolly's *Once Upon A Christmas*. Dolly Parton has such a fun spirit it just makes you feel good and you can't help but sing along.

I have a lot of serious Christmas CDs but you likely have those too – Josh Groban, Barbra Streisand, Celine Dion and lots of other expected beautiful singers. I also have some that are just instrumental and one favorite is Ottmar Liebert's *Poets and Angels*. He is an incredible guitar player and his CD is so very nice. I also love *A Smoky Mountain Christmas* which features dulcimers and the mandolin which make for a most joyful unique sound.

A couple years ago we went to see Flash Cadillac sing with the Grand Rapids Symphony. They had a hit in the sixties and are still a viable group. I bought their Christmas CD, *Ghosts of Christmas Past*, and enjoy it so much.

I think my favorite of the last few years, if I had to pick one, is by Chris Isaak - *Christmas*. Who'd a guessed he would have such a wonderful holiday album, but he does. His sexy voice comes through and every song is a keeper.

So, as you decorate, shop, bake, write cards and wrap, take some time to listen to some good holiday tunes and have yourself a merry little Christmas.

Can We Keep Christmas?

Isn't it interesting what Christmas has become? We've come a long way from the Christ child being born in a stable, to standing in line at stores at 3 a.m. to Christmas shop for bargains. How did we get here? How crazy it has all become!Christmas is a wonderful time of year: holy; festive; celebratory; special music; special clothes; special foods; lots of la-de-dah.

We cut down trees, haul them into our homes and decorate them. We have boxes and boxes of stuff to garnish them with.

That isn't enough, though. We decorate our entire homes. Inside. Outside. Lights. Greens. All kinds of decorations. Some lovely. Some old, worn, and very loved, full of our history and memories.

We fill our schedules with church events, parties and gatherings, trying to cram it all into a few short weeks.

And then there are the gifts. We buy for folks we love and for some we like a lot. We buy for people we don't know. We buy when people don't need anything and we don't have a clue what to buy them. That doesn't stop us. We still buy.

We send cards and letters to people we aren't in touch with any other time of the year. We buy special stamps. Photos go into the cards. Even with the rise in the cost of stamps, we still send. It is, after all, an important way of staying in communication with friends and family. Priceless, to be exact.

And then we eat. Of course, if we are celebrating with gifts, decorations, cards and all – food has to be a part of it. And, boy, is it! Somewhere, sometime, someone must have decided that we needed to fatten up and Christmas was the time to do it. Everyone seems to be on a mission to get all the candy, cookies and treats they can tuck into their bellies. Ho, ho, ho.

Add to this all the special TV shows, movies, concerts and programs - way too many to see or attend.

Yes, we Christians celebrate the birth of Christ, but we have certainly made it into a lot more than just celebrating our faith. And even though it's a lot of work and causes stress and busyness, we love both parts of Christmas. Hopefully, we connect with our faith, our family and our friends all in a special and personal way. It is the blend of our faith rituals and our secular routines that gives us joy and peace over the holidays.

Years ago my Grandmother sent me the words of Henry Van Dyke.

"Are you willing . . .

- to forget what you have done for other people, and to remember what other people have done for you;

- to close your book of complaints and to look around you for a place where you can sow a few seeds of happiness;

- to stoop down and consider the needs and desires of little children;

- to remember the weakness and loneliness of people growing old;

- to bear in mind the things that other people have to bear in their hearts;

- to try to understand what those who live in the same home with you really want, without waiting for them to tell you;

- to trim your lamp so that it will give more light and less smoke, and to carry it in front so that your shadow will fall behind you;

-to make a grave for your ugly thoughts, and a garden for your kindly feelings, with the gate open;

- to believe that love is the strongest thing in the world – stronger than hate, stronger than evil, stronger than death – and that the blessed life which began in Bethlehem so many years ago is the image and brightness of the Eternal Love?

Then you can keep Christmas."

This is a pretty tough assignment but definitely something to strive for and to put at the top of our holiday lists. These thoughts may be the perfect gift for us to bring to the Christ child.

On America

Presidential Encounters Of The First Kind

"The whole day was incredible and it truly was an out-of-body experience. I still can't even believe it happened to me!"

President Obama & Christina Beckman

That is a quote from Christina Beckman who introduced President Obama as he spoke recently at the University of Michigan. "This was a dream come true and something I'll never forget! It's one of the best days of my life and I'll be talking about it forever."

"President Obama asked me how school is going for me and what I am majoring in. It was a very normal conversation. He said, 'I can tell you're going to do a great job . . . see you up there.' That comment was one of my favorite memories of the whole experience! Regardless of political affiliation, meeting the president and getting a chance to speak with him is an honor. It's a once-in-a-lifetime opportunity and something almost anyone would be happy to be a part of!"

As I chatted by email with Christina, I wondered about other people I knew and if they had had personal encounters with U.S. Presidents. Wow, I never expected so many responses. It proved my theory true, that these encounters stay with us forever, imbedded colorfully in our minds.

Some weren't so excited. Marty said, "I saw a president once in California, but I can't remember who it was." Then, later, she remembered. "Oh, yeah, it was Nixon. I think I've tried to forget it."

Barb, in Illinois, said, "I met Hubert Humphrey once . . . a golden memory I'd like to forget." These reminded me that my husband went into a men's restroom and saw a sign above the urinal which read, "Deposit Goldwater here." That was during the presidential race of Goldwater and Johnson.

Carolyn was a stewardess for United Airlines and chosen to work the charter flight for Spiro Agnew as he was running for Vice President with Nixon. She talked with him quite a bit and he reminded her to vote as he got off the plane.

I have known Gary for many moons and he has often talked about how his MSU commencement speaker was President Harry Truman and how tremendous he was. Recently, Gary and Connie visited the Truman Presidential Library to cap off this great memory.

Margaret said, "My aunt used to lunch at the White House with Mamie Eisenhower. They were college friends." Even though it didn't happen to Margaret, I thought it was a great story and proves these encounters are proud memories that pass through generations.

When WW2 ended, General Dwight Eisenhower was courted by both Republicans and Democrats to run on their ticket for president of the country. He refused and became president of Columbia University. Gerry was a student there. Eisenhower would come in each month and talk with Gerry's class of 25 students. Ike shared his war experiences and was very laid back, friendly and patient. He often said he had a fear of a military-industrial-congressional -complex becoming a reality in peacetime. In 1952 he was elected U.S. President as a Republican. At his farewell address, he again warned of the danger of a military-industrial-complex, but he left out the word "congressional ". His advisers said it might offend too many congressmen with military contractors in their districts. How very interesting!

Harriette, a New York girl, saw Eisenhower in 1953 in Manhasset Long Island, riding in a convertible in his military uniform, waving as he campaigned for president. "Amazingly impressive and I still have the visual in my mind."

This is the first in a three part series. I'm going to close this part with something Steven Wright said, "When they asked George Washington for his ID, he just took out a quarter." We gotta end with a laugh, right?

****

Marcy was a college student working at a hotel in Des Moines. John Kennedy stayed there. When he left the hotel, the staff stood around in the lobby. He came over to her, shook her hand and said, "You did a very good job." Marcy says, "He was so darn good looking, sun bleached hair and very tan. He was casual and friendly. I have never seen a photo of him that was able to portray how handsome he was. My whole life, I have pretty much told everyone I have ever met, 'I shook hands with Kennedy!' "

Charlie was stationed at the Naval Air Facility across from the Naval Academy where Kennedy gave a commencement address. When Kennedy's helicopter landed, it was Charlie that was out on the landing site directing him where to go. No matter who the president, I know there are always people who want to tell him where to go!

On Friday, October 14, 1960, Ann, Mary and Bill went to see John Kennedy when he was campaigning in Grand Rapids. After his speech, Mary chased his convertible all the way down Division Street to shake his hand. She said it might not have been a real shake. It might have been only a touch, but it was very memorable just the same. Bill pushed through and got his autograph. Sadly, he lost it later, but the memory remains.

Fred, our cousin, was a sophomore at Catholic Central High School and not particularly enamored with politics or Kennedy. He was, however, on his way home from school as the motorcade went by. Fred was very shy, but stepped to the curb to watch with the crowd. Kennedy was sitting on the back of a convertible with secret service lining both sides of the car to keep people back. Without planning to, Fred jumped off the curb, went between the guards and right up to JFK to shake his hand. Kennedy was a bit surprised but shook hands with him. It only took five seconds and the guards let Fred go.

Later, Fred remembers he cried when he heard Kennedy had been assassinated. He realized this experience had a much bigger effect on his life than he realized. Though very shy, this chance encounter gave him confidence to tackle other things that he had been afraid to do. He believes his brief brush with JFK triggered a change in his confidence level that lasted his entire life and affected all his future decisions.

With Gerald Ford having been our congressman for many years, plus a Grand Rapids all around guy, many people had memories of him. Roseanne remembers being at the old Civic Auditorium when Ford was speaking. He came into the foyer where they were and her mom giggled and waved to him as he went by. Roseanne said she almost died of embarrassment at her mother. Some things never change, right, fellow mothers?

Don and Diane were in Krakow, Poland, in 1975, with GVSU. Betty Ford was outside and they went up to her. She looked at them with a vacant, dull, distant look. She appeared buzzed. They chalked it up to the rigors of traveling. Shortly thereafter, she admitted herself to a rehab program, which became the Betty Ford Clinic. As Betty was so honest about these things, we decided it was okay to include that.

Terri met her when Betty spoke in Grand Rapids in 2000. She said, "She was such a friendly, engaging woman and won their hearts!"

Bill and Harriette also visited with Gerry and Betty Ford in Vail at a Xmas tree lighting ceremony. Bill told them he knew John Heintzleman, Bill's Greenville high school football coach, who played ball with Ford. Betty and Harriette discussed a mammogram Harriette had just had at the Betty Ford Clinic. "It was all surreal."

Rae's dad was a local dentist. He always said his claim to fame was that he had tackled a young high school football player who later became President. Of course, that was Jerry Ford.

I will close this part with a campaign slogan by Pat Paulsen, who ran for president many times without success. "We've upped our standards. Up yours." Perhaps he should have won just because of his sense of humor!

****

When our daughter, Colleen, graduated from Marquette University in Milwaukee, Barbara Bush was her commencement speaker. She wore a blue dress with pearls and everyone loved her! She was so charming and warm and I quote her to this day. One thing she said was that she was "going to share the secret of parenting . . . when your child wants to lick the beaters, be sure to turn off the motor." It brought the house down.

Gary has "worked with President Jimmy Carter on several Habitat for Humanity projects. Roslyn was always at his side. They are down to earth. Most importantly, so many in the world have safe, decent and affordable housing because of him."

Roseanne's "parents were republicans, but once attended church in Plains, Georgia, and went to Sunday school taught by Jimmy Carter. Some walls came down that day!"

Gunder met Ford, Reagan and Carter. He says, "The visit to the Carter Center was the most meaningful because President and Mrs. Carter were so gracious and unhurried with us. They have a genuine interest in community colleges and public service. I can see why Jimmy Carter is regarded as the best ex-president we have ever had."

Bonnie and Hal were having dinner in Hawaii in 1980. "Men in suits came into the dining room, looked everything over and a few minutes later, President and Mrs. Carter came in and had dinner. It was definitely an unforgettable moment."

Cathy and Ken went to the Lansing airport to greet Bill and Hillary Clinton in 1992. Ken said to Hillary, "Thank you for running." She replied, "Someone's got to do it!"

Terri heard Bill Clinton speak at an Economic Club in Grand Rapids. "He was a bigger than life individual. He opened his speech by asking us to thank the wait staff at our table. This set the tone to include all people in our nation."

Dee "met several presidents during her time as trustee at Michigan State University.

They were each very memorable and almost overwhelming events. The presidents were all very special, gracious and charming. However, Bill Clinton was on another level in terms of how he connected with people. No matter the circumstances, he looked you directly in the eye and made you feel as though you were the only person in the room and the only one who mattered.

President George W. Bush & Brian DeKraker

"Brian went with his son, Greg, who was covering a campaign stop with George W. Bush in Ionia. "I got to shake hands with him like we were old college buddies."

Al met every presidential candidate since Reagan. "What I remember most is how distinctly different their personalities and persona were. Reagan was affable, personable, warm, approachable and truly "present" when talking with me. George H.W. Bush was extremely professional, very bright, seemed deeply committed to the issues. Barbara was absolutely charming. Bill Clinton perfected the town hall meeting and is obviously very bright, but a bit slick. George W. is a real Texan – hardy, less formal than the others, less articulate than the others. Still, he exuded trust, the kind that comes from believing in a handshake deal. When Laura was with him, she stole the show. The two Bush men sure married fine ladies. Finally, Barack Obama, the most charismatic of them all, is absolutely masterful with a town hall audience. He has tremendous people skills and is very personable and caring."

My own presidential encounters amounted to seeing Jerry and Betty Ford as they led the Cherry Festival Parade in Traverse City. It was a long time ago. I remember that because I only had two little kids! I also remember thinking it was funny that the secret service is secret but so obvious with their suits, sunglasses and ear pieces. I also saw Obama speak in Grand Rapids. Just seeing a president or first lady of the United States with your own two eyes is an event to remember.

I will end this with a thought. When we see a U.S. President, it doesn't matter if they are Republican or Democrat. What we see is a real person that loves this country. Wouldn't it be wonderful if we could transfer that awareness to this divided nation. God bless America!

We Remember . . .

Edward Colegrove,
Maureen's Grandfather

Walter Empey
Maureen's Father

Today is my grandson, Louie's, birthday. He is six. It is also the 70th anniversary of Pearl Harbor. I watched the news tonight. They were honoring 120 of the men who survived Pearl Harbor. It made me think of how that history is going fast. Those survivors are in their late eighties. How will this history stay alive? How will little Louie know what it is all about? It will stay alive because we will remember and we will pass it on. It is our familial and civic duty.

I was born after World War II ended and am one of the first baby boomers. We got this label because the men came home from war and got the women pregnant. I only know about our family in the wars because the stories have been kept alive. For that I am grateful.

As I grew up, I always heard about cousin, Bobby. He went down with the Arizona, I was told. Bobby Colegrove was a young good-looking sailor serving on the USS Arizona in Hawaii. He was my mom's first cousin.

It was just before 8:00 a.m. on a Sunday in beautiful Hawaii. The USS Arizona battleship was the first one hit by a squadron of Japanese aircraft. The ship exploded into fires. Most of the crew were either killed by the explosions and fires or were trapped by the rapid sinking of the ship. In all, 1,177 of the crew died on that ship. Of course, cousin, Bobby was one of them. The total number of Americans that died during the Pearl Harbor attack was 2,400. 2,399 were just names to me, but one, just one, is part of my family story. I must pass that on to my children and grandchildren.

Both Bobby's dad, Bill, and his brother were career military and retired with high military ranks. Uncle Bill's two brothers, one was my Grandpa, were also in the military and served during World War I.

On my father's side, he and his two brothers all served in the Navy during World War II. I often have thought of my Grandma worrying about her three sons fighting in other lands. There is a wonderful photo which ran front page in the Rochester, New York, newspaper. It showed all three sailors looking in the window of their home. They had been allowed to come home together to surprise their mother for Christmas. Happy holidays, indeed.

One of them, my Uncle Bill Empey, is the only one left. He was recently honored in Washington, D.C. as a survivor of World War II, among other honorees. An entire trip was done to honor these heroes in every way possible. When they got on the plane, they were each given three personal letters written by school children thanking them for their service. There were many stories told, many memories shared, many laughs and many tears. My uncle is on dialysis three days a week and is frail. My aunt went to the airport to meet him when they returned from Washington, D.C. She was sure he would be in a wheel chair, but he surprised her. As they came off the plane and into the airport, there were hundreds of people to greet them, all cheering. My dear, fragile and wonderful uncle walked all the way on his own, saluting and smiling to all. He was so proud to have served and to have been honored! This is part of a national project to honor all living World War II veterans. When that is completed, they will begin doing the same with Viet Nam and Korean Veterans.

Way back in 1883, another uncle, Arthur Guy Empey, was born. He served in World War I with the US Cavalry. I have always heard about his bestselling book, "Over the Top: by an American soldier who went". It is sold on Amazon today and has a 5 star rating. It is touted as "the first book about real war life that offers a unique description of trench warfare during World War I". I have found copies for my children to help them realize that history touches each of us through our relatives. We just need to remember it and pass it on.

Think about your families and what stories you have to share about them and their military history. What do you need to pass on so that it will never be forgotten? What do you need to pass on so that it will honor the service and the lives that were given? In our church there is a hymn I love, We Remember. We must.

Our family stories continue on my husband's side and also with good friends. They continue through other wars. Our son was named after a good friend and a marine, Dan Jaskewiecz, who was killed in Viet Nam. Our son has been told Dan's story of service. He's also been to The Wall in Washington, D.C. and felt Dan's name etched in the memorial. We have kept Dan's story alive in our family history.

Today at Pearl Harbor, an 88 year old survivor spoke. "Freedom isn't free, never has been – looks like it never will be." He sums it up. It is a story that goes on and on through generations. Let us never forget those generations from our own families who fought and served. By honoring and remembering them, we honor ourselves and our families today. Take time to pass the memories and stories and photos on. It is the least we can do.

How Are We Doing?

I was talking with a friend about books. I mentioned one about Vietnam and he said how the war ended before he was old enough to really be aware of it. That struck me.

Viet Nam was such a big, horrible thing in our lives that I forget that it is truly just history to most of the adults alive today. Vietnam ended in 1975.

This week we celebrated the work of Martin Luther King as a national holiday. That is likely just history, too, to most Americans alive today. But I remember living through the work of Dr. King.

I remember having a friend, Dorothy, come to our wedding. Dorothy was my first black friend. We worked together in an office in Grand Rapids. I was excited to have her as a friend. I had never known any blacks, really. In Coopersville, I don't think there were any. When I met Dorothy, she invited me to her home for dinner. I remember we had sweet potato pie, my first taste of that. I also remember how very kind and inviting her mother was to me.

That was the sixties. Race problems and riots were common in the nightly news. Martin Luther King was leading his odd non-violent movement. As violence had always been a tool used in these circumstances, his philosophy was hard to understand.

I think of that time. I think of that movement. I am struck by their non-violent grounding. I am pretty sure I wouldn't have thought of going about it that way. I think I might have been drawn more to the eye for an eye philosophy. But as Gandhi said, "If we all live by an eye for an eye and a leg for a leg, everyone will end up blind and without legs." Hmmm. Good point, Gandhi.

Race, sadly, is still an issue in so many ways. I often try and imagine what it must feel like to be black in a room full of white people.

Sunday we had a black priest from Africa. He did a wonderful job and was a great man – you could tell. But there he was, up at the pulpit, talking to a church full of only white folks. There are many times that I am aware of these situations and I always wonder how they feel when they are still a minority in cases like this.

Minority is always palpable when you are the minority. I lived as a minority with my religion. It didn't feel good. I have worked at times as a minority, being female in a male working world. It has not always felt good or fair. Sometimes, now, I feel in a minority with my age. That doesn't always feel good either.

I think we are doing much, much better than we did previously in these areas. However, in many ways there is still room for improvement.

I have been on a golf course in the area and heard the foursome in front of me using the "N" word. I have been at a local restaurant and heard the guy in the booth behind me saying horrible racist things. What upset me the most about that one was he had children with him.

But, I see hope, too. I remember when my grandson had a young black friend and never seemed to notice that they had different color skin. Hope is beautiful when you see it as reality.

So, this week we celebrated the birthday of Martin Luther King, Jr. We closed banks and didn't get our mail. Hopefully, we also took it a step further and did some evaluating of where we are with our own little worlds, where we are with our great big world, and if there are any changes we could make to refine the way things are today.

We profess we believe in racial equality. That must go further than thinking. It must also go into how we act, how we treat others and if we respect others. Are we where we want to be as a society? Are we where we want to be as a community? A family? An individual?

Once Mahatma Gandhi was asked what he thought of Western civilization. He replied, "I think it would be a good idea." I'm sure we all agree.

The Liberty Bell

Come On Rise Up!

There is a special sadness in your heart when you see young men and women going to war. They look so young. Because they usually are. They look like such good people. Because they usually are.

Many of us were at the parade and waved support and caring to the 1073rd as they prepared to go to Iraq. That morning I was leaving water aerobics. As I hauled all my gear out, hair wet, no make-up, I was surprised and deeply touched by the bustle of activity in the lobby. It was full of people in uniform, members of the 1073rd, and their families. They were talking, eating, enjoying each other. Love and fellowship was in the air. Until that moment, I hadn't thought about the fact that most of them are not from Greenville. Their families had to come and stay for the sending off celebrations.

I spoke to a couple of the men in uniform and told them thank you for doing this brave service for America and that we would be praying for them every day, and praying hard. In a second, we connected in a special way. They politely said, "Thank you, maam."

That night, in the parade, amongst the crowd, I saw those men and our looks remembered that encounter. I was touched, once again, by what wonderful men they seemed to be.

Tonight, I left Meijers and God blessed me in a special way. As I went to get to my car, Ben was walking by. He was in his National Guard uniform and is one of the 1073rd heading to Iraq. I couldn't believe it as I had wanted to see and talk with him and hadn't had the chance yet. I felt I wouldn't get it as I didn't want to impose on his family time in these last precious days before his deployment. We gave each other giant hugs and I wished him well and told him how very happy I was to get to see him and have a second with him.

Ben was dear friends with our daughter. He was our neighbor and in high school they would often walk up to the playground and swing together and talk.

You know how parents are about friends of their kids. Those friends hold a special place in your heart. You watch them grow up. You share this journey, the good and the bad, with their parents. It bonds you in a special way. Of course, we have always loved Ben's parents so the bond was pretty special.

Ben and his dad, Jerry, went to Iraq together the last time our guards went. It was a mighty happy time when they all came home. It will be a mighty happy time when all of these wonderful soldiers come home too.

I don't like powerlessness. I hate that we watch them go and it is out of our hands. But, then again, we aren't really powerless. We have prayer. We have faith. We have caring and love in our hearts. And we have each other.

Ben is just one of the many going. He leaves behind a two year old, a seven year old and a lovely wife. Most of the people going leave loving families too. War affects many, many lives. And then there are the parents, the extended families, the many friends, and even the parents of the friends.

In my head is playing one of my favorite songs by Bruce Springsteen. It feels like an anthem as I write this.

"I pray Lord ... with these hands ... for the strength Lord ... with these hands ... for the faith Lord ... with these hands ... I pray Lord ... for the strength Lord ... with these hands ... for the faith Lord. .. with these hands ... Come on rise up ... Come on rise up ... rise up."

May each of the members of the 1073rd rise up to meet the challenges they are being given. May they feel the strength and the faith.

May each of us rise up to support them in a variety of ways. May we rise up to support their families who are left behind. May we take our hands, our faith and our strength and help them to rise up to get through this difficult time.

"Come on rise up ... rise up ... with these hands ... for the strength Lord ... for the faith Lord. Rise up."

God bless each of you soldiers. Rise up and know we lift you with prayer. And know that it is a mighty power indeed.

For Your Reading Pleasure

Maureen's 2012 Summer Reading List

Danny Burns

Ah, summer is about to begin and with it the promise of relaxation. Hopefully, you will find some time to read a book or two or three. This is my sixth annual summer book list.

Sally "reread *The Buffalo Soldiers* by Chris Bojalian. It's one of my favorites. I really liked Ann Patchett's *Patron Saint of Liars*, Anne Jean Mayhew's *The Dry Grass of August*, Paula McClain's *The Paris Wife* (about Hemingway), *The Descendents* by Kaui Hart Hemmings and *Townie* by Andre Dubus III, a memoir - all were very good."

Margaret said, "*Astrid and Veronika* by Linda Olsson is a powerful poignant novel". Jonelle suggests "*The Forgotten Garden* by Kate Morton - a multigenerational saga full of family secrets and a touch of mystery."

Missy favored "*The Angel Makers* by Jessica Gregson - very interesting with lots to think about afterwards".

Ann "enjoyed *Wildflower Hill* by Kimberley Freeman, reminded me of *The Thorn Birds* - also, *Blackbird* by Jennifer Luack, an amazing story of survival, and *This Burns My Heart* by Samuel Park – very engrossing."

For some non-fiction, Bob "found Steve Jobs and Man of the House: *The Life and Political Memoirs of Speaker Tip O'Neill* with William Novak, both interesting". Terry said, "*American Sniper: The Autobiography of the Most Lethal Sniper in U.S. Military History* by Chris Kyle is expertly explained, full of rare honesty and conviction."

My husband liked *Over the Top* by Arthur Guy Empey, a relative of mine. It is the first book to describe actual trench warfare. Written in 1917 after WWI, it was a New York Times best seller and is available on Amazon and free on Kindle. If you liked the T.V. show, *Downton Abbey*, this is an addition to that time period.

If you liked the Dragon Tattoo series, *Entertainment Weekly* suggested two other Norwegian authors – Henning Menkell and Jo Nesbo. Friends and I tried and liked them. We began with Faceless Killers by Mankell – an easy engrossing read. *Redbreast* by Jo Nesbo was voted "best Norwegian crime novel of all time". I read it and then sat down and read it again to see if I had it all straight. The sequel is *Nemesis*. The Norwegian authors certainly have a different style than American crime writers. Try 'em. I'm guessing you'll like 'em.

Jodie liked *Ali in Wonderland* by Ali Wentworth, who was a regular on *Oprah* and is married to George Stephanopoulos. "It is well worth the read – short (read it in one sitting) and belly-laugh funny!"

Deb suggests, *"Ender's Game* by Orson Scott Card (a sci-fi, first of a series), *Inheritance* by Christopher Paolini (fantasy, semi-medieval, last of a series) and the Inspector Lynley mystery series by Elizabeth George (layered, complex and British – love these books".

Rosemary liked *Heaven is for Real* by Todd Burpo. "It's an inspiring glimpse at the realities of heaven and a great read for teens and adults". Judy added, "I found this book to be a comfort to many who have lost family members. The innocence and purity are refreshing."

Maureen suggested *The Warmth of Other Suns* by Isabel Wilkerson. It is a powerful account of the Great Migration of blacks to the north in the U.S. and a captivating history tracing three black persons' life stories and spanning six decades.

Harriette "loved *The Art of Fielding* by Chad Harbach. It's baseball but not just baseball." She added, "Ann Patchett's *State of Wonder* is interesting and different, takes place on the Amazon with lots of intrigue. An older, but oh, so good book is *Open* by Andre Agassi. You think it can't possibly tell you anything you don't know, but it is extremely well written and full of wonderful stuff."

Many really loved *The Hunger Games* trilogy by Suzanne Collins. I thought they were hard to put down, fast and easy. Of course, the books are better than the movie.

Gregg really likes the Prey series by John Sanford and Linda liked *The Hour I First Believed* by Wally Lamb. Bev reminded us of the great one, *The Art of Racing in the Rain* by Garth Stein.

Don liked *A Governor's Story* by Jennifer Granholm, *American Icon: Allan Mulally and the Fight To Save Ford Motor Company* by Bryce Hoffman, *In the Garden of Beasts: Love, Terror and an American Family in Hitler's Berlin* by Erik Larson, *Destiny of a Republic: A Tale of Madness, Medicine and the Murder of a President* by Candice Millard.

Drea recommends *"Wild* by Cheryl Strayed – about a woman dealing with profound grief and doing a solo hike. It taught me that everyone has a story and is on a journey."

Eron says, "Educators may like the books by Chip and Dan Heath – *Switch and Made to Stick"*. She also suggests *Drive* by Daniel Pink, *Brain Rules* by John Medina and *Predictably Irrational* by Dan Ariely.

Katie said, "I read *Loon Feather* by Iola Fuller every summer. It is set on Mackinac

Island and full of adventure, romance and lots of Michigan history. I also suggest *The Flight of Gemma Hardy* by Margot Livesey – haunting and captivating and *Those Who Save Us* by Jenna Blum, harrowing and hard to put down."

Don liked two recent John Grisham's, *The Litigators* and *Calico Joe*.

Don and I also suggest *The Invention of Hugo Cabret* by Brian Selzer, an illustrated unique story about a real life character that can be read very quickly. We were captivated by the artwork. We also liked 11-22-63 by Steven King. Don't let the size deter you. It's an easy read that skillfully takes you back to a life you remember.

Darlene "really liked the Outlander series by Diana Gabaldon - time travel, wars, love and Ireland. Though not fast reads, they are very intriguing."

The Book Thief by Markus Zusak was a hit with many. I think it may be my favorite book of all time.

Two previous One Book One County selections were recommended again - *Lay that Trumpet in Our Hands* by Susan Carol McCarthy and *My Sister's Keeper* by Jodi Picoult'. Both are great reads.

Deb also encouraged us to read the Stephanie Plum series by Janet Evanovich and *A Tree Grows in Brooklyn* by Betty Greene. Shelly found *"Roses* by Leila Meachum to be intriguing and difficult to put down". It is a *Gone with the Wind* type, modern day family saga.

Connie liked *The Lucky One* by Nicholas Sparks. Diana was excited about *Sarah's Key* by Tatiana de Rosnay, *The Piano Teacher* by Janice Y.K.Lee, *Hotel on the Corner of Bitter and Sweet* by Jamie Ford, and *The Guernsey Literary and Potato Peel Pie Society* by Mary Ann Shaffer and Annie Barrows. Mary and Sally both "liked *Fish and Grits* by Tina Smith-Brown – excellent characters with every emotion evoked".

The History of Love by Nicole Karuss was recommended by Kelsi. " I read it over and over – it's playful and delightful." Hollie liked Secret Daughter by Clare Vanderpool, *Moon over Manifest* by Shilpi Gowda, These is my Words by Nancy Burner and *A 1000 Mile Walk on the Beach* by Loreen Niewenhuis, about a woman who walks the whole way around Lake Michigan.

"If you thought I wouldn't mention *Fifty Shades of Grey* (called mommy porn), you're wrong. Stores can hardly keep it in stock. Deb says, "I'm not ashamed to say I liked it and read all three books twice. I couldn't put them down. You will either like it or hate it". The other two are *Fifty Shades Darker and Fifty Shades Freed* by E.L. James. Toni says, "Not every book has to be a Pulitzer Prize winner. These are great entertainment and easy summer reads". Toni cautions, "Don't read them next to your grandma and don't let your kids look over your shoulder". I haven't read them but last week at my grandson's ball game, I noticed three moms reading them. Hmm.

Major Pettigrew's Last Stand by Helen Simonsont is the 2012 One Book One County Montcalm selection. It is quite delightful. I'll close with a quote on fiction by Herman Wouk. "Income tax returns are the most imaginative fiction being written today." I'll bet he's right! And here's a great quote from Andy Rooney. "The two biggest sellers in any bookstore are the cookbooks and the diet books. The cookbooks tell you how to prepare the food and the diet books tell you how not to eat any of it." I miss Andy Rooney. Happy Reading!

Maureen's 2011 Summer Reading List

Donna, Don, Drea & Dan Burns

Summer is coming and that means it's time for my 5th Annual Summer Reading List, which is perfect all year long.

Gail shares, "The best book I read this year was *Cutting for Stone* by Abraham Verghese –intrigue, drama, love and hope. I couldn't put it down."

Joyce reread *Animal Farm* and *1984* by George Orwell and got more out of them now. Darci recommends *The Sparrow* by Mary Doria Russell. "It is sci-fi with interesting characters. I read it years ago and loved it." Another sci-fi comes from Jim, "*Mercury Falls* by Robert Kroese is hilarious". Dan liked the Jack Reacher series by Lee Child. The latest, *61 Hours*, precedes 12 or so. John Grisham's *The Confession* is one of his best.

In the thriller/mystery genre, *Vanished* and *Power Play* by Joseph Finder and *The Godfather of Kathmandu* by John Burdett. Linda enjoyed *The Lion by Nelson DeMille, a sequel to The Lion's Game.*

Hollie was enchanted with *The Hundred Foot Journey* by Richard C. Morais, which takes place in France.

Bev favored *The Mayflower* by Nathaniel Philbrick and *The Gift of Rain* by Tan Twan Eng. "Both are excellent historical reads, engaging characters, never dull." Many said *Unbroken* by Laura Hillenbrand, author of *Seabiscuit*, is an unbelievable page turner. Don said "The Civil War" trilogy by Bruce Catton is a classic for any Civil War buff. He also recommends *Field of Honor* by Edwin Bearss and James McPherson.

Skeet suggested *Saving Cee Cee Honeycutt* by Beth Hoffman, "powerful and a quick read". Rena loved *The Next Place* by Warren Hanson, "beautifully illustrated and comforting for anyone grieving".

Missy says *Breaking Night* by Liz Murray is great. I read it in two days and was absolutely changed." She also endorses, *Bitter in the Mouth* by Monique Truong, "well written and quirky. *Let Me Go* by Helga Schneider is a touching and shocking short memoir."

My daughter, Donna, loved the learning in *The Immortal Life of Henrietta* Lacks by Rebecca Skloot and also *The Kitchen House* by Kathleen Grissom.

A book club member suggested, *A Man Called Intrepid* by William Stevenson, about the intelligence operations involving Winston Churchill during World War II, "Exciting, complicated, extremely interesting!" Tim found *The Given Day* by Dennis LeHane "a great read with great character development – a historical novel which ties in Boston, law, crime, baseball, Babe Ruth, etc." Les thought the new biography of George Washington was "especially interesting", *Washington: A Life* by Ron Chernow.

Eron offers Blink by Malcolm Gladwell, *The Other Queen* by Philippa Gregory, *The Lotus Eaters* by Tatjana Soli and *Madonnas of Leningrad* by Debra Dean. Several suggested *Half Broke Horses* by Jeanette Walls.

Gary says mature readers would like *Leisure Seekers* by Michael Zandoorian. Pastor Joel calls *Prodigal God* by Tim Keller among the top 5 books I've ever read, a refreshing look at the Prodigal Son parable. Also, *The Five Dysfunctions of a Team* and *The Four Obsessions of an Extraordinary Executiv* both by Patrick Lencioni are quick, refreshing reads – very good."

Eric recommends: *Hitch 22*, a memoir by Christopher Hitchens; *Home Game: An Accidental Guide to Fatherhood* and *The Big Short: Inside the Doomsday Machine* both by Michael Lewis; and *Daniel Patrick Moynihan: A Portrait in Letters of An American Visionary* by Steven Weisman.

Jim enjoyed No *One Would Listen* by Harry Markopolos, who first uncovered Bernie Madoff's ponzi scheme. Ed suggests, *To Account for Murder* by William Whitbeck and *Decision Points* by George Bush.

I was recently in New Orleans and everyone told me to read *1 Dead in Attic* by Chris Rose. They said it was the best book on Katrina.

Jim suggests, "*Cleopatra – A Life* by Stacy Schiff, excellent, and *A Visit from the Goon Squad* by Jennifer Egan, which may get a Pulitzer."

Don flew through *Moneyball* by Michael Lewis, called by *People* magazine, "...the most influential book on sports ever written. If you're a baseball fan, this is a must." He also raves about *The Things They Carried* by Tim O'Brien, a short book called "as good as any piece of literature can get and the definitive book on Viet Nam. Darrin suggests White Noise by Don DeLillo, Once a Runner by John L. Parker and *The Sound and the Fury* by William Faulkner.

Don says, *In Stitches* by local boy, Tony Youn, now a nationally known plastic surgeon, "is really quite good. His characterizations of life in Greenville and his family are very honest."

The 2011 One Book One County choice, *Look Me in the Eye* by John Elder Robison is worth the read and helps us understand others.

To close, a question to ponder, "When a book and a head collide and there is a hollow sound, is it always from the book?" – George Lichtenberg. Happy reading!

Maureen's 2010 Summer Reading List

Don Burns

This is my fourth annual list of summer book ideas. Are you ready? Let's go!

I just finished the Harry Potter series and am in total awe of J.K. Rowling. How she can write in such creative detail, keep it all straight, and bring it to a close after seven very large books is beyond me. She's a terrific writer. You may think these books are just for kids, but you would be wrong. I intend to read the whole series again, when I get older and have lots of time. I recommend them to adults as well as younguns.

Last year we mentioned *Loving Frank* about Frank Lloyd Wright. Well, if you liked that, *The Women* by T.C. Boyle is a great book, very well written with terrific insight into this creative, wild man.

Several local book clubs, as well as my family, have read *Zeitoun* by Dave Eggers, a true story about Katrina and New Orleans. A fast read, educational, and billed as a must read for everyone.

There has been a west Michigan buzz about *Mennonite in a Little Black Dress* by Hope College professor, Rhonda Janzen. My husband and I found it interesting and it reads quickly.

My favorite book of the year was *Double Bind* by Chris Bohjalian. I loved it, lots of thriller aspects to it. Trust me.

Friends mentioned *Suite Francaise* by Irene Nemirovsky. They said it was very good and very touching.

Several said they loved *Tisha, a Young Teacher in Alaska*. Carole said she "was sorry to see it end" and Gisela said it is one of her "favorite books of all time". Gayla read *Portrait of an Unknown Woman* by Vanora Bennett and really enjoyed it.

Linda liked *South of Broad* by Pat Conroy. Judy said she loves anything by David Baldacci for summer thriller reading and encourages everyone to read *Gifted Hands – the Ben Carson Story*. I saw the movie and loved it. I even cried.

Linda said her book club loved *City of Thieves* about the siege of Leningrad by David Benioff. She said it is funny, sad, touching and educational - a good combo. Gisela suggested *Shanghai Girls* by Lisa See.

Bev loved *Olive Kitteridge* by Elizabeth Strout and it won the Pulitzer too.

Tim mentions this every year - *Night* by Eli Weisel. It's a must for all.

Mudbound by Hillary Jordan is a very fast good read. My husband kept talking about three books he loved: *The Speed of Trust* by Stephen R. Covey; *The Healing of America* by T.R. Reid; and *My Stroke of Insight* by Jill Bolte Taylor. They were quick reads and full of great stuff for us to learn and benefit by.

For fun, remember what Dana Carvey said, "I'm thirty years old, but I read at the thirty four year old level."

Relevant Recipes

Every once in awhile, I throw a favorite recipe into my columns.
I have included all of them in this chapter, so enjoy!
I only share the best. Trust me!

Just for fun, but a true story - a friend, Jill, took Slim Fast to diet, but found she gained weight. Later someone told her she wasn't supposed to be taking one with each meal, but instead of a meal. Ohhhhh!

Maureen's Margaritas

1 large can frozen Limeade

1 large can tequila (use limeade can)

1 large can triple sec (use above can)

Blend with crushed ice till frothy.

Chill stemmed glasses. Rub rims with lime juice or limes.

Invert rims of classes in coarse salt to coat.

These are quite strong so I use ½ or 2/3 of the tequila and triple sec.

If you use it full strength, be prepared!

Enjoy!!

(This recipe came from Bea Doser.)

Lage's Margaritas

2 parts tequila

1 part simple syrup

2 parts rose's lime juice

1/3 part orange curaco

1/3 part grand marnier

1/3 part triple sec

Salt rim of glass, fill with ice cubes, add above with a wedge of lime.

(Recipe from friends, Larry and Marcy Lage)

Sun-Dried Tomato Dip

1/4 cup sun-dried tomatoes in oil, drained and chopped (about 8 tomatoes)

8 oz. cream cheese, room temperature

1/2 cup sour cream

1/2 cup mayo

10 dashes Tabasco

1 t. kosher salt

3/4 t. pepper

2 green onions, thinly sliced - use both green & white parts

In food processor, puree all but onions.

Add onions for just a couple pulses.

(Recipe came from my daughter-in-law who is a wonderful cook.)

Donnie's Blue Cheese Burgers

Serves 4.

2 T. steak seasoning (like mccormick's montreal)

2 T. red onion, finely minced

2 # ground sirloin

½ # blue cheese, crumbled

One and ½ t. kosher salt

1 t. freshly ground black pepper

Heat grill. Mix well in bowl: steak seasoning, onion, & beef.

Form 8 patties and put 2 oz. blue cheese on top of each of 4 patties,

Then top w/ remaining 4 patties, sealing edges very carefully.

Season each side w/ salt and pepper.

Grill both sides, being careful not to break the burgers.

(Recipe from my friend, Donnie Muzzall)

Donna's Herb & Cheese Stuffed Burgers

4 servings

¼ cup shredded cheddar cheese

2 T. cream cheese, softened

2 T. minced fresh parsley

3 t. Dijon mustard, divided

2 green onion, thinly sliced

3 T. dry bread crumbs

2 T. ketchup

½ t. salt

½ t. dried rosemary, crushed

¼ t. dried sage leaves

1 # lean ground beef

4 buns

In small bowl, combine cheddar, cream cheese, parsley and 1 t. mustard – set aside.

In another bowl, mix onions, bread crumbs, ketchup, salt, rosemary, sage and rest of mustard.

Crumble beef over mixture and mix well. Shape into 8 thin patties.

Spoon cheese mixture onto center of 4 patties and top w/ rest of patties.

Press edges firmly to seal. Grill over med. heat for 5-7 min.

Per side or till 160 degrees in center and juices run clear.

(Recipe from my daughter, Donna)

French Bread

2 PKG dry yeast   2 cup warm water

Dissolve & mix water and yeast.

2 t. salt   ¼ cup melted oleo   2 T sugar

Stir in salt, oleo and sugar.

Flour -   add 4 – 5 cups to make soft dough, closer to 4 is best

Let rise 2 x and punch down. Shape into long loaves w/ water & flour on hands –
go over loaves & dust w/ cornmeal.

Rise ½ hr. Bake 370 degrees for 25 min.

(From the Grand Rapids green Junior League Cookbook)

Chocolate Banana Bread
Makes one loaf

1 ¼ cup all purpose flour

1 t. baking soda

¼ cup alkalized cocoa powder

½ cup unsalted butter, soft

1 cup sugar

2 large eggs

3 ripe bananas, mashed

1 t. vanilla

½ cup sour cream

6 oz. - 70% bittersweet chocolate, finely chopped

1. Preheat oven to 350. Butter or pam bread loaf pan.
2. In med. bowl, sift together flour, bk. Soda and cocoa powder. Stir to combine.
3. In big bowl, use mixer to beat butter & sugar at med/hi speed til light, about 2 min.
4. Beat in eggs one at a time, beat well after each, scrape down sides as needed.
5. Add bananas & vanilla at low speed, mix till combined.
6. Add flour mixture in 3 additions, alternating it w/ sour cream in 2 additions.
7. Add chocolate and blend just for a few seconds.
8. Put into prepared pan & smooth top.

Bake 55-60 min., till toothpick inserted in center comes out clean (except for any melted chocolate it might have on it). Cool bread for 15 min.

(This recipe came from "Chocolatier Magazine".
I make it exactly as it says. Perfecto! Enjoy!)

The Hansen Family Aebleskivers

3 eggs, separated

2 cups buttermilk

2 cups flour

1 teaspoon baking soda

1 teaspoon baking powder

2 tablespoons sugar

1 teaspoon salt

1 teaspoon vanilla

1/4 teaspoon nutmeg

Beat egg yolks and buttermilk together.

Sift all dry ingredients together.

Mix the above with the vanilla.

Beat the egg whites until stiff.

Fold them into the batter.

Here is the tricky part. Get your aebleskiver pan hot. You need an aebleskiver pan to make these. In each well of the aebleskiver pan, put about 1 teaspoon of Crisco. When that melts, put in about 1 teaspoon of butter. When that melts, put the batter in to fill 2/3 of the well. Batter should bubble and it should move on its own. With a tooth pick, flip it around and around cooking it evenly. Do this procedure with the Crisco and butter each time you cook a batch. Be careful not to burn the butter.

To eat, roll in brown sugar, powdered sugar or dip in jelly. Sue, the Hansen's daughter, said they break them open and eat them with butter and jam. This was something I did not need to know. I don't need anymore ideas. Personally, I like to roll them in a mixture of brown and powdered sugar. No matter what you choose, you can't go wrong with a hot aebleskiver. This recipe makes maybe 3 dozen.

(Recipe came from Shirley and Gay Hansen family and has been handed down through the generations. They are friends and a wonderful Danish family.)

Black Bottom Strawberry Cream Pie

1 refrigerated pie crust (15 oz.)

2/3 cup hot fudge topping

8 oz. cream cheese, softened

1 cup powdered sugar

1 pt. (2 cups) fresh strawberries, quartered

½ cup strawberry pie glaze

½ cup whipped cream, if desired

Heat oven to 450. Do pie crust as directed for one shell using 9" glass pie plate. Bake 9-11 minutes or until lightly browned. Cool completely, about 15 minutes.

Spread hot fudge topping in bottom of cooled baked shell. Chill one hour.

In small bowl, beat cream cheese and powdered sugar with electric mixer on medium speed until smooth. Carefully spread over fudge layer in shell.

In medium bowl, gently mix strawberries and pie glaze. Spoon evenly over cream cheese layer. Chill until firm, about one hour.

Just before serving, top with whipped cream, if desired. Store in refrigerator.

8 servings.

EASY! Great! Yummy! Everyone loves!

(This recipe came from an ad in a magazine.)

Bittersweet Cookies

Mix - 2 ½ cup flour
1 cup butter
1 cup powdered sugar
2 t vanilla

Put into balls the size of cotton balls,
Indent w/ thumb

Bake 350 degrees 12-15 minutes
While baking make filling

Filling - Mix- 1 cup coconut
1 cup walnuts (or pecans) – ground
1 t. vanilla
8 oz cream cheese
2 cups powdered sugar
4 T flour   -   Keep at room temperature

While cookies are warm, fill indentation with this mixture
Put 1 t. or so in each cookie

Glaze - 1 cup semi sweet chocolate chips
4 T water
4 T butter

Mix and heat in microwave or on stove until melted
Add 1 cup powdered sugar
Glaze each cookie with ½ t or so

When I made these, I made them too big. So my advice . . . make them small.
They are fabulous! So unique!

(Recipe comes from my friend, Donnie Muzzall)

Lavender Tea Cookies

350 degrees   Makes 30

Line Cookie sheet w/ parchment paper

1 c. unsalted butter

2/3 cup minus 1 T. superfine sugar

1 egg, beaten

1 ¼ cup minus 1 T. self-rising flour

1 T. fresh lavender flowers (I use dried)

Preheat oven. Cream butter and sugar, add egg and beat well.

Stir in flour and flowers. Drop teaspoonful on parchment, spacing widely for spread.

Bake 15-20 min. until pale golden and edges tinge brown. They will be soft until

Cooled on waxed paper.

Store in airtight tin.

(This is one of my favorite recipes to serve at tea parties.)

Naughty Bars

2 sticks butter

2 cups firmly packed brown sugar

2 t. baking powder

1/4 t salt

1 t vanilla

2 c. flour

2 lg. eggs

350 oven. Grease 9 x 13 pan.

Melt butter in microwave until almost completely melted.

Mix in brown sugar until
completely mixed.

Add baking powder, salt and vanilla - mix well.

Gradually add flour, mix well - it will be stiff.

Whisk the eggs in small bowl and then add to batter. Mix all well.

Bake until golden brown around the edges and center is still soft, about 30 min.

DO NOT OVERBAKE!!!

Cool completely before cutting into small squares. Serves 15 or so.

These are great for pot lucks or picnics and go quickly.

(This recipe came from a cooking magazine.)

Triple Layer Lemon Bars

*(Recipe comes from a bakery in Evanston and I begged for it.
It takes some work but is well worth it.
Cream cheese definitely takes it to a higher level.)*

Shortbread Crust:
1 stick salted butter, softened

¼ cup confectioner's sugar

1 t. vanilla extract

1 cup all purpose flour

Lemon Curd:
4 large egg yolks

1 T cornstarch

¾ cup granulated sugar

¾ cup water

2 med. lemons grated for 2 t. lemon peel &
squeezed for ¼ cup fresh lemon juice

2 T. salted butter, softened

Cream Cheese Filling:
8 oz. cream cheese, softened (not whipped

1 ½ cups confectioner's sugar

1 large egg

1 t. lemon extract

Topping:
2 T. confectioner's sugar

Preheat oven to 325 degrees.

Shortbread crust: Cream butter & sugar in med. bowl. Add vanilla & mix well. Add flour & mix at low speed until fully mixed. Press dough evenly into bottom of 8 x 8 pan. Chill until firm, approx. 30 min. Prick shortbread crust w/ fork and bake for 30 min. or til crust is golden brown. Cool on rack to room temp.

Cream Cheese Filling: In med. bowl, beat cream cheese & sugar until smooth with electric mixer on high speed. Add egg and lemon extract and beat on med. speed until light and smooth. Cover bowl tightly and refrigerate.

Lemon Curd: Blend the egg yolks w/ the cornstarch and sugar in med. non-aluminum saucepan. Place over low heat and slowly whisk in water and lemon juice. Increase heat to med-low and cook, stirring constantly, till mixture thickens enough to coat the back of a spoon. Remove from heat. Add lemon peel and butter and cool for 10 minutes.

To assemble: Spread chilled cream cheese filling evenly over cooled shortbread crust. Spread lemon curd evenly over cream cheese filling. Place pan in center of oven. Bake 30 -40 min. or until edges begin to turn light golden brown. Cool to room temp on rack. Chill one hour before cutting into bars. Dust top w/ confectioner's sugar.

Note - *I follow this exactly. It will look like it isn't set enough when it is time to take it out of the oven, but it will set as it chills. Enjoy!*

Books By Maureen Burns:

On My Mind . . . Or What's Left Of It

Contains 136 new and favorite columns, including her Associated Press winners.

"A treasure. People who read Maureen simply enjoy their lives more and I don't know any higher praise for an author."
- Brent Cushman, Stand-up/writer, San Diego

Looking And Laughing At Life

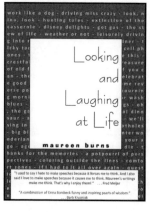

Rated "A" in Grand Rapids "On The Town" magazine. Contains 130 of her most popular columns.

"A combination of Erma Bombeck funny with inspiring pearls of wisdom." - Barb Krusniak

"Maureen's writings make me think. That's why I enjoy them!"
- Fred Meijer

Run With Your Dreams

Over 100,000 sold internationally!

" . . . One of the most powerful tools I've read to change your life for the better." - Og Mandino

"There is no greater gift to bestow than to encourage people to follow and develop their positive dreams. This book does just that. Read and be inspired!"- Dr. Robert Schuler, Author, Inspirational Speaker, Pastor

Forgiveness / A Gift You Give Yourself

Featured in "Reader's Digest" and "McCall's" magazines.

"Wonderful! Very moving and direct." - Norm Nickle, therapist, Seattle

"This book is an invaluable tool for forgiving others and forgiving yourself." - Jim Doughty, therapist, Tennessee

"Without a doubt, Maureen's best! A timeless master. Vital." Rudy Bengtson, businesswoman, Tucson

Cara's Story

Coping with life, death and loss. A True story. For children and all ages.

Featured on National Public Radio.

"This book is very valuable. I recommend it to all parents." Elisabeth Kubler-Ross, M.D.

"Third grader's book about life, death called hit!" Lansing State Journal

Getting In Touch . . . Intimacy

A book about people, love and caring. Vital message. Easy format. Practical ways to enhance relationships in your life - with yourself, mate, children, family and friends.

"Excellent! Made me re-evaluate my life." - J.H.

To Order Books and CDs/Tapes:

Books:

On My Mind . . . Or What's Left Of It $12.00
    (Also available as e-book)

Looking And Laughing At Life $12.00

Forgiveness / A Gift You Give Yourself $15.00

Cara's Story $10.00

Run With Your Dreams $10.00

CDs or Audio-Tapes:

Maureen Burns on Humor $5.00

Maureen Burns on Forgiveness $5.00

Maureen Burns on Motivation $5.00

Maureen Burns presents "Change Happens" $5.00

Maureen Burns presents "Stress Busters" $5.00

To Order: Email maureenburns@maureenburns.com or
call 616-754-7036.

Visit our website www.maureenburns.com

Maureen's books are also available on Amazon.com.

Maureen Burns is an international professional speaker and author of six books. She writes a weekly newspaper column for The Daily News and a monthly column for Faith Magazine. She has won two Associated Press awards and a first place award for the Catholic Associated Press.

She is married with four grown children, two wonderful grandsons and an extremely gifted dog.

Visit her website at www.maureenburns.com
For speaking engagements or to write her, email
maureenburns@maureenburns.com